HARVARD EAST ASIAN SERIES

HARVARD EAST ASIAN SERIES, 17

The Origins of Entrepreneurship in Meiji Japan

The East Asian Research Center at
Harvard University administers projects
designed to further scholarly understanding
of China, Korea, Japan, and adjacent areas.

THE ORIGINS OF
ENTREPRENEURSHIP
IN MEIJI JAPAN

Johannes Hirschmeier, S.V.D.

HARVARD UNIVERSITY PRESS

1964 · CAMBRIDGE, MASSACHUSETTS

Distributed in Great Britain by Oxford University Press, London

Preparation and publication have been aided by a grant from the Ford Foundation

Library of Congress Catalog Card Number: 64-20973

Printed in the United States of America

TO MARY

PREFACE

This book has grown into its present shape over a period of five years. When I started to write a dissertation on Meiji entrepreneurship, I had only a vague idea of the problems involved. In the course of my research my own viewpoints changed repeatedly, and my material and its arrangement had to be altered accordingly. I know of no research works of a similar kind that might have served as a model, and in Japan the study of entrepreneurship is still in its infancy.

One of the greatest difficulties was to find a meaningful balance between writing a general history of Meiji industrial development and presenting detailed biographical data on individual business leaders. I became increasingly convinced that the two must be synthesized because Meiji industrial development was contingent upon the dynamism of its entrepreneurs, while the entrepreneurs themselves were a product of the social, political, and economic conditions of their time. It therefore became my primary objective to point out this interplay between outside forces and the initiative of individuals. The first two chapters and part of Chapter Four stress the social and political conditions of the late Tokugawa and early Meiji periods. Chapter Three and the second part of Chapter Four put greater emphasis on economic development. The rest of the book focuses on private entrepreneurship.

I am indebted to many who helped me during my research and writing. First of all I want to express my gratitude to Professor Alexander Gerschenkron who as thesis adviser provided firm guidance, especially during my initial groping with unfamiliar material. I am equally indebted to Professor Edwin O. Reischauer, who was of great help in redressing imbalances of interpretation.

While rewriting for publication I received untiring help from Professor Albert M. Craig of Harvard University. I profited greatly from discussions with Professors Henry Rosovsky and William W. Lockwood, both of whom I had the pleasure of meeting in Tokyo. I am grateful also for very useful suggestions given me by Professors Benjamin I. Schwartz, Fritz Redlich, and Arthur H. Cole, all of Harvard. I should also like to thank the East Asian Research Center and notably Mrs. Elizabeth Matheson for all their help in editing and preparing the manuscript.

During my prolonged research in Japan I had the pleasure of frequent discussions with Professor Tsuchiya Takao, and I also received good advice from Professors Miyamoto Mataji and Yamaguchi Kazuo. My colleague and friend Suma Chikai of Nanzan University was always ready to help out with his vast knowledge of the Tokugawa period.

Through the most pressing months of thesis writing I enjoyed the generous hospitality and stimulating discussions of my friend Robert L. Hamman, who at that time was working on his own dissertation.

I thank Yasuike Masuya for so ably assisting me for a year in the collection of material. Library facilities were generously extended to me by Tokyo University and Hitotsubashi University. Special thanks are due Kato Chiye for her patience in typing and retyping the manuscript.

Finally, I am grateful to the Society of the Divine Word for financing my trip to Japan and my stay there from 1957 to 1959. Without that generous sponsorship I could not have written this book.

JOHANNES HIRSCHMEIER, S.V.D.

CONTENTS

THE ORIGINS OF
ENTREPRENEURSHIP
IN MEIJI JAPAN

Nor is new wine put into old wine-skins; if that is done, the skins burst, and there is the wine spilt and the skins spoiled. If the wine is new, it is put into fresh wine-skins, and so both are kept safe. Matthew, 9.17

INTRODUCTION

The economic development of Japan since the Meiji Restoration of 1867 has caught the imagination of the Western world, because Japan has been the only non-Western nation to succeed in breaking through the barrier of backwardness that still entraps most of Asia. Less than a hundred years have passed since the dawn of Japan's new era, and yet this dynamic nation is beginning to extend a helping hand to her Asian neighbors in an effort to lead them, too, on the road to vigorous economic growth.[1]

The economic development of Japan has many fascinating aspects, and the literature on modern Japan, particularly on its industrialization since the Meiji era, has assumed monumental proportions. This book is not intended to repeat or improve on existing accounts of the course of Japan's development. It will focus instead on entrepreneurship, in the broadest sense of the word. All the material presented is designed to throw light on the important question of how Meiji Japan generated the power to make her economy run uphill, leap unbelievable hurdles, break down centuries-old barriers, and finally arrive at self-sustained industrial growth. Japan succeeded so well because she had exceptional leadership in both the government and the private economic sector. The combination of governmental guidance and private industrial initiative has many facets, and I am aware that I have been able barely to scratch the surface of the matter.

The role of entrepreneurs in economic development is today a much discussed subject, but unfortunately it is an unwieldy one. We cannot limit the discussion of it to quantitative variables but must also include sociological and political forces. This is particularly necessary in the early phase of economic development, prior to the industrial "take-off," when statistical data are hard to come by and when cool economic rationality is often swamped by political and social upheaval. If the economist is to treat of entrepreneurship, he has to examine the bewildering kaleidoscope of variables and from them derive a coherent theory of economic development. He cannot willfully restrict his model to those variables that are statistically tractable if others also occupy a strategic position in the developmental process. Myrdal remarks on this problem: "Also, the distinction between 'economic factors' and 'noneconomic factors' will likewise have to be discarded as illogical and, consequently, misleading. Economic analysis will have to deal with all the relevant factors if it wants to be realistic; general economic theory will have to become social theory. I believe that the main hypothesis for this new theory will then be the assumption of circular causation between all factors in the social system resulting in a cumulative process." [2]

For a long time it was thought that lack of capital was the real villain preventing economic growth. Once sufficient capital was provided — from within or without — to overcome the "low-level equilibrium population trap," economic growth would issue forth and feed on its own impetus, so the argument went. If nations provided loans and grants to underdeveloped countries, all would be well.

Recently increasing attention has been given to entrepreneurship as a key factor in the entire process. The will to develop, to invest, to take risks, and to break with traditional business attitudes may be of greater strategic importance than the availability of capital. Of course, a minimum of savings is required to set in motion modern economic growth, but this does not mean that savings hold a logical or causal priority. Hirschman thinks that capital supply may often behave passively and that it is, over a wide range, a positive function of entrepreneurship.[3] Sufficient potential capital for a vigorous start may already exist in various disguised forms. A classic example in support of this theory is Japan, where sizable amounts of disguised capital were activated by vigorous entrepreneurship. Then, as the developmental process gained momentum, more capital was formed as a result of economic and social reforms, and also as a result of the initial success of the pioneering ventures. All this was done without any foreign capital to speak of.

According to this theory, whether a country succeeds in making its big leap forward will depend largely on its ability to supply sufficient "entrepreneurship" — the determination and ability to invest, independent of the question of private versus public initiative. The government can and should, in the initial phase, go a long way not only to provide guidance, but also to build the social and economic overhead. But unless the country intends to acquire a completely planned economy, in the Soviet style, its planners must recognize the need to stimulate private entrepreneurship of a high quality and make it one of their chief tasks to do so.

Entrepreneurship, seen in this context, becomes at once a matter of paramount importance as well as one that resists quantitative analysis. It is not enough to insist that entrepreneurs are necessary for economic development; we need to know more about the factors that influence the supply of entrepreneurs. Is there anything that can be done to stimulate the emergence of business leaders in backward countries? What are the main obstacles preventing capable young men and potential industrialists from devoting their energies to private business pursuits?

Schumpeter assigned the key role to the entrepreneur in his theory of economic development. The entrepreneur is the Faustian element in the economy; he disrupts the equilibrium circular flow by introducing new combinations and thus drives the economy to ever higher levels of performance. He destroys the old and builds the new, and it is he alone who reaps profits in the proper sense.[4] There appears to be no particular scarcity of the Schumpeterian type of entrepreneur in the economically advanced countries. Even where the individual innovator is being replaced by research teams and decision making is being delegated to a managerial group,[5] the will to innovate and the eagerness to exploit all possible profit opportunities cannot be said to be in short supply. Modern capitalist societies not only provide monetary rewards for economic success but often make idols of their successful businessmen. Societies in which generals and civic leaders of the first rank retire into top business positions without any loss of prestige will easily draw capable and ambitious men into industry and business. The economically backward countries, on the other hand, frequently have an almost diametrically opposite scale of values, in which business pursuits automatically cause a man to lose his social respectability. In countries where the merchant class has been notorious for cheating and ruthlessly exploiting its customers, the very idea of business easily becomes abhorrent to the most talented people in the society. In the course of this book we shall see that this inherited value system presented one of the most persistent obstacles to the formation of a dynamic business leadership in Meiji Japan.

The approach adopted in this book represents a middle way between what can be termed macroanalysis and microanalysis. The Japanese literature abounds in biographies of all types and degrees of reliability on the Meiji "heroes," among whom are many of the top business leaders. But we gain little by simply compiling biographical sketches without attempting a macroanalytic view of the whole entrepreneurial situation. We need, above all, conclusions that are neither complete generalities (as, for example, "entrepreneurship is necessary for economic development") nor too closely limited to the conditions existing in a particular industry at a particular time. We cannot answer the question of who introduced "the new mode of production" to Japan with clichés, for then it is possible to get bogged down in attempts to find out who or which class was really "bourgeois" in Meiji Japan. The whole bourgeois or not-bourgeois problem must be left aside for a while so that we may start fresh, without looking all the time for Western prototypes.

Despite this rejection of a pat class model, my first three chapters will deal with the economic and entrepreneurial function of the three groups that occupied key positions in the process of growth prior to the Meiji Restoration and afterward. At the same time, these chapters are intended to provide general background information on the economic and social conditions of the period. The third and fourth chapters examine the all-important initiative and help that came from the center, as well as the need for and the emergence of private pioneering and independent entrepreneurship. ("Center" stands here for government in the broadest sense: it includes direct investments as well as policies, political pressures as well as official and semi-official influence on popular attitudes; particularly significant is the influence of the Restoration itself.) The last two chapters provide numerous examples of the unique interrelationship between the center and the private sector. The ample biographical material also serves as a basis for a few generalizations on the prerequisites for the emergence of modern entrepreneurs in Meiji Japan. The choice of individual entrepreneurs has been made with considerable care to lend my conclusions as much general validity as possible.

A final word needs to be said on the use of the term entrepreneur throughout the book. I use it to denote all businessmen of the modern type who excelled in some way in the fields of industry, trade, or banking. The test is their actual contribution to the building of Japan's industrial economy. It may require no less ingenuity and daring to introduce imported methods of business or production into an economically backward country than it does to introduce the primary innovations into advanced countries. Thus, such a broad use of the term seems well justified even in the Schumpeterian sense.

I

THE MERCHANT CLASS

Feudal Japan shared many social and economic features with feudal Europe. There was an aristocracy whose power was based on the ownership of all land and which lived on taxes levied on the farming population. There was also a merchant class that collected in the castle towns (*jōka-machi*) of the feudal lords (*daimyō*).[1] In these castle towns the townsmen (*chōnin*) organized their trade by supplying the consumers in the towns and cities with the products of the primary producers and craftsmen in the villages. They developed guilds with objectives and characteristics similar to those of medieval Europe.[2] If things had gone according to the European model, the merchants eventually would have become an energetic and progressive element, introducing innovations and gradually spearheading a complete change of the social as well as the economic system.

But history did not run that way in Japan. The merchant class did not rise to the top and did not display the requisite leadership; instead it succumbed to the stagnating influences of tradition and to the rigidities of Tokugawa social policy.[3] In the early seventeenth century, just as the merchant class became crystallized, Japan's military dictators (*shōgun*) closed the country to foreign intercourse, and it remained protected from external influences for almost two hundred and fifty years. When the forced seclusion was terminated by Admiral Perry's arrival in 1853, the merchants were caught unprepared for the enormous task of bridging Japan's economic backwardness. The entrepreneurial task put before the Meiji industrialists required attitudes and capabilities that the merchants, by and large, were untrained for.

This should surprise no one. It is one thing to move ahead step by step, using previously acquired skills and experience as a foundation; it is quite another to face, all at once, a set of completely unknown variables. Entrepreneurs in a country that is a latecomer to industrialization have to tackle formidable problems, and business experience may not be the best answer. We know that in latecomer countries in Europe leadership in the pioneering of large modern enterprises fell to the banks and the state, since the traditional merchants or manufacturing groups lacked the necessary capital and experience. The greater the backwardness that has to be overcome, the greater will be the guidance and help required from the state; correspondingly, the wider will be the difference between the type of entrepreneur who can be expected to pioneer successfully in the private sector and the European prototype of the bourgeois merchant. At least, this is what the case of Japan would suggest. In the following section we shall see why and to what degree Japan's "bourgeoisie" remained committed to the past and why it failed to assume economic leadership in industrialization.

The Commitment to the Past

The Guild System

The guilds in England, and even in France and Germany, had lost their importance and power before they were finally dissolved officially. New products and new methods of manufacturing sprang up which did not fit into the traditional guild structure and therefore could not be regulated by the guilds. The new spirit of liberalism and a revolutionary critique of the established political and social hierarchy undermined the strength of the guilds from within. In Japan, at least in the cities, the guilds were not eroded by economic changes or undermined by a liberal ideology; they continued a relatively vigorous existence until the Meiji Restoration. The essential character of the guilds was the same as that of their counterparts in medieval Europe: they exercised regulatory functions with regard to the prices and quality of goods, and guaranteed the stability of the market by restrictions on membership and on output or sales per enterprise. Finally, they were social groups which protected the interests of the group and gave the individual a place in society. The guilds exercised a stabilizing influence on economic and social relations, and in this respect they were welcomed and protected by the shogun's government (*bakufu*).

Throughout the two hundred and fifty years of its existence, the bakufu's overriding objective was to keep the country at peace and all social groups in obedience and contentment. Japan was to remain like the dream castle in the Sleeping Beauty tale, ever unchanged and undisturbed by the evil influence of the Western "barbarians." Actual changes in economic conditions were ignored, and the classes remained forcibly frozen in their seventeenth-century molds. The guild system was not only tolerated but was promoted as one of the best expedients to keep the merchants under control and to preserve their conservative attitudes. The bakufu even sold guild charters and monopoly rights for hard cash, which was but one of its many ways of extorting money from the prosperous merchants.

The bakufu did not mind the merchants' becoming rich

through monopolies, so long as it could benefit from those riches. By the beginning of the nineteenth century, the guild merchants had succeeded in accumulating great wealth simply by relying on their chartered rights and their exclusive trading privileges; they had offered almost nothing in the way of innovations or productive contributions. But they had also earned the hostility of the hard-pressed samurai (the military class) and of the peasant population. A series of natural disasters and famines in the 1830s caused large-scale peasant uprisings and general social unrest, which was directed mainly against the merchants. The bakufu gave way to pressures and abolished the guild system in 1841–42, after it had tried in vain to make the merchants lower their high prices. But the cure turned out to be worse than the disease. Abolition of the controlling guilds was followed by chaos in the business world, with adventurous business undertakings, rampant speculation, and frequent bankruptcies. The bakufu was forced to reintroduce the guilds in 1851, and they lasted from then until their second and final abolition in 1872. Decrees against monopolistic practices and restrictions on membership were issued repeatedly, but without noticeable effect.[4] Yet from 1851 on there existed merchants outside the guild system, and their numbers increased rapidly after the opening of Japan's ports in 1858.

The opening of the ports to foreign trade, which was enforced by the Western powers, introduced a wedge into the protective guild system. The port cities attracted new men from all strata of society, men with daring and imagination, adventurers and moneymakers who cared little about rules and traditions. Former samurai without a coin in their pockets or seasoned rural manufacturers would start a business in Edo or Yokohama, fascinated by the prospects of trade with the barbarians.[5] Leading entre-

preneurs like Asano Sōichirō, Yasuda Zenjirō, Ōkura Kihachirō, and Amamiya Keijirō started their careers in Yokohama.

The guild merchants suffered heavy losses through these
new adventurer-merchants of the port cities because the
latter would buy their supplies directly from the producers
without following the usual route from local wholesaler
to city wholesaler, then again to local wholesaler, and
finally to the retailer. In their distress the guild merchants
of Edo appealed to the bakufu, which decreed that a number of export goods must be moved to Yokohama via the
Edo wholesalers, notably raw silk, seaweed, oil, wax, and
fats.[6] This decree was also aimed at the control of exports
and at price stabilization. In the last decade of the Tokugawa period, then, the guilds did break down in practice
before they were officially abolished by the Meiji government. But they had been able to exercise a determining
influence on the nature of the merchant class until ex-
terior forces destroyed the protective system.

The support accorded the guilds by the bakufu, however,
only partly explains their long, unchallenged continuance.
We may well ask why economic opportunities arising outside of the rigid system did not weaken the guilds much
earlier, as they did in most European countries. If the re-
strictive and conservative character of the guilds blocked
the emergence of vigorous entrepreneurship, why did not
a counterwave of entrepreneurial innovations shatter the
confining chains of an ancient, clearly outdated system?
The answer to this question reveals some of the marked
differences between Japan's economic development and
that of the advanced Western countries. It also brings into
relief the salient features of the Meiji entrepreneurs, who
emerged only by breaking radically with business traditions. Entrepreneurs are, to be sure, innovators by defini-

tion, and therefore also "new men"; but we usually visualize them as building at least in part on the experiences and traditions of the existing business leadership. In Japan entrepreneurship emerged through an emphatic break with all that might have constituted such a line of continuity. Because the economic and the ideological situation within the merchant class was hostile to change, the guilds were able to continue and any major innovational drive was stifled. What were the conditions primarily responsible for the stagnation of the entrepreneurial spirit among the bourgeoisie of Tokugawa Japan?

Osaka: The City of Wealth

The heavy stress on capital availability as a necessary condition for economic development tends at times to obscure the other requirement — that potential investment capital must become available to men who are able and willing to initiate productive investments. The mere concentration of wealth in terms of gold, banknotes, or debt holdings in the hands of a certain economic group may not in itself set economic development in motion, since such claims against national income can be used in a variety of ways: they may be hoarded, squandered in luxury consumption, reinvested in traditional trading, or lent out as consumer loans. None of these uses of capital is conducive to economic growth. As long as such avenues of unproductive investment remain attractive, merchant wealth may not become available for real capital formation. It is therefore necessary that productive investments become more attractive; where the difference in profit rates between productive and unproductive uses of wealth does not become convincingly large, other strong inducements in terms of prestige or power may be needed in order to channel wealth into capital formation.

The merchants of the big Japanese cities, where the nation's wealth was centered over the Tokugawa period, generally preferred to invest unproductively in trade and in consumer loans, and they conspicuously shunned the risks of innovations. There were exceptions — merchants who invested heavily in land reclamation and in rural manufacturing. But the tendency was to stick to the easy and well-trod path of monopoly trade and consumer lending. How did the accumulation of wealth take place, and what proportions did it assume?

At the turn of the seventeenth century, the merchants became the beneficiaries of the separation of the large samurai population from its rural base and its concentration in the castle towns.[7] Trade relations between town and village necessitated the spread of money, and with it came possibilities to make profits. The merchants knew how to handle money and how to use it for the spread of luxury consumption. The monetization of the economy thus moved the economic power away from the feudal class (daimyo and samurai) over to the growing merchant class. Contemporary writers warned against this trend, as the following passage shows:

Because everyone from the greatest feudal lords down to the lowest samurai uses money, the merchants make huge profits. In prosperity they far outstrip the samurai class, and enjoy far more conveniences and amenities of life. Without moving an inch, they supply the necessities to all provinces, they act as official agents of the ruling classes down to the lowest samurai, changing money, handling rice and all other products, even military equipment, as well as providing facilities for travel, horses and trappings, etc., and merchants are indispensable for any kind of ceremony.[8]

But the trend toward urbanization, and with it the great opportunities for the merchant class, could not be stopped by such critics.

Three cities became consumer centers: first there was Kyoto, the emperor's seat; then Edo, the shogun's administrative capital; and finally Osaka, a city of trade and commerce. Edo grew rapidly from a small town into the world's largest city by the beginning of the nineteenth century, with a population of between 500,000 and a million.[9] About half of its population were samurai attached to the daimyo residences,[10] and the other half were merchants. Osaka came next in size after Edo, with a population of some 350,000 at the outset of the nineteenth century.[11] At the shogun's court in Edo the daimyo and the samurai vied with each other in displaying their importance through pomp and extravagances. This was all to the benefit of the merchants, who throve on luxury trades. The merchants of Edo themselves started to dissipate their easy profits, and they became proverbial for their amusements and gay life.

Osaka was different. It was a city of merchants with few samurai, and there the merchants developed an almost puritanical sense of thrift. Osaka became the main supply center, storehouse, and trading entrepot for the whole country. The city's favorable position on the shore of the Inland Sea gave it a unique advantage as a wholesale center; rice and other staples were transported by ship from all parts of the country to Osaka's storehouses, and from there they were channeled to the main consumer centers, notably Edo and Kyoto. Wholesale trade was the mainstay of the Osaka business world.

In 1715 Osaka had no less than 5,655 wholesale establishments (tonya).[12] Among the various wholesaler groups the Twenty-Four Wholesalers Union gained national fame and through its financial power dominated the Osaka business world. Along with trade came finance, the second pillar of Osaka's economic strength. Toward the close of

the Tokugawa period, popular opinion had it that about
70 percent of the nation's wealth was concentrated in the
hands of the Osaka merchants and financiers.

Osaka gained unchallenged leadership as a financial
metropolis during the Tokugawa period because of the
close relationship between wholesale trade and banking
that developed out of the monetary confusion of the time.
There was a bewildering variety of paper and coin money
in existence: the bakufu had its own gold, silver, and
copper coins, and so did the various han. The printing
of paper money and the debasement of currency added to
the confusion and made long-distance trade extremely
difficult.[13] This is why the merchants welcomed the services of specialized money exchanges (ryōgaeya) which
would reliably and expertly exchange one type of coin
for another. These money exchanges came also to serve
as clearing houses in large business transactions and as
deposit banks. Finally, they issued their own notes, which
circulated like money in the cities and even throughout
the whole country, like present-day bank notes. It is said
that the notes of the very large money exchanges enjoyed
higher prestige and confidence than the official government
money. For one thing, the wealth of the leading exchanges
seemed to provide perfect security and, for another, the
bakufu was always ready to back up the money exchanges
by prosecuting, with top priority in the courts, any case
of counterfeiting.[14] Among the 1,340 money exchanges
that existed in Osaka around 1850, the top group of Ten
Money Exchanges had the best reputation. Its services were
requested for official transactions by the government or
the han; it enjoyed such privileges as tax exemption; and
its notes circulated throughout the country.[15]

The high degree of liquidity and confidence among the
Osaka financial institutions had its effect on the interest

rates in that city. When the rates in the rest of the country varied between 10 and 15 percent, the large merchants and money exchanges of Osaka kept them as low as 5–6 percent.[16] The bakufu knew well that it should accord protection and favors to the Osaka merchant princes and financial magnates. Whenever the bakufu's coffers became depleted, it sought of these men forced loans (goyōkin) and special "donations" (myōgakin), and obliged them to buy up rice for the sake of price stabilization. A few examples will illustrate the magnitude of these various forms of taxation, which in themselves are a measure of the wealth of the Osaka financiers.

When the price of rice dropped to rock bottom in 1806 and threatened to cause unrest and misfortune among farmers and samurai, the bakufu ordered 318 Osaka merchants to purchase and store up over 1.2 million koku of rice (one koku equals 4.96 bushels). On that occasion the house of Kōnoike was forced to buy no less than 73,000 koku.[17]

In 1843 a large forced loan was demanded from a group of Osaka merchants, amounting to 1.14 million ryo, which corresponds to about 1.14 million koku of rice, or the sustenance of over a million people for one year.[18] Although such levies were imposed on the merchants of other cities too, Osaka always bore the heaviest burden. The curious fact is that many wealthy merchants or money exchangers actually became embarrassed if their portion of the levy was too small relative to their importance. These widely publicized contributions to the government were viewed by the merchants as the best advertisements of their financial soundness and of public confidence in them.[19]

The accumulation of so much wealth among the top echelons of the Osaka financiers and merchants might lead one to expect that these same groups would have initiated economic advances and social change. But the truth is that we find no major efforts among this city bourgoisie to break the constraints of the feudal economic system, one which had assigned them the lowest rank in society. Instead of becoming strongly antifeudal, the city merchant class tended to become even more conservative toward the end of the Tokugawa period.

At the beginning of the seventeenth century, the bakufu had divided the population into four classes: samurai, peasants, artisans, and merchants (*shi, nō, kō, shō*).[20] The rigidity of this status division was enforced by various devices and was given an ethical sanction through the Confucian doctrines on social relations. These were promoted by the bakufu and became something like an official ethic of Japanese feudal society. In the West in the Middle Ages, the merchants had also stood at the bottom of society, but they eventually succeeded in acquiring not only wealth but also prestige and a liberal outlook. In Japan a number of factors combined to prevent such a development, among them the seclusion of the country from foreign influences and the impossibility of engaging in foreign trade. Another factor was the control system devised and operated by the bakufu, with its detailed prescriptions governing all aspects of living, down to food and clothing, for the various classes of society. In spite of shifting economic power, social positions had to remain unchanged and they had to retain their basic characteristics and external appearance. Frequent decrees proscribed luxury among the merchants and tried — apparently in vain — to force upon them frugality and simplicity, as befitting the lowest social class.

With the help of the feudal class, the bakufu did succeed in denying the merchants access to a social position commensurate with their economic strength. Money was power, power over the samurai and the daimyo, but money remained something "dirty," and the merchant class in Tokugawa Japan could not rid itself of the stigma of social inferiority. Consequently, the merchants were most attracted by any kind of activity or investment that might open the way to social recognition and even to the ranks of the feudal class itself. Two avenues of escape presented themselves to the rich merchants and financiers: lending money to the daimyo and samurai, and land reclamation. I shall now examine the lending activities, leaving land reclamation until Chapter Three.

Lending to the Daimyo

One of Osaka's chief sources of revenue was the management of warehouses and trade transactions connected with warehouse goods. The warehouses were usually owned by merchants, but many were rented out to daimyo who wanted to store their han products, especially rice, in Osaka either for sale in the market there or for shipment to Edo. These daimyo warehouses (*kurayashiki*) were like extraterritorial castles of the han, and samurai were placed in charge of them. The number of warehouses in Osaka kept increasing, from 25 in the 1760s to 125 in the 1830s. By the beginning of the nineteenth century, an annual average of some 3 million koku of rice, or 10 percent of the total rice production of Japan, thus came into the Osaka warehouses as daimyo rice and wholesale rice.[21]

The merchants who handled the business transactions of the daimyo warehouses (*kuramoto*), and the merchants who acted as financial agents of the daimyo (*kakeya*), came into a quasi-retainer relationship to the daimyo. Such merchants not only reaped handsome profits from their monopolistic business deals with the warehouses, but they frequently were accorded special honors and privileges: they might, like samurai, receive rice stipends and be permitted to assume family names and carry swords similar to those of samurai (this was called the *myōji taitō* privilege).[22] Family names and swords were highly coveted by the merchants, as titles of nobility had been by the European bourgeoisie.

The *kakeya* had to extend loans to the daimyo on request. The interest rates charged were usually lower than those prevailing on the market; sometimes, instead of interest, a new right or privilege was granted. Repayment of the loans was usually assured — so long as the daimyo was solvent — by the particular economic hold that the merchants had over their daimyo creditors. If a merchant sensed a danger of default, he might confiscate and sell the warehouse goods. Nevertheless, cases of default increased considerably toward the end of the Tokugawa, when the han economies were in trouble. Occasionally, when the daimyo and samurai were in great distress, the bakufu decreed total abolition of samurai and daimyo debts to merchants; the merchants countered this danger by lending under the name of some temple, since temple debts could not be nullified. Despite the insecurity involved in daimyo loans, the advantages seem to have remained great enough to induce an ever-growing involvement of the Osaka merchants in feudal lending.

The House of Kōnoike is typical of such a development. Starting as peddlers and sake brewers in the rural districts, the Kōnoike family extended its trading activities throughout the country and became one of the wealthiest merchant families in Osaka. Gradually they concentrated on daimyo lending and turned away from pure trading. The Kōnoike records show that in 1670 credits to merchants constituted 59.3 percent of the total loans extended, against only 19 percent in daimyo loans. By 1706 the daimyo loans had risen to 65.8 percent, and by 1795 they were as high as 76.9 percent of the total loans extended.[23] Kōnoike at one time was involved with 32 daimyo and received stipends of 10,000 koku of rice, more than many a daimyo could boast of having. The interest rates on the Kōnoike loans to daimyo varied widely from as high as 8 percent a month on short-term loans to no interest at all on long-term loans that were to be repaid in installments over 10 or even 30 or 70 years. Of 338 loans negotiated by Kōnoike, 56 were interest-free.[24] On the whole, interest rates were low in comparison with the current rates of between 10 and 15 percent a year. It is therefore quite obvious that the chief attraction of daimyo lending lay in the honors, privileges, monopoly rights, and stipends that the daimyo extended to their creditors.

The negotiation of the loans was a constant source of annoyance to the feudal lords. The merchants were not always willing to grant the requested loans; they haggled and often split the total loan among each other. The daimyo had to send their highest samurai administrators to negotiate a loan, and these agents had to treat the *chōnin* to elaborate geisha parties and make deep bows to them before they would consent to the loan. Such humiliation of samurai by *chōnin* drew criticism from writers of the time, but this had little effect on the merchants themselves.[25]

Whereas daimyo lending was considered a safe investment in the earlier part of the Tokugawa period, it became risky toward the close of the eighteenth century, when the han economies were pushed to the wall and when defaults or cancellations of outstanding loans by the bakufu often occurred. Some sober Osaka financiers warned against involvements in daimyo lending, but the extramonetary considerations of economic power over the feudal lords, acquisition of a family name and the sword, continued to attract a large stream of capital into further consumer lending.[26] By the time of the Restoration, the House of Kashimaya of Osaka had some 9 million ryo in outstanding loans with daimyo and samurai; [27] and the entire economy of Sendai han is said to have been controlled in this way by the House of Masuya of Osaka.[28]

The merchants, by extending loans to the feudal leaders, not only gained a strong hold on the oppressive and over-bearing warrior class; in the end, many a merchant suc-ceeded in entering the samurai class through his creditor position. Numerous samurai sold their status privileges to merchants when they were unable to pay the interest on their heavy debts, or they adopted merchant children and obliged the merchant father thus honored to bail them out. Actually, samurai positions had something like estab-lished prices in the last decades before the Restoration — 50 ryo for the adoption of a commoner's son into samurai rank of 100 koku of (nominal) rice stipend.[29]

It may be entirely possible to conclude that the mer-chants had little vested interest in the abolition of the feudal system. Indeed, when feudalism was abolished, and with it most of the daimyo and samurai debts, many credi-tor merchants were ruined. A good deal of the merchants' passivity toward the Restoration movement,[30] and their outright hostility to the modernization policies of the Meiji government, can probably be explained by the peculiar financial and trade relations that existed between the mer-chant and the feudal class. Economically the merchants did not stand to gain much from a change which they were not prepared for and did not understand.

The Ideology of the City Bourgeoisie

European capitalist development received a vital stimu-lus from an economic ideology which Max Weber has associated with the Protestant ethic. Whether or not the Protestant ethic was the real cause of the change, there can be no doubt that this new capitalist spirit gave a tremendous impetus to economic development. Without the scientific and rational approach to economic problems which Rostow calls post-Newtonian thinking, Western capitalism as we know it would have been unthinkable.

It has been suggested that the development of a spirit of capitalism, of economic rationality, and of a "sensate" value system should be viewed as a universally valid condition for effective economic development in any country.[31] It is therefore meaningful to ask if a similar break-up of feudalism and of traditional values and thinking patterns occurred in Japan before the Meiji Restoration, and, if so, who was responsible. If things had gone according to the Western model, it would have been the city merchant class, the bourgeoisie, that championed a liberal and individualist economic rationality. However, the official Tokugawa Confucian ideology retained a very strong hold on all of Japanese society because of its strict political enforcement and because Japan lacked direct contact with foreign countries. Confucian philosophy decreed that the hierarchical structure of society was unchangeable, God-given, the expression of a divine plan.

Filial piety and adherence to the wisdom of the ages were embodied in the sacred traditions, and to break with tradition was an offense against these two highest virtues of the Confucian ethical code. Loyalty found its loftiest expression in the relation between feudal lord and retainer, daimyo and samurai; but ties of loyalty pervaded the whole of Japanese society and gave unique social coherence to the nation even when it was torn by civil warfare. Finally, the institution of the imperial throne gave a sense of family fealty to the nation: although many of the emperors were obscure and insignificant persons, they were symbols of authority, embodying a line of tradition down from the gods.

Loyalty to one's class and profession and adherence to tradition were sanctioned by the fixed division of society into the four classes of samurai, peasant, artisan, and merchant. Peasants were associated in groups of five families (*gonin-gumi*) which were responsible for one another. The guilds similarly united the merchant class, strengthening loyalties to class and tradition. To fulfill one's duty as a merchant meant to discharge one's obligation to the whole of society; this justified the protection and the other benefits that one received in the feudal scheme.[32] Within the individual merchant enterprise, loyalty found eloquent expression vertically in the *oyakata–kogata* (parent–child) relation through which the master commanded absolute respect among clerks and apprentices. The *oyakata* not only exercised his leadership in business matters, but remained a person of authority for life: the former clerk made courtesy calls on him, assisted him in times of need, and gave him respectful precedence even in social and family affairs.[33]

The master in the enterprise was also the living embodiment of ancestral wisdom. Confucian precepts demanded that the teachings of the ancestors, and hence of the head of an enterprise or family, never be questioned. Rational criticism and the introduction of new ideas were out of place. To say that a merchant had deviated from the practices of his ancestors and "innovated" was to cast an aspersion upon his honor. The Mitsui family rules contained the following prohibition: "Do not put your hand to any type of activity that has not been done before." [34] The rules of many other merchant houses included similar statements. According to merchant ideology, all things were to remain unchanged.

Honesty and business ethics within the guilds were a

direct outgrowth of feudal class consciousness and group spirit. In loyalty to his group and to his inherited store, the merchant had to keep his good name. If the merchants were socially the lowest and most despised group in Tokugawa Japan, they nevertheless found self-respect in the big cities — in Osaka, for example, they were "honorable townsmen" (o-chōnin-san). They made a point of being absolutely honest with one another and of fulfilling contracts whether or not they were put in writing. Among often-quoted principles governing merchant behavior, we find strong exhortations to honesty: "It is on the straight road that the god of happiness comes; evil and dishonest ways are shortcuts to hell." [35] A merchant had to keep the name of his store (kanban and noren) [36] undefiled as an obligation to the guild and to his ancestors. How strong this sense of obligation to the past was can be gleaned from the fact that members of the old merchant houses that had been located in Osaka for centuries still put their rural place of origin on official documents as late as 1868.[37]

The merchants' group consciousness created a double standard: honesty toward the fellow merchant, notably of the same guild, and unscrupulous exploitation of the outsider. According to contemporary critics, the merchants had no scruples about cheating outsiders and charging them arbitrary prices. Thus, to many the merchants were known for their cheating and dishonesty. None of this could fail to discourage public confidence in tradesmen and commercial activity. And this in turn hampered business growth.

The remarkable fact about the Tokugawa bourgeoisie was that it perpetrated the kind of stifling atmosphere that effectively prevented the rise of energetic innovators. Even the great houses of Kōnoike, Mitsui, Sumitomo, and Hirano, which had entered the merchant class from the ranks of the samurai before the four classes had been frozen, produced no outstanding business leaders in the two centuries before the Restoration. The great enterprisers who built up the fame of these houses lived in the early part of the Tokugawa.[38]

Emphasis on practical business training and an avowed aversion to book learning became additional deterrents to entrepreneurship in the merchant class. It was mainly through books that Western ideas and industrial technology were introduced into Japan before the Restoration and during its first decade. Entrepreneurship required not only an understanding of a single technique, but a grasp of the whole idea of industrial production, of a new economic organization for Japan. Recognition of this need required a level of education and intelligence for which the routine activities in the merchant stores were poor preparation.

The merchants scorned book learning not only as useless but as downright harmful. A man who engaged in scholarship was regarded as playing with bankruptcy. There was nothing about business to be learned from books; all was laid down by tradition. Thrift, calculation, and business talent (shimatsu, sanyō, saikaku) received paramount attention. Thrift was the fundamental virtue, as indicated by these rules for merchants: "simplicity and thrift are the ground on which house and barn are built"; "luxury and splendor prepare the banquet for the god of poverty." [39] To invest savings profitably and to calculate profits, the merchant had to know how to use his abacus: "consider the abacus as your only child and embrace it even in your sleep." [40] Business talent, of utmost importance for entrepreneurial activity, did not go much beyond a clever handling of customers, shrewdness, and politeness. "Do not quarrel with anyone, no matter what a man may say; do not lose your temper or use harsh words, but address him always in polite terms." [41] This sentence from the Sumitomo house rules may perhaps be considered typical. Careful study and loyal observance of all inherited rules and practices was the "way of the merchant"; learning and theoretical education were for the samurai. Scholars were given lip service but were actually regarded as "hungry gods." When a few entrepreneurs after the Restoration built schools for business and industrial education, the merchants laughed at the whole idea. [42]

It cannot be denied that Osaka had its own Confucian scholars and that they did find interested students among the merchants. In 1725 a group of five wealthy merchants built the Kaitoku Dō, the largest private school in Japan, and invited the famous Confucian scholar Miyake Sekian to teach there. [43] Many merchants did achieve a high level of education in the late Tokugawa period. They were often criticized for indulging in such luxuries as private teachers for their children. But education was not their status symbol; on the contrary, they sought education in emulation of the feudal class, to gain self-respect. Learning remained essentially unconnected with business practices; it had no direct bearing on day-to-day commercial activities, which remained pointedly tradition-bound.

The *shingaku* philosophy represented a major effort to better the education and raise the social standing and self-esteem of the merchants. Originating in the first half of the eighteenth century, its first purpose was to rehabilitate the merchants' ethics after a time of luxury and dissipation in the preceding Genroku period (1688–1703). [44] It had been customary for Confucian scholars to deride the merchants' activities and call them parasites because they made profits out of others' toil. [45] The scholars could not grasp the idea that selling was a service and that a samurai in Edo could not live on the rice that a peasant in northern Japan kept in his barn. Japanese Confucian scholars were not unique in regarding commercial transactions as exploitation; the scholars of medieval Europe thought in quite the same way and attached a moral stigma to buying and selling. In a stationary feudal society based on agricultural self-sufficiency, merchants were a disruptive element and the objects of suspicion; the elite of society defended its position with the only weapon that was left — contempt. But the *shingaku* philosophers proclaimed that the merchants' profit was as much a reward for service to society as was the samurai's stipend. They even turned the tables and called the aristocracy merchants: "To sell rice is nothing more or less than a commercial transaction. It may therefore be said that all the people, from the feudal lords of the great provinces down, are in a sense engaged in commerce. . . . Commerce is absolutely indispensable in daily life, hence it is wrong to despise money or hold commerce in contempt. There is nothing shameful about selling things. What is shameful is the conduct of men who fail to pay their debts to merchants." [46]

For a while the *shingaku* philosophy seemed to initiate liberal thinking and to inspire something akin to the Western spirit of capitalism. It did enhance the self-respect of the city bourgeoisie, but it was no match for the deeply ingrained Confucian traditionalism. Even at its best the *shingaku* movement did not go beyond the confines of status concepts. Ishida Baigan equated the "way" of the samurai and the "way" of the merchant by insisting that in either class the degree of fulfillment of one's divinely predetermined obligations decided a man's worth. In effect the *shingaku* was nothing but an adjustment in Confucian thinking designed to incorporate the merchant class into the feudal framework, to make it follow with closer steps,

albeit with more pride, the beaten path of tradition. Filial
piety, honesty, loyalty, were its central themes; loyalty
meant faithfulness to tradition and to the ancestors; thus
loyalty and filial piety had a common base.[47] With the beginning of the nineteenth century, the bakufu used the
shingaku schools to inculcate its own political doctrines
and to teach the merchants their duties to the central government. Even the central objective of the *shingaku* movement, to establish the view of business activity as a service
to society, was not achieved. The leading entrepreneurs of
the Meiji era still found it necessary to proclaim that their
activities had no connection with the profit making of the
merchants of old.

The Merchants after the Restoration

General Reactions

The Meiji Restoration of 1867 was the important step
toward the modernization of Japanese society and toward
the building of large-scale industry.[48] But the opening of
Japan to foreign trade had preceded the Restoration by fifteen years and had already stimulated efforts by the bakufu,
and by some daimyo, to push ahead with various modernization programs. Moreover, prior to 1867 it had been the
bakufu that had pursued a policy of intercourse with foreign nations, forced by the ominous presence of American,
British, and French warships. The sharp turn of the Meiji
government toward the West could not have been clearly
anticipated by the people prior to 1868, because the slogan
of the antibakufu forces prior to the Restoration had been
"restore the emperor; expel the barbarians." It would be
a mistake to think that those who fought against the bakufu
in the Restoration movement were all progressives favoring the opening of the country and the modernization of

the economy. On the contrary, many of the most vocal elements within the Restoration movement were intransigent reactionaries.

As far as the merchants and the people were concerned, there was no way to resolve the contradictions that arose from loyalties to the established government and loyalties to the emperor, from han rivalries and hatred for the barbarians, and it was even more difficult to perceive constructive plans for reform. A collection of letters written by merchants in the years of the Restoration struggle reflects the perplexity and confusion that prevailed among the people. The merchants sensed that the old peace and security were crumbling, but they could not see the new horizons. They prayed for peace and order, and placed the increasing hostilities in the same category as previous peasant or samurai revolts or as natural disasters from which the gods should save them.[49]

Attempts have been made to assess the merchants' attitudes as progressive or conservative on the basis of their financial contributions to the bakufu or to the Restoration party prior to its final victory. But we know too little about the motivation behind those more or less forced contributions. Most contributions were undoubtedly made under pressure, out of former han loyalties, or because of previously established creditor connections. The Osaka merchants had become accustomed to heavy forced loans to the bakufu in times of emergency. Since Osaka was bakufu territory, it was quite natural that most merchant contributions went, at least initially, to the support of the bakufu army. The House of Mitsui, which had its stores in Osaka, Kyoto, and Edo, did make a genuine decision in favor of the Restoration party, but this decision resulted almost exclusively from the political acumen of Mitsui's head clerk, Minomura Rizaemon, and his personal friendship with Inoue Kaoru, one of the leaders of the Restoration party.[50]

The first few years following the victory of the Restoration party proved disastrous for the merchants of the cities, particularly in Osaka. They had suffered greatly from the opening of the ports and the rise of the new merchants; heavy taxes and forced loans had been demanded of them for the armies of both sides. After the Meiji government was established, the guilds were dissolved and the daimyo warehouses disappeared with the abolition of the han system. (The han were abolished in 1871 and the country divided into prefectures, in order to facilitate central control over the country.) Osaka's local silver coins were abolished when the national gold standard was established. Finally, the large daimyo debts were almost completely nullified: debts contracted by the han prior to 1843 were abolished; debts originating between 1844 and 1867 were to be repaid by the government within fifty years at no interest; and han debts contracted after the Restoration and before 1871 were to be repaid within twenty-five years at 4 percent interest. All this spelled ruin for the financiers and merchants of the cities. In Osaka twenty-six of the old established merchant houses collapsed in the early years after the Restoration.[51]

After the abolition of the guild system in 1872, the merchants and the money exchangers were very much at sea. They were told to compete, to start foreign trade, and not to band together for group security. But they were not used to competing; they had been brought up in a world of stability and order, where each merchant was assured his livelihood and his profits. The merchants' habits of mind were still worlds away from assuming a belief in a "harmony of interests" and an "invisible hand" that would make competition mutually beneficial. Normally they were peace-loving people, and now business was supposed to be a fight (*kyōsō*, the newly adopted word for competition, means "running and fighting"). Suddenly insecurity was to be the basic principle and struggle the means to survival, a situation that could not be expected to spark much enthusiasm among the former guild merchants.

After the abolition of the guilds, the government tried to establish a new company system. Apparently most of the small shopkeepers, and even managers of merchant enterprises of all sorts, had not the vaguest idea of what this meant. They understood little more than that from now on their stores were to be called "companies"; there was nothing simpler than to change the *kanban* from *dō* or *ya* (store) to *kaisha* (company). A "company-foundation boom" swept the cities, especially Tokyo and Kyoto, but little is known of the actual details. Each company had to secure a charter, which gave it official backing and increased prestige. In Kyoto some three hundred companies were chartered in the first few years following the Restoration, but they simply continued trade as before, dealing in cotton, salt, copper, and similar articles. These companies banded together, as they had under the guild system, and in 1871 the Kyoto city administration dissolved them all because of their monopolistic policies.[52] Among forty applications for company charters in Tokyo in 1873, we find such names as Roadsweepers' Company, Singing Girls Managing Company, Translating Company, Beef Trading Company, Carrot Company, Umbrella Company.[53] The applications apparently became so numerous and nonsensical that the city administration asked the Ministry of the Interior whether all must go through the cumbersome chartering procedure or whether masseurs, fortunetellers, and the like could be left to call themselves "company" without application.[54]

At the same time, the merchants made a strong effort to reintroduce some guildlike organization in order to stop the confusion, and this resulted in the establishment of *kumiai* (unions). Business morale was sinking to a new low, if we are to believe the assertions of Shibusawa Eiichi, an entrepreneur of the new type. Shibusawa complained of the dangerous abuse of trade names, especially in the sale of foodstuffs and medicines.[55] He wrote about the attitudes of the older merchants, exaggerating drastically in order to drive home the point that there was a difference between new "entrepreneurs" like himself and the merchants: "The merchants of the time [early Meiji] were men who had almost no feeling for things like rules and written regulations. Furthermore, it seemed as if the officials of the Meiji government and the merchants of Tokyo, Osaka, and Kyoto were men of an entirely different kind. One had only to look at their faces to recognize that they were almost like beings of a different species. It was only too clear that this work [economic modernization] could not be carried out with such people [the merchants]." [56]

The Drafting of Merchant Capital

Immediately after the Restoration, the government faced a pressing need to establish trading and banking facilities that could cope effectively with foreign trade. The Japanese were perplexed and disturbed by the fact that in the port cities the initiative was left entirely to foreigners. As late as 1874, Japan's foreign trade was conducted by foreign companies for 99.97 percent of her imports and 99.45 percent of her exports.[57] Specie was flowing out at a rapid rate, and the balance of trade moved increasingly against Japan. The experienced merchants with capital showed little desire to take risks in direct dealings with foreigners; and the adventurer-merchants who thrived in Yokohama,

Nagasaki, and Hyogo (Kobe) lacked the necessary experience and capital. When the government established an official exchange market in Yokohama, it summoned Osaka men to teach the Yokohama merchants the rudiments of the exchange business. It did the same in Hyogo, for the new merchants had "nothing but courage." [58] The British consul wrote in a report of 1869 on the passivity of the Osaka merchants: "Few of the wealthier native merchants have turned their attention to foreign trade: indeed, this class of the people in Osaka is the last to recognize any benefit in foreign relations. They do a good business among themselves by advancing money on produce, and trading in other ways; and their fear seems to be that foreign merchants will deprive them of a portion of the profits that have hitherto accrued to themselves alone." [59]

Actually, the Meiji government expected much of Osaka as a port city (it was opened to trade in 1868). Osaka was to become the center of foreign trade as it had been the commercial metropolis in the Tokugawa period. Some officials even suggested making Osaka the administrative capital instead of Edo because of the city's economic strength. Ōkubo Toshimichi [60] and others expected that Osaka would become the nation's center of trade and modern industry.[61] In 1868 the government set up a trading center in Osaka that was to operate with official inconvertible notes; the notes were to be loaned out to han trading companies and official han merchants. This scheme would have been a repetition of what the individual han were already doing, but now under the auspices of and coordinated by the new Restoration government. The scheme failed because the han did not trust the government paper money which they were supposed to repay with specie.

A more ambitious trading operation was started in 1869 under the auspices of the Ministry of Transportation and

Trade (Tsūshōshi).[62] This time reliance was to be placed on private initiative among the merchants. In eight key cities, exchange companies were set up to finance this large foreign-trade drive. Associated with these finance companies were trading companies that were to direct, assist, and finance the operations of many subordinate trading enterprises in company form. According to a survey of 1872,[63] the exchange company of Tokyo had a total share-capital of 948,500 ryo, that of Osaka 197,800 ryo, and that of Kyoto 238,500 ryo. The main participants were the rich merchant houses, chief among them Mitsui, Ono, and Shimada, which had become the official government financiers in the first years of the Meiji. Mitsui paid up 145,000 ryo, Ono 135,000 ryo, and Shimada 90,000 ryo. How much capital the trading companies had is not known, but their composition was similar to that of the exchange companies.

The government used both the carrot and the stick to push through its foreign-trade program. The members of the trading companies received various privileges, among others that of borrowing from the exchange companies without security deposit and that of monopolizing the lucrative importation of rifles; the exchange companies had a monopoly on transporting and marketing the han products, former functions of the daimyo warehouse merchants.

Of special importance were the social distinctions granted to the presidents and main shareholders of the new companies. The presidents were given the privilege of the sword and family name. They were appointed by the government, as officials were. A president could walk directly into the room of a government official while common people had to wait and squat outside the building. Many other minor privileges were granted. Indeed, the government encouraged anyone who entered foreign trade. Yet for the most part the merchants remained unenthusiastic, and many of them participated in the scheme only under pressure. In Tokyo the government threatened noncooperating merchants with exile to Hokkaido.

There was much misunderstanding about the objectives of the trading and exchange companies. The merchants had received so many blows from the new policies and developments that they assumed a capital contribution to these companies to be nothing but a disguised goyōkin (forced loan). Katō Yukichi, a government official, tried to promote the new idea and wrote that one should not think it difficult to contribute to these companies: it would be like contributing to the building of a shrine or a temple. Shrines and temples were for the purpose of strengthening the faith and thus giving happiness to each individual; the trading companies would stimulate trade and thus earn immediate profits for everyone.[64] It is doubtful that this comparison had encouraging effects.

Eventually more than seventy trading subcompanies came into existence in Osaka. Most of them were not directly involved in foreign trade and were similar to the old establishments of the guild period in that they joined their stock only partially. The actual operations of the scheme are not of particular interest here. The strong government controls apparently discouraged free initiative and, at the same time, encouraged irresponsible action. The exchange companies initially printed bills without restrictions, and it was understood that the final guarantee, as well as the resulting losses, were to be carried by the government. Thus the shareholders were to take only the honors and the profits. After approximately two years, the entire scheme collapsed in bankruptcy for all but the Yokohama exchange company.

Once more the central government drafted merchant

capital and experience, this time to establish joint-stock banking in Japan. It was decided to establish national banks in an effort to introduce order into the confused monetary situation. Many kinds of debased coins were in circulation. Furthermore, the government, in the first year after the Restoration, had issued 32 million ryo of inconvertible notes as loans to daimyo, merchants, and wealthy peasants and later had paid the army with an additional 14 million ryo of such notes.[65] The depreciation of these inconvertible notes and, above all, strong protests from foreign consuls induced the government to set up a new system of national banks in 1872, on the American model; the banks were to deposit 60 percent of their share capital in inconvertible notes with the government and receive the same sum in bonds with 6 percent interest attached. These bonds were to be deposited with the government as security for the issue of bank notes. Forty percent of the capital was to be kept as reserve in specie.[66]

The government had received many applications for the establishment of private banks before 1872, but when the wealthy merchants were invited to establish joint-stock national banks, they were reluctant. The House of Shimada, one of the three official money agents of the Meiji government, flatly refused to cooperate, and it was only as a result of considerable pressure that Ono finally joined with Mitsui and other Tokyo merchants to set up the first national bank with a total of 2.44 million yen, of which 2 million came from Mitsui and Ono.[67] Three other national banks were established in a similar fashion: one was a direct continuation of the Yokohama exchange company; one was established in Niigata with a rich landowner as its principal spareholder; and one was founded by a group of nobles and samurai from Satsuma.

The merchants of Osaka and Kyoto did not establish national banks of their own, although an attempt was made by Kōnoike and ten other merchant houses of Osaka; they failed to reach an agreement and abandoned the project. Their application for a charter, however, is full of flowery phrases on the new era and the need for cooperation to build up the national economy:

As we live presently in the era of civilization and enlightenment we feel ashamed to follow the old foolish practices of each one considering nothing but his own profit. Now we have to be of one mind and unite for the building of a solid foundation of great enterprises. We have been cherishing already for some time the desire to shoulder our share, as far as our weakness permits, of the burden to promote the progress of civilization. When we consider, in all humility, the national banking act, we are overwhelmed with joy because of the unification of the system, the public as well as private advantages and the building of solid enterprises, that will result from that act. Instead of empty applause, however, we, enlightened by the banking act, shall immediately work for the establishment of a bank, and we hope to raise about 1.5 million yen in all. We shall, as always, observe strictly the rules of the banking act and never deviate from it.[68]

These phrases indicate sufficiently that the establishment of a bank was thought to be a burden and at variance with the "old foolish" profit-making idea. In spite of their assertions to the contrary, men who had been brought up with the abacus could not be expected to feel enthusiasm and to exercise entrepreneurial initiative.

Modern Industry in Osaka

Manufacturing had never been important in Osaka during the Tokugawa period. Merchant capital had flowed into cotton spinning and weaving and other domestic manufacturing in the rural areas, especially in the vicinity of

Osaka, but not in the city itself. There are records of only
a few minor manufacturing establishments in Osaka: sake
breweries, bleacheries, and establishments producing wax,
soy sauce, and soybean cheese (*tōfu*). In connection with
the economic reforms of the han induced by the pre-Restoration military threats and the impasse reached in the
daimyo economies, some modern enterprises had sprung up
in and around the city, such as the Sakai Spinning Mill,
founded by a Kagoshima samurai and financed by the
daimyo, or the Hōrai Company, which started modern
paper manufacturing, founded by Gotō Shōjirō, one of
the economic reformers of Tosa han.

A strong influence on the modernization and industrialization of Osaka was exerted by Godai Tomoatsu, a government official from Satsuma han who took up residence
in Osaka in 1868. He was not only a capable and energetic entrepreneur but a pioneer of the era of Civilization
and Enlightenment (*bummei kaika*), who had gathered information on the operation of modern industry during a
study trip to England before the Restoration. He initiated
the construction required to open the Osaka harbor to
ocean-going vessels and the building of residences for foreign consuls and trade representatives. When some of his
opponents succeeded in effecting his transfer to Yokohama,
he resigned his government post so that he might stay
in Osaka and help to make it a flourishing industrial city.[69]
Godai established a refinery in which he separated the
silver and gold content in coins bought up from the han
and then delivered the gold and silver to the government
mint, at considerable profit to himself. He achieved his
greatest success in mining, buying up and modernizing a
string of copper and silver mines. For the administration
of his growing mining empire, he erected a large office
building in Osaka, the Kōseikan, which, with its modern

methods and over two hundred employees, became one of the wonders of Osaka.[70] Godai's most outstanding pioneering enterprise was the building of an indigo factory with a government loan of 500,000 yen in 1876.

The government mint, established in Osaka in 1869, became the center and rallying place of all modern and progressive elements. The machines for the mint had been brought in from Hongkong. The bricks for the buildings also had to be imported, and the problem then arose of finding bricklayers, since nobody in Osaka had ever built a brick house. When the building was finished, after two years of construction, a grand banquet was given for which the cooks were brought from Yokohama and Kobe. The men employed at the mint had to wear Western dress and had to cut their hair short, as symbols of the new era.[71] Although its main purpose was to coin a standard currency that would be acceptable at home and abroad and would replace the debased coins still in circulation, the mint soon became involved in a whole string of associated enterprises.

In the process of refining copper, sulphur was obtained, and this the mint marketed. Since the mint had to use large quantities of fuel, it built a plant that produced coke and gas — the coke it used for fuel. The gas was used for lighting the mint buildings and the streets of Osaka; 65 lamps were put upon the streets and 621 in private houses, mostly the homes of officials and foreigners.[72] The mint initiated construction of a telegraph and a telephone line and a horsedrawn railway line that connected the important points of the city. A school for the children of mint employees and of other townsmen taught English and physics, and thus constituted another important modernizing factor in this city of tradition and practical training.[73] All of this happened rapidly, during the first few years after the Restoration, when the rest of the city was still very much weighed down in the slump of a depression.

It is typical of Osaka that, until about 1892, almost all the initiative in the building of modern industry came from outside — through direct government enterprise as in the case of the mint, through men from Tokyo or other places, and through foreigners. Westerners and Chinese were prominent as entrepreneurs in Osaka during the first fifteen years of the Meiji era. A steel factory with 240,000 yen capital, established in 1881, was planned by an American named Hunter, living in Kobe; he also supplied most of the capital, but was wise enough to make a Japanese the formal owner.[74] Some Chinese established a match factory which was also nominally owned by a Japanese. Fujita Denzaburō and Ōkura Kihachirō entered the Osaka industrial world from outside; each established a large tannery, in 1877 and 1879 respectively, and later they combined them into a single factory with over three hundred workers.[75] Fujita became one of the industrial leaders of Osaka in the second decade after the Restoration, together with Godai, Sumitomo's Hirose Saihei, Matsumoto Jūtarō, Nakano Goichi, and others.

One can, of course, exaggerate the point that outsiders were predominant in Osaka until the industrial breakthrough was achieved. A survey of 1886 showed that only forty of the more important businessmen in the city were natives; the majority of the leading men in all fields of business and industry were immigrants.[76] This survey included men like Hirose Saihei and Matsumoto Jūtarō as immigrants. But Hirose had been with the Sumitomo Besshi copper mine in Osaka since boyhood, and Matsumoto Jūtarō had been a merchant's apprentice in Osaka since he was thirteen. They were not born in Osaka, however, and perhaps had a somewhat different outlook for this reason, taking a certain pride in the fact that they were different men, progressive men. As mentioned earlier, Osaka's real swing toward industry came only in the 1890s, primarily in cotton spinning, and this was a result of the great success of the Osaka Spinning Mill, founded by another non-Osaka man, Shibusawa Eiichi.

In addition to those already mentioned, there were a few other large-scale enterprises in Osaka prior to the mid-1880s: the Osaka Copper Manufacturing Company, established by Hirose Saihei and Godai Tomoatsu in 1881 with a capital of 200,000 yen, foreign technicians, and imported machinery; a paper mill that struggled on close to bankruptcy for many years; the Osaka Printing Type Manufacturing Company (Ōsaka kappan seizō sho), established by a native of Osaka who had traveled to China to study printing processes and had been influenced by the pioneering work of Hirano Tomiji and Motoki Shōzō of Tokyo.[77] Shipbuilding was at first entirely in the hands of foreigners who either built new yards or were invited to take over and modernize existing yards. It was not until 1886 and 1891 that two large modern yards were built by Japanese in Osaka, who were inspired by the great success of Mitsubishi's Nagasaki shipyard.[78] Small workshops multiplied in the manufacturing of matches, leather, and soap. At one time there were forty-four workshops producing leather bags; by 1892 their number had increased to over one hundred.[79] Soap and match production came under the control of merchant capital, and Japan began to export these two articles as early as the 1880s.

If we compare the industrial development of the country as a whole during the first two decades of the Meiji era with that of Osaka, the former merchant metropolis, we find that Osaka lagged. In terms of industrial capital, only

10–12 percent was invested in Osaka between 1885 and 1890. In 1891–1892 the percentage rose to about 25; in 1895 it rose again to about 27 percent of the nation's total industrial capital investment.[80] The remarkable thing, however, is that at the same time that the percentage of Osaka's industrial capital relative to the rest of the country moved up from 10 to 25 percent, its relative share in trading capital also jumped from a previous 16–18 percent in the years 1888–1890 to 34–35 percent in 1892–1893, and to almost 50 percent in 1894–1896.[81]

The reason for the overall rise in Osaka's participation in industry and trade after 1890 is rather obvious. The source from which my figures are drawn indicates only the capital of corporate enterprises, meaning that Osaka's capital moved into corporate enterprise relatively late; this was especially true in trading. A jump from 16–18 percent of the national total to 50 percent within six years signifies a tremendous change. It indicates Osaka's final turn toward a modern form of enterprise, and the eventual success of the early efforts to establish joint-stock trading. While Osaka thus remained primarily a trading city, its share of the nation's industry was an impressive 25–27 percent in the 1890s, second only to Tokyo; at the same time, it retained an absolute lead in the field of trade. These figures are also a commentary on the frequent assertion that Osaka lacked capital for large-scale enterprise. It may be assumed instead that large amounts of Osaka capital were held back and used in the traditional forms of merchant business, and that they were poured into large-scale enterprise only after pioneering efforts had proven beyond doubt that these were safe and profitable investments.

Osaka, then, did rebound after its period of slump. But it never gained leadership as a center of industry and capital; the position was ceded to Tokyo. This was, of course, not solely because of the merchants' traditional outlook. For one thing, Osaka's harbor proved unsuitable for large ships, and foreign merchants soon turned to Kobe. Thus one of the most stimulating influences — foreign trade and contact with Westerners and their ideas — all but bypassed Osaka. Furthermore, the very fact that the Meiji government made Tokyo its administrative capital concentrated the progressive elements in that city. In the first two or three decades of the Meiji era, when political connections and motivations were highly important stimuli for starting industrial enterprises, Osaka was in a severely handicapped position. If Ōkubo's suggestion to make the city the center of trade, as well as the political capital, had been carried out, the Osaka bourgeoisie might have bestirred itself to show more initiative.

But even when all this is said, the main point of my argument remains unshaken. The Osaka bourgeoisie — and we may take this group as representative of the Tokugawa city merchants in general — lacked most clearly the required set of attitudes, the mentality, for launching modern business. This stifled the emergence of entrepreneurs from their ranks. Entrepreneurship must be viewed as a result both of individual personality and of the favorable economic and social conditions provided by the group and the cultural milieu. If there is too wide a distance between the new goal and the established standards of the group, even strong and talented persons will achieve the goal only with great difficulty: "Changes must be accepted. New habits and attitudes must be learned. New relationships to people must be established. If personality and culture are unfavorable to such changes, economic development may take place only slowly, if at all." [82] What is to be remembered about the city merchant class of Tokugawa Japan is that its mentality and its culture both resisted change; and this made the emergence of entrepreneurs all the more difficult.

II

THE SAMURAI CLASS

To many Westerners — and to many Japanese, for that matter — the samurai have become something of a legend. Together with the few samurai swords that are handed down as family treasures go tales of battle and harakiri, of feudal loyalties and chivalry. The Meiji Restoration was wrought by this same knightly class, which rose renewed from the ashes of its own decay and rejuvenated a nation as well. The samurai not only fought the battle that made Japan a new country; they imbued her with a new spirit, which somehow seems to live on — from the self-immolating kamikaze fliers of World War II down to the intricately detailed code of honor in daily life.

Unquestionably the samurai — the lower samurai, the experts will add — carried out the Meiji Restoration; they also supplied the administrators for the new government. It was the samurai who provided the essential dynamic force that turned Japan away from the Tokugawa status-quo policy and toward rapid modernization. Further, the "spirit of the samurai" not only determined official policies but during the Meiji era also became something of a standard public attitude: a happy mixture of militant patriotism and economically rationalized Confucian ethics.

The striking differences between the merchants and the samurai and their role in the Restoration have led to conclusions about their relative contributions to economic growth in Meiji Japan. Lacking detailed knowledge, which is indeed difficult to come by, one is tempted to construct a theory. The trouble with general statements of this kind is that they are as difficult to verify as they are to refute; they only leave the reader with an uncomfortable feeling of over-simplification. What I propose to do here is to examine the actual contribution made by the samurai class to the entrepreneurial achievements of Meiji Japan, particularly in the first half of the Meiji era when things were the most difficult for the new entrepreneurs.

Two principal schools of thought exist on this subject, and they flatly contradict one another. The first is expressed in the words of Herbert Norman: "The lower samurai . . . could not embody any new mode of production. The representative of the new mode of production which was gradually supplanting feudalism was, of course, the great *chōnin* class. Its members were, however, so immature as industrial entrepreneurs and so inexperienced in statecraft that they had to rely on the state to develop industry and on the members of the former feudal class, especially the samurai, as administrators and statesmen." [1] How could the samurai introduce a "new mode of production" when capitalism is supposed (by definition) to be spearheaded by the bourgeoisie? But since Norman, with his vast knowledge of Japanese history, could not deny the backwardness of the bourgeoisie, he had to offer the formula that the state coached the bourgeoisie until it was ready for its historically predetermined role.

The second line of thinking is expressed by George B. Sansom: "It was these men [samurai], and not the bourgeoisie, who laid the foundations of a capitalist structure and at the same time developed a political system that bore little resemblance to those which came into force in the advanced industrial countries of western Europe under the influence of a powerful moneyed class." [2] For Sansom it is not a matter of course that Japan must have repeated exactly the Western model, and he is ready to agree that the samurai played a dominant role in the private sector as well as in the government. Many present-day students of economic development will be in basic agreement with Sansom's statement.

The theory behind the statement might be drawn up something like this: The samurai had suffered continuous impoverishment throughout the Tokugawa period. Many of them had become economically ruined while still maintaining their social and educational advantages. The events following the Meiji Restoration did not improve their economic condition; on the contrary, they were robbed of almost everything by being made common citizens, with no special economic advantages. As a class that had enjoyed high standing and was trained for achievement, they were bound to compensate for their losses by striving for economic power. Yet traditional types of business were barred to them because of their deep-seated prejudice against engaging in trade and also because of the greater business experience of the entrenched merchants. The obvious avenue, then, was the new enterprises, for here the samurai had a twofold advantage over the merchants: the superior education that was essential for learning new techniques and better connections with samurai officials in the government. Working closely with the government in modern enterprises could provide prestige in the eyes of the public at a time when the building of industry was proclaimed as a supreme national duty. The samurai, therefore, were motivated by a unique combination of economic necessity and patriotism.

Although this theory seems neat and almost flawless, it will not stand up. Facts have an unpleasant way of destroying nice theories. The chief flaw in this one is that it assumes the samurai class to have been strictly homogeneous both in background and in reaction. In some directions the samurai did react very much according to the theory — as in the founding of the national banks, which will be discussed later. But in other areas one would tend to pick the rich peasants or even the merchants as "typical" representatives for introducing the "new mode of production." The last decades of the Tokugawa period had done much to blur class distinctions with respect to education, patterns of thinking, and economic activity. And even where class images and handicaps did remain, they were not the only factors that decided entrepreneurial activity.

Instead of working out another theory, I shall proceed with a review of the relevant historical facts. In this way we may see in proper perspective the development of the samurai class and its contribution to the process of economic modernization in Meiji Japan. Ultimately we may be obliged to abandon altogether the notion that Japan's entrepreneurs derived from any one social class.

THE ECONOMIC IMPASSE OF THE SAMURAI

It is ironic that the class of professional men-of-arms was officially established by Hideyoshi (in power from 1582 to 1598) only at the end of a long period of internal warfare and at the beginning of the Great Peace which was to last two hundred and fifty years.[3] Many former peasant-militiamen now became members of a feudal class that gathered in large numbers around the castles that had begun to be built under Oda Nobunaga. This new class developed its own code of ethics, in which the principal virtue was absolute loyalty to the feudal lord. Obligations of feudal loyalty were extolled to the extent that they even took precedence over filial or paternal duties. A samurai worthy of his name had to be ready to give not only his own life but the lives of his family to protect the honor of his daimyo. The Japanese recount with awe and admiration stories of dutiful samurai who lived up to this code, unflinchingly allowing their whole families to be slaughtered by the enemy rather than utter a word that might compromise the safety of the lord. These ideals were developed during a century of warfare. In the prolonged peace, however, the martial virtues lost their original and practical meaning to a great extent, as did the two samurai swords that were symbols of their status. The ties of loyalty between samurai and daimyo became increasingly theoretical. Many samurai of low rank never even met their lords and had no occasion to demonstrate their loyalty with heroism. The samurai became a cultured leisure class whose main purpose was to justify their superior social position by physical prowess, literary pursuits, and adherence to an elaborate code of ethics. Benevolence, honesty, and erudition became important virtues.[4]

For the service rendered to their lords, the samurai were entitled to regular payment in rice. Their lives were devoted to the preservation of peace and order, a pre-eminent social duty. This public function, according to Confucian teaching, raised them high above the common crowd of those engaged solely in economic pursuits. The peasants ranked next to the samurai because it was through their labor that the samurai could live. The samurai were strictly forbidden to engage in any kind of mercantile activity for it would degrade the men of the sword. There were occasions when the bakufu meted out severe punishment for infringements of this rule.[5] Any association with business activity, even with such a simple act as shopping, was

considered by the samurai as unclean and unworthy of his
class. Fukuzawa Yukichi wrote: "According to the con-
vention among the warrior class, they were ashamed of
being seen handling money. Therefore, it was customary
for samurai to wrap their faces with small hand-towels
and to go out after dark whenever they had an errand to
do. — I hated having a towel on my face and have never
worn one. I even used to go out on errands in broad day-
light, swinging a wine bottle in one hand, with two swords
on my side as becomes a man of samurai rank." [6] Fukuzawa
also observed that his father did not want his children to
be taught arithmetic because numbers were the "instruments of merchants." [7] It is doubtful whether these attitudes were general throughout the whole samurai class.
Much of the disdain for handling money and engaging
in any sort of business seems to have vanished toward the
end of the Tokugawa period.

It was severe economic pressure that led to the gradual
crumbling of the samurai code of ethics. The daimyo became unable to pay the stipulated amounts of rice to their
samurai. In the course of the Tokugawa period, the samurai were caught in a squeeze, especially after the Genroku
era (1688–1703) which became known for its luxury and
the rapid rise of the merchant class. Various devices came
into vogue for cutting the samurai stipends — for example,
the *hanchi* system, whereby the daimyo "borrowed" half
of the samurai's stipend. Sometimes the samurai would
receive only 40 percent of the amount due them.[8] Luxury
consumption, which spread through the *sankin kōtai* system of alternate residence in Edo,[9] and the increasing
monetization of the economy led naturally to the transfer
of economic power from the feudal class to the merchants.

Exhortations to the samurai to practice simplicity and
forbearance increased. The spartan frugality of the warrior

class became proverbial, but it had physical limits. They tried to maintain pride and dignity: "Even if a samurai has nothing to eat he will pretend with a long toothpick" (*bushi wa kuwanedo takayōji*) runs a proverb from the late Tokugawa. They were obliged to sell their household treasures, paintings, even their armor, ceremonial dress, and furniture, and to dismiss their servants.[10]

Those samurai who resorted to borrowing became completely dependent upon merchant moneylenders or rich peasants and saved themselves in the end by selling their samurai titles or adopting merchant children as heirs. Both practices were in vogue before the Meiji Restoration and were severely criticized by contemporary writers. These developments varied somewhat according to the general economic positions of the individual han. Some han managed to carry out drastic reforms and started their own trading and even "industrialization" programs.

The social cleavage between upper and lower samurai gradually became complete.[11] The two groups almost never intermarried; they used different styles of speech and writing; and they built their houses differently (the houses of the upper samurai had *genkan* [porches]). The telling difference, of course, was the size of their rice stipends. According to Fukuzawa's description of his own han of Nakatsu, Kyushu, the upper samurai received 100 koku of rice or more; since some 20–30 koku were needed for the sustenance of one family, they could live comfortably on their allotments. The lower samurai in the same han received only 7 to 15 koku.[12]

Although the fortunes of all samurai declined drastically in the later Tokugawa period, the lower samurai had to work. The upper samurai could go on living as a leisured class, though with fewer luxuries and less display. The

more impoverished samurai were forced to start some
kind of home employment perhaps as early as the middle
of the eighteenth century; it was already common practice
in the first decade of the nineteenth century. They sold
goldfish and carvings, made paper fans and lanterns, lacquer ware, umbrellas. They also entered widely into the
production of sugar and tea and the manufacture of porcelain. Silkworm raising, spinning, and weaving were their
most common occupations.[13]

Some samurai who did not find their way into these
forms of production severed their allegiance to the feudal
lord and became *rōnin* (roaming men), offering the service
of their swords to anyone who would pay them. Or, as
reckless political fanatics, they threw their support behind
the opposing forces in the Restoration struggle. The plight
of the samurai after the opening of the ports in 1853 is
vividly described by a contemporary critic: "Although
cheap money is abundant in the world, the Shogun's sustenance rate to his direct retainers remains the same.
Driven to the wall, these samurai are now given to greed,
cheating their superiors and tyrannizing over the common
people. They have no time to show loyalty to the Shogun.
They are in mind baser than merchants." [14]

Although the Restoration cannot be regarded as an
achievement exclusively of the lower samurai, it cannot
be denied that the success of the movement and the post-
Restoration ascendency of many lower samurai into leading governmental posts kindled great hopes for economic
betterment among the poor samurai. Restoration meant
for many, first of all, the return of the emperor to power;
with this, it was thought, the old glory of feudal Japan
would be restored. These hopes were ruthlessly crushed
by subsequent events. The government had no intention

of restoring the old; it moved with determination into a new era, using the Western countries as its model. In the new Japan of the Meiji government there was to be no room for feudal privileges. The swords had become obsolete when guns decided victory or defeat.

The brief Restoration war and the ensuing changes in Edo spelled ruin for those samurai who had remained in Edo even after the *sankin kōtai* travels of the daimyo had been abolished. The merchants had left the city in a hurry and thus the central rice supply was all but cut off. Many samurai followed the abdicated shogun to Shizuoka (his family domain) as a matter of loyalty. Those who stayed set up teahouses in their front yards or little shops and sold their last possessions to prevent outright starvation.[15]

From the very start, the new government aimed at a strong central administration, and in 1871 the han were abolished and replaced by a prefectural system. Thus, by the stroke of a pen the old loyalty relationships were suspended: there were now neither feudal lords nor han for the samurai to belong to. Instead, they were citizens of prefectural units. For the time being they retained their titles, though even these were treated rather haphazardly by the new government, with willful regroupings and simplifications of the elaborate scales and degrees of rank.[16] However, the samurai were now free, like all other citizens, to pursue any type of work.[17] They still received their rice allotments, although these were sharply reduced. The central government took over the burden of paying the samurai and urged them to accept commutation of their stipends into lump sums in cash.

The cash awards were granted at about five times the market value of the rice stipend. With their new capital the samurai were supposed to start some kind of business.

Only a few were willing to trust this new approach, however. Economic conditions were not at all promising for new enterprises, and the samurai's deep antipathy to business remained strong. When the commutation became law in 1876, there were still 312,775 samurai families on the stipend system,[18] probably close to 75 percent of the total samurai population. One could argue that voluntary commutation by some 25 percent indicates a considerable degree of initiative to start new business enterprises. But the disappearance of samurai from the list of stipend receivers by no means indicates that these men had received commutation payments before they were enforced by law. Many simply disappeared from the samurai registers without applying for commutation of stipends; they were absorbed into the ranks of artisans, small peasants, and employees. Their stipends had fallen to such a pittance that they did not consider registration and collection of the allowances worth the trouble. It is claimed that, for this reason, the number of samurai in Sendai dropped to but a few families of stipend receivers by 1873.[19] All the evidence points to a great reluctance to commute and to enter business. It also indicates that there was no vigorous spirit of enterprise among the samurai class as a whole.

In the early years after the Meiji Restoration, the real income of the average samurai continued to decline. In view of the back-door exodus from the samurai ranks on the one hand, and the steep rise in consumer prices on the other, it is most difficult to determine any exact percentage for the fall in real income per capita. The following list gives the unadjusted totals of samurai incomes between 1867 and 1876, according to government statistics.[20] Even if the gradually diminishing number of samurai stipend receivers lessens the per-capita decline, it must

have become practically impossible for all but a few upper
samurai to sustain themselves on their receipts.

Pre-Restoration payment in rice, money value, 1867	34,621,583 yen
Payments of rice stipends in 1871, money value, 1871	22,657,948 yen
Value of the yearly interest paid on commutation bonds, 1876	11,568,000 yen

The value of the stipends for the han samurai who became
prefectural samurai in 1871 amounted in that year to
15,300,000 yen, a very large sum if compared with the
total government expenditure of 42,470,000 yen for the
same year; [21] thus the expenditures for samurai were more
than 36 percent of the budget. The government clearly
had to find a solution to this fiscal problem, and it determined to enter the jobless stipend receivers into the production process.

The commutation of 1876 was paid in interest-bearing
bonds with a total face value of 174 million yen, a sum
about four times that of the total government revenue for
one year. The system was very involved, and the rate of
interest varied according to the class of samurai and the
type of stipend rights. The payments themselves ranged
from five to fourteen times the market value of the yearly
amount of rice, while the interest was fixed at 5–7 percent.[22]
This drastic decline of samurai incomes became the samurai's only reward for the support many of them had given
to the Restoration movement. In addition to their economic straits, their pride was hurt by the abolition of old
status privileges and of the right to carry swords. In protest some samurai carried wooden replicas of their weapons
on the streets.[23] Discontented samurai became ringleaders
in the peasant uprisings which plagued Japan in the first
decade of Meiji. Some groups of samurai staged revolts of

their own. In 1874 a large group of samurai took to arms in Saga han. They were defeated, eleven ringleaders were beheaded, and all participants were expelled from samurai rank.[24]

Other rebellions broke out in Kumamoto, Akizuki, and Hagi; finally the dissatisfied elements rallied for a last stand in the Satsuma Rebellion of 1877. Although the immediate reason for the rebellion was political (the rebels objected to the weak stand of the government in the Korean affair [25] and its excessively pro-Western policies), it was the bitterness and disappointment stemming from their economic misery and social degradation that led these samurai of southwestern Japan to defy a modern army of conscripted commoners.[26] The samurai were dealt a crushing defeat and were thus shown in realistic terms that the time of the sword and its privileges was over, once and for all. It now remained the government's task to find a way of using the samurai for constructive purposes, a way that would not only give them a living but would fit easily into their background and their peculiar mentality.

In spite of the government's ruthless suppression of samurai revolts and its liquidation of samurai privileges, the Meiji leaders were not without sympathy for their former compeers. Moreover, being samurai themselves, they were better aware than anyone else of the invaluable qualities that remained the distinctive mark of that class, such as education, social responsibility, self-respect, and devotion to duty. The Meiji leaders hoped that, once the opposition of the samurai to the inevitable changes was broken and once they had realized that the new era and the new economic conditions were here to stay, they would become the most important entrepreneurial element in the nation. The government's task was to restore the samurai to a position of leadership, this time in the economic field.

THE DRAFTING OF SAMURAI FOR MODERN ENTERPRISE

The National Banks

The commutation bonds of over 174 million yen created a grave monetary problem. Unless the bonds were absorbed quickly, they would flood the market and depreciate, thereby depriving the samurai of their last hope for economic survival and of their confidence in the government. It was felt in government circles that virtue ought to be made of necessity by turning the bonds into foundation capital for new banks. An improvement of the banking system was sorely needed. Under existing regulations, the four national banks in operation were unable to cope with the inconvertible government notes. Furthermore their number and total capital were considered insufficient for the overall needs of the gradually rallying economy. In 1876 a new banking act was passed. Its regulations on share capital and reserve requirements were designed to enable the samurai to join in the founding of new banks.[27] By the old regulations, national banks had to pay 60 percent of their cash holdings to the government. They received securities from the government in return, bearing 6 percent interest. The banks were permitted to print and circulate convertible banknotes up to the total value of these securities, but they suffered heavy losses because the notes were required to be converted at parity while they were actually depreciating rapidly. Consequently the banks virtually stopped the issue of banknotes.

The revised banking act of 1876 provided that 80 percent of the banks' capital be paid up to the government. In return the banks were to receive government bonds bearing 4 percent interest, purchased at market value. The banknote issue could be made up to the total face value of these securities.[28] Actually the commutation bonds were made the main part of the new banking capital and thus, in practice, up to 80 percent of the value of the commutation bonds invested as banking capital could circulate as paper money. By 1879 the national banks had a total capital of 40.62 million yen, of which over 29 million was in commutation bonds, the rest in currency. Against this total paid-up capital, the banks circulated 34.4 million yen in paper money.[29] Because of the favorable conditions granted the banks, they were supposed to charge less than the market rate of interest on loans — the regulations provided for 12–20 percent according to the size of the loans. But many of the new banks charged more.[30]

Along with the publication of the revised banking act of 1876 went a drive to stimulate participation of the samurai in founding new banks. The investment of bonds and cash in the establishment of banks was propagandized as a service to the country. Bankers were declared to be patriots who contributed to the building of a strong national economy.[31] Thus they were not associated with the much hated and despised money exchangers of Tokugawa days. The response to the government's drive for bank establishments surpassed all expectations. Within two years, 153 banks were founded and chartered as national banks. The Ministry of Finance stopped the rush and set a ceiling at this number in 1879. The total share capital of these national banks had risen from 2.55 million in December 1876 to 40.616 million in December 1879.[32]

From 1879 on, private banks mushroomed as the national banks had done previously. By 1883, 204 private banks were in operation, in addition to the 153 national banks.[33] Many samurai eagerly grasped the unique opportunity to invest their bonds in enterprises that received close governmental attention and were thus considered quite safe and, at the same time, gave them the distinction of being

progressive patriots. Banks were founded, as the businessmen would often boast, to "prevent the influx of foreign
goods," to "promote enterprise," and to "promote the
cause of civilization and enlightenment." Sometimes even
destitute samurai became promoters of national or private
banks, urging their compeers as well as commoners to contribute share capital. They tended to play down the risks
and to emphasize the idealistic aspects in reference to the
national economy.[34] Sometimes outright pressure was applied. In Sendai all samurai were compelled to offer their
bonds as foundation capital, and 308 samurai gathered a
total of 83,865 yen in bonds and cash.[35] In 1877, a year
after the publication of the revised banking act, the Ministry of Finance sent a rescript to all local authorities
cautioning against the use of compulsion: "It seems that
our instructions concerning the establishment of national
banks have been very well propagated among the people
at large by the local authorities. . . . We cannot avoid
noticing, however, that many a samurai thinks he has now
by all means to compel his fellow classmen in his district
to join in the foundation of companies. Thus it happens
that even those who have no interest at all are forced to
cooperate in the establishment of banks. The local authorities are herewith enjoined to prevent such bad practices." [36]

The rush of the samurai to found banks stands out in
striking contrast to the attitudes of the wealthy merchant
houses, which had to be forced to establish the first four
national banks in 1872. Correspondingly, in this early
phase the merchants also fell far behind the samurai as
contributors of capital to the whole banking system. A
report of the Banking Bureau in 1879–80 gives the following picture of percentage distribution of capital supply by
classes for the national banks.[37]

Nobility	44.10%
Samurai	31.86
Merchants	14.85
Peasants	3.45
Artisans	0.12
Others	5.62
	100.0%

Records of individual banks indicate that even where merchants had supplied a majority of the capital, the initial drive toward foundation had come from samurai. The national banks were very successful. Until their charters expired, in 1898–99, only four banks closed and fourteen amalgamated. After 1898 a total of 122 continued as private banks, the reduction in their number being due to amalgamations or closings in 1898–99.[38] The private banks did not fare quite so well, undoubtedly because of less stringent supervision by the government; this in turn resulted in reduced public confidence. Between 1876 and 1892, a total of 410 private banks came into existence, of which 86 closed in the same period.[39]

The all-important breakthrough in the field of banking — and it was a real and lasting one — was thus achieved by the samurai in combination with the nobles, although the large amounts of capital held by the nobility tends greatly to exaggerate their share as participants. The most famous and largest of the national banks was founded by 480 nobles with 17.8 million yen of share capital, almost all in commutation bonds. As of 1881, the 147 other national banks then operating had only a total of 26 million yen. This bank enjoyed various privileges and favors from the government until 1883.[40]

The fact that the samurai had had little choice in the matter does not detract from the greatness of their contribution in the banking field. In declaring that the establishment of banks was in the interest of the country and therefore quite distinct from ordinary profit making, the government had managed to strike a note to which this class had long been accustomed to respond. Undoubtedly, at this early juncture, the arduous entrepreneurial task had to be supported by political motivations and government guidance. We can see that already a dichotomy existed in the Japanese business world. On the one hand there was "enterprise for the sake of the country" and, on the other, "business for profit." The feudal class carried its own social pride into the economy by refusing, at least outwardly, to become "merchants."

The national banks succeeded for several reasons. They inspired confidence because of government backing and were able to draw on the savings of the local population. Most of their loans were to minor local entrepreneurs and businessmen. Operation of the banks was not complicated, and the bankers received not only supervision but careful coaching and detailed instructions. Shibusawa, as president of the Dai Ichi Bank, played a major role here. He invited representatives of local banks to learn at the Dai Ichi Bank, and over twenty banks responded. Shibusawa saw to it that in times of difficulty these new banks would be supported; he also intervened for them with government officials when the inexperienced bankers misinterpreted regulations. Booklets and instructions were printed and distributed in which all operations, from banknote issue to interest-rate calculations and bookkeeping, were explained.[41]

This kind of operation was almost tailormade for the samurai, who were naturally prone to behave like officials, follow regulations, and act with a sense of public responsibility. The average director of a small or medium-sized

national bank did not need much entrepreneurial vision
and creativity, as Shibusawa himself once admitted. Of
course, there were great entrepreneurs among Japan's
bankers, but they did not, as a rule, emerge from this
group that rushed into the founding of national banks.
The leading bankers were far more independent men
and more often than not connected with a string of industrial operations.

The chief contribution of the samurai to the success of
the national banks was their willingness and ability to
learn new things, qualities that were conspicuously absent
in large segments of the merchant class. The samurai's
willingness to start something new was of course the result
of bitter necessity, but the new venture was made palatable
by the appeal to patriotism. Their ability to learn hinged
largely on their literacy. By 1876 Japan could no longer
be called an illiterate country; perhaps 30 or even 40 percent of the population had received some schooling and
could read. But the samurai were still the educated class
par excellence. Between 1863 and 1871 Keio Gijuku, the
college established by Fukuzawa, was attended by only 40
commoners as against 1,289 samurai.[42] Furthermore, the
samurai were generally more open-minded, since their educational tradition was formal and philosophical. It is
common knowledge that direct job education and practical
training make the mind less flexible than a general education will. Thus the impractical outlook of the samurai
actually became an asset in the face of completely new
phenomena like modern banking, which had to be learned
from printed material.

The Samurai Companies

Throughout the first twenty years of the Meiji era, the
problem of samurai employment received priority in the

government's policies. The deposed samurai class was not only an object of humanitarian concern; it constituted a real political danger. If properly directed, the samurai could eventually become a great asset to the economy. The drive to establish national banks was only one of various elements in the government's program for coping with the economic difficulties of its elite class. Roughly from the time of the Restoration on, samurai were urged to settle on small farms and reclaim land or to emigrate to Hokkaido. But by 1879 there still must have been approximately 1.5 million destitute samurai. The government planners then set out to direct the highly valued capabilities of these men toward the foundation of large-scale enterprises in company form. Iwakura Tomomi, one of the leaders of the Restoration movement and a champion of the company-foundation program,[43] expressed his expectations thus:

The samurai will be able to display a strength of character which has been groomed through the ages, and will thus enter successfully into a hundred fields of activity. Giving full sway to their mental vigor they can stand up in competition with the foreigners. In the present state of affairs there is none but the samurai who can, endowed with training in many fields, bring the enterprise of the country to a head. . . . If we take the rest of the population, excluding these high-class families, we still find much wasteland. It will take some twenty to thirty years until their strength will suffice to compete with foreigners.[44]

In 1874 the government granted a loan of forty yen per household to rebellious samurai of Saga han, after crushing their revolt. They were given this loan on the condition that they invest it in companies.[45] This precedent was followed by a larger program initiated in 1878. Loans were granted to samurai for the purpose of investment in either agriculture or manufacturing of some sort. The

choice of venture was left to the imagination and skill of
the individual; it also depended largely on the economic
conditions of the region. But there was one invariable
stipulation: the enterprise must be a joint-stock venture,
with samurai as members.

This government program was not the only one. The
prefectures had their own employment projects; wealthy
merchants and peasants sometimes also made sizable contributions to help samurai families or to get a samurai
company started. A few spinning mills, owned by groups
of samurai, were established with substantial subsidies
from prefectures or private individuals. Information on the
prefectural subsidies and private loans is very difficult to
come by. According to the original bill submitted by
Ōkubo, the central government was to spend a total of
10 million yen in loans to start samurai companies; in
reality only 5,256 million yen were spent over the whole
period from 1879 to 1889, when the program was terminated.[46] According to a survey of Kikkawa Hidezō, 257
companies received loans from the central government between 1879 and 1885; 176 received the loans free of interest.[47] Of these companies 47 were agricultural enterprises; 78 were in raw silk or silkworm rearing; 33 could
be called "modern" enterprises, with 14 of them in textiles. Again, it must be pointed out that this is only a
partial list of the companies that began under central-
government auspices.

If we consider that, at this early date, joint-stock enterprise was all but unknown in Japan and that modern business ventures were few, we can estimate the economic and
entrepreneurial importance of this vast program. The
shareholders in these companies were often numerous.
Giant "all-purpose" companies tried to combine the advantages of bigness, capital and scale of operation, with

the use of diversified skills and opportunities. In some instances a few thousand families would join in a single company, but they usually failed after a short time. It is not possible here to give detailed statistics on the total outcome of the program. Approaches and results varied greatly from place to place and from company to company. Usually the agricultural companies and tea-growing and silkworm-rearing establishments were relatively successful, at least for a while, but most of those entering into modern types of manufacturing fared very badly.

Generally the samurai had participated in the program out of hard necessity, to avoid starvation, and consequently many enterprises were founded upon resentment rather than enthusiasm. In Akita in 1882 a group of about 250 samurai founded a reactionary newspaper favoring the restoration of the old order. The paper went out of business for lack of popular support, and the government then granted the same samurai a loan of 20,000 yen to establish a silk-weaving company.[48] The samurai problem had become a national emergency that concerned the whole population. Many merchants or wealthy peasants felt an obligation to join the government in trying to provide a livelihood for the esteemed cream of the nation. Do-gooders of all types became founders or promoters of samurai enterprises. In the Nagasaki area [49] 17 samurai companies of various types were founded between 1881 and 1888, ranging over a wide field of activities including silkworm rearing, spinning, tea growing, cattle rearing, the manufacture of porcelain, wax, sugar, and gelatine, and iron casting. One silkworm-rearing and cattle-breeding company comprising 7,308 samurai families started with 10,000 yen of share capital, a government loan for the same amount, and a subsidy from a private source of 20,000 yen. It was a fair success for at least a decade. The records of most companies are very scanty and do not permit precise statements as to their success. One company that took up fishing, raw-silk production, and porcelain manufacturing soon collapsed, whereas another engaged in silk and sugar production, and numbering 294 shareholders, operated successfully for some time.

Shizuoka prefecture had been hit especially hard by the Meiji Restoration. Following the shogun's resignation, his direct retainers were given a threefold choice: they could become retainers of the emperor, follow the former shogun into exile to his own territory of Shizuoka,[50] or become ordinary citizens and renounce their samurai status. Some 7,000 to 8,000 samurai chose to follow their feudal lord to Shizuoka, thus increasing the stipend receivers in that territory to about 15,000 families.[51] Not unnaturally, this group was anything but enthusiastic about the new era and its programs.

In spite of the large number of samurai in Shizuoka, records show only eight companies that formed there, of which two tea-growing companies were large, one with 800 samurai members and the other with 200.[52] The larger company had started in 1869 and was organized into groups of families according to their former military regiments; the superior ranks held the managerial positions. The company was fairly successful until 1882, distributing yearly profits per family of 30 to 65 yen, an equivalent of 4–6 koku of rice. After 1882 the profits fell to an equivalent of one half to one koku.[53] On the whole, the Shizuoka enterprises in tea production, silkworm rearing, cattle breeding, and umbrella manufacturing fared worse than those in Nagasaki prefecture; perhaps Nagasaki's proximity to foreign influence and the generally progressive conditions there were partly responsible.

But there is not much point in stressing differences in

progress and entrepreneurial approach among the various regions. Many other variables were in operation simultaneously, and all combined to make the entire samurai-company plan a vast failure. After a few years most of these companies collapsed. Their capital was too thin to carry the blundering and experimental undertakings over the years of losses. With the deflation of currency initiated in 1881 by Minister of Finance Matsukata, they tumbled wholesale. The regions with the lowest per-capita loans usually showed the poorest results, a sign that scarcity of capital was an important reason for their collapse. Shimane prefecture, which had the lowest loans (0.4 yen per capita, as against 1.8 yen for Tottori and 1.5 yen for Okayama, which had the highest rates),[54] reported in 1880 that 94 percent of all its samurai bondholders had either sold their bonds for cash or had invested in company enterprises that had gone bankrupt. Three years later, Shimane prefecture reported that approximately 20 percent of all its samurai had neither employment nor savings to fall back on, and that they survived through the help of friends or relatives.[55] A survey of Osaka district in September 1881 indicated that of a total of 3,434 samurai households only 31 percent had some kind of employment.[56] An 1883 report by Hiroshima prefecture gives the following picture: only about 20–30 percent of the samurai succeeded in entering gainful employment between 1875 and 1883. In 1883 the total number of samurai households was 7,735. Of these, 1,720 had achieved economic subsistence, 4,374 scarcely had the necessities of life, 1,167 were in severe straits, and 474 were completely unable to sustain themselves.[57]

The samurai as a class did not manage to achieve a breakthrough in manufacturing, as they did in joint-stock banking. The reason was that in banking, at that time, the most important requirements were enthusiasm and strict observance of set rules — the establishment of manufacturing and trading enterprises required much more experience and imagination. The great majority of entrepreneurs of stature had more than enthusiasm; they had acquired precious practical experience and had freed themselves from the past and its traditions. Indeed, willingness to accept change may have been at the root of the different fates of the banks and the samurai companies. The banks came first and probably attracted those who were most ready to change, to accept the economic challenge. The samurai companies then were left to gather in those who "had not jumped before." The courageous volunteers who constituted the real entrepreneurial timber and had a positive attitude toward economic change were by and large already engaged elsewhere.

Within the first two decades of the Meiji era, roughly speaking, the samurai were transformed from nonproductive consumers into productive agents. Through the mechanism of commuting their consumption into bonds that were invested, actual savings were raised by almost the same amount. By the end of the Tokugawa period, the daimyo and samurai consumed most of the tax revenue, which was as high as 25–30 percent of the gross national product. Now the Meiji government was in a position to use almost all of its tax revenue for its own purposes because the interest on the daimyo and samurai bonds, which were depreciating very rapidly, became a negligible burden in a time of high inflation. The samurai could not live on bond interest and, in order to earn a living, were forced to become productive.

Perhaps, in a sense, the most important contribution of the samurai class to Japanese economic growth was, paradoxically, its abolition as a privileged and passive consumer group. In view of the quest of underdeveloped countries to raise the rate of domestic capital formation, the case of the samurai points to an interesting and probably very important possibility: the liquidation of consumer-group privileges and the transformation of the unearned incomes of such groups into savings. Even where such passive consumer groups do not exist, a similar process is feasible through the transfer of the disguised unemployed from the farms where — theoretically at least — they do not earn, but consume, into the production process of modern industry or other types of manufacturing. I need not elaborate on this possibility here because it is often mentioned in treatises on economic development.[58]

But there is something else that tends to be overlooked in discussing the theoretical possibilities of capital formation. The mechanism of social and economic transfer must also provide stimuli and incentives for the declassed or transferred groups that will break down their initial resistance and eventually make them cooperate in the program. Moreover, privileged groups of passive consumers, like the samurai in Japan, more often than not have superior qualities in terms of education and leadership capabilities, and these must not be lost to the economy by the creation of a permanent sulking resistance. The uniqueness of the Meiji experience is that the samurai were declassed by compeers who were extremely anxious to activate the best qualities of that elite class, and succeeded in doing so. Thus the samurai were able to generate a good deal of entrepreneurial dynamism and eventually provided the modern entrepreneurial elite with a new status image, based on the old vibrant "spirit of the samurai."

III

RURAL ENTREPRENEURSHIP

It is common knowledge that the burden of financing industrialization in its early stages falls heavily on the agricultural sector, unless large-scale foreign aid can be obtained. The agricultural sector must provide an initial surplus to feed the new industrial labor force and must finance by exports the required imports of capital. How did Japanese agriculture provide the necessary basis for the vigorous industrial development that started in the Meiji era? How much had agricultural productivity risen above the subsistence level during the Tokugawa period, and what were the forces that made such an achievement possible? We shall see that it was the entrepreneurial elements in the rural sector that must be given particular credit for the creation of the agricultural surplus, mainly through the reclamation of new land and the introduction of cash cropping, new farming techniques, and domestic manufacturing.

RURAL ENTREPRENEURS IN TOKUGAWA JAPAN

The Tokugawa System of Agriculture

Tokugawa agriculture rested on the nominal ownership of all land by the feudal overlord (*ryōshu*), who had the right to levy taxes on the peasantry.[1] The amount of tax was left to the lord's discretion and it varied from han to han, but as a rule of thumb about four parts of the value of the produce were collected as tax and six parts were left to the farming peasants. The greater part of the payment was made in kind, chiefly in rice, but another part was paid in money, to which were added various kinds of services, such as upkeep of roads and river embankments and — along the highways — the emergency supply of horses and messengers.

Land, according to an edict of 1643, could not be sold, and partition of land below two cho was also prohibited.[2] One cho produced on the average somewhere between twelve and fourteen koku of rice, and one koku of rice is equivalent to minimum subsistence for one person for a year. The prohibition against partition of land was apparently aimed at keeping a few farmers in each village above subsistence level, in order to strengthen the village community. Peasants were exhorted to live frugally and not to consume the surplus owed to the lords. They were not to eat much rice but rather millet, barley, sweet potatoes, and radishes, and they were to drink water and not tea or sake.

The village was administered by the headman, who was responsible to the overlord not only for the prompt deliveries of tax rice but also for general discipline. He carried a sword and had a family name, as signs of honor, and his position was hereditary. The village was subdivided into groups of families, usually five (*gonin gumi*); each group had to pay the tax as a unit, though the amount was reassessed at regular intervals of five years or more, according to the productivity of each plot. Within the village and the *gonin gumi*, land ownership was unequally distributed. A few families were rich, owning some four to

five cho; at the other extreme were the poor peasants with
no more than a quarter of a cho. The poor were forced
to lend labor services to the rich and were in turn assigned
some additional marginal plots to cultivate for themselves.
This relationship between wealthy and poor peasants, the
oyabun–kobun relationship, constituted another important link of social interdependence. The *oyabun* was not
only the employer but also the protector and councilor of
the weak *kobun*. The social control exercised by the village headman, the *gonin gumi*, and the *oyabun-kobun* relationship were all perfectly designed to keep the Tokugawa village in subordination and to suppress initiative
and change.

Beginning in the second half of the eighteenth century,
however, it became increasingly obvious that even a bakufu
bureaucracy could not legislate against the laws of demand and supply. Village life began to change markedly.
Improvements in agricultural techniques and the increased
power of money destroyed the static economic and social
stratification in the villages. Rural merchants and rich
peasant-manufacturers gained prominence, and they did
so not only by exploiting their co-villagers and reducing
them to tenant position, but even more by their own entrepreneurial activity. Indeed, in the last century of the Tokugawa period, the principal entrepreneurial stirrings occurred not in the large cities but in the villages. First,
however, let us examine briefly the achievements that are
usually credited to rural entrepreneurship in this period.
How much did agricultural productivity rise during the
Tokugawa period?

We sometimes hear statements that Japan's agriculture,
by the end of the Tokugawa, was close to subsistence level
with no surplus for industrial investments. Some people
apparently assume that Japanese agriculture "must have

been" at subsistence level until the beginning of industrialization, which in turn was made possible by an unbelievable squeeze on the peasant population.

Some indicators do suggest such an interpretation — for example, the combination of almost stationary population combined with an increasing frequency of peasant uprisings. There are no precise population figures, but we may not be far from wrong in assuming the total population to have risen by no more than 10 percent over the 250 years of Tokugawa rule. Between 1721 and 1846 Japan's population is supposed to have risen by no more than 900,000, from 26 to 26.9 million, and to have fallen off during the great famines of the 1830s by 300,000.[3] We have to realize, of course, that official figures did not include unregistered people who may have constituted over 10 percent of the population. Consequently we may assume with Irene Taeuber that by 1853 Japan's total population stood at about 30 million; we must raise the earlier figures correspondingly, with the same result of a very slow population increase. The number of peasant uprisings increased steadily and accelerated in the first half of the nineteenth century.[4] We may question the accuracy of the early records and try to explain away this rising rural unrest, but it is well known that the bakufu became seriously concerned about the uprisings. Although there appear to have been, especially in the decades immediately before the Restoration, a good many political causes for the uprisings (the antibakufu forces gained extensive support among the rich peasants and rural samurai), the main cause was economic. The uprisings were directed against the exploitation of the peasants by the merchants and rural magnates.

It is theoretically possible that, in spite of rising overall productivity, the real income of the lower stratum of peasants could have declined in absolute terms. But such a postulate is not needed to explain the lack of population growth and the frequent uprisings. Even if the low-income farming population had in fact improved its absolute level of living, the introduction of new consumer goods, and the amassing of economic power by the merchants and rich peasants while many poor peasants were being reduced to tenant status, must have created widespread discontent and made the slight actual improvements appear as losses when compared to the incomes of the new village capitalists.

As for the stable population, the population rate was controlled by infanticide. Once population control becomes an accepted custom, as it did in Tokugawa Japan, it can become a habit and cannot always be assumed to be an indicator of subsistence living standards. The Tokugawa peasants in a way defied Malthusian theory; the Meiji government at times had to resort to rather drastic measures to eliminate infanticide.

There was, furthermore, a substantial rise in agricultural productivity in the Tokugawa period, and it resulted from land reclamations, land improvements, new techniques, and specialization. The total cultivated area increased constantly throughout the Tokugawa years, although it is difficult to interpret reasonably figures that suggest an increase of 300 percent, from 1.5 million cho in 1598 to almost 4.5 million cho in 1880.[5] What probably happened was that a substantial amount of cultivated land in the seventeenth and eighteenth centuries was concealed in order to avoid taxation, which was based on yield per cho of land. We know that even the first cadastral surveys of the Meiji era permitted a certain amount of concealment or undermeasurement. Another factor may have to be considered when we read of the enormous increase in cultivated land: when new land is simply added to the old, the result may be a higher set of figures than reality warranted. Sufficient cases are recorded wherein old land was abandoned by peasants because of erosion or floods, or because it was subject to a heavier tax than new land.[6]

According to a survey of the han, conducted under the auspices of the Meiji government in 1869, the total value product of all han had risen on the average from the base 100 to about 150 between 1614 and 1869, varying widely, of course, from han to han and from region to region.[7] A rise of 50 percent over 250 years cannot be considered a high growth rate, and, taking the population rise during the same interval to have been about 10 percent, it does not indicate a remarkable surplus available for industrialization. The fact of the matter is, however, that we are probably misled again by purposeful concealments: the survey was carried out by the han administrations for the central government, and it is anybody's guess how honest the administrators were when they had reason to fear that the findings might be used as a basis for tax assessment. Agricultural output is said to have risen from 18.5 million koku in 1598 to 30.56 koku in 1842.[8] This means approximately an increase of 60 percent, and it leaves out the last 25 years of the Tokugawa period when economic growth was most pronounced. So it may not be unrealistic to assume a near doubling of agricultural output in the course of the 250 years of the Tokugawa period.

Recent thinking tends toward the belief that by the end of the Tokugawa period Japanese agriculture was by no means at the subsistence level; that instead it showed every sign of a quickening growth and the capacity of supplying the initial surplus for industrialization. Wealth came into the villages through manufacturing, crop specialization, and trade. Although the distribution of income became increasingly skewed in favor of the manufacturing and commercial group, the average peasant was not completely bypassed by the rising productivity. One sign that this was so is the spread of elementary education among the peasants. By the end of the Tokugawa about 30 percent of the total population had received some elementary education. Literacy is an almost certain sign of a rise above subsistence levels.

In the following sections I shall not pursue further the question of the exact amount of potential investible surplus supplied by agriculture at the beginning of the Meiji era. The primary emphasis will be on the various factors that contributed to its emergence, particularly on the entrepreneurial elements operating in rural Japan.

Land Reclamations by Merchant Capitalists

The bakufu encouraged land reclamation, especially after the disastrous famines lasting from 1783 to 1788. A bakufu rescript dated 1790 decreed that for newly reclaimed land the tax should not be higher than 10 percent on the yield.[9] The daimyo took similar measures in their own territories. The process of reclaiming swampy river land or forests was costly, and only the wealthy capitalists, mostly merchants, could afford long gestation periods for their investments. But these investments were lucrative indeed. The new landlord was free of all burdens except the stipulated 10 percent tax. The new land was often more fertile than the old paddies, and the landlords sometimes received as much as 65–70 percent of the yield as rent, leaving the peasant only 30–35 percent.[10] This is certainly proof of high fertility because from the old land, on the average, about 40 percent of the yield was required to maintain a tenant.

The inducements to engage in land reclamation were

many. The land laborers who were employed in the reclamation project came into a tenant relationship with the
new landlord. They were provided with tools and working
capital, and were freed from the bonds of control and
interdependence that existed in the old village; instead
they became completely dependent upon the new landlords. These quasi-overlords came into opposition with
the older feudal class; yet the feudal lords welcomed them
and, at least initially, gained by their activities.

The Osaka merchants were well represented among the
new landlords. The Kagaya family of Osaka, between 1745
and 1841, reclaimed a total of 120 cho in new land by
draining the swamps between the Yamato and Kitsu
rivers.[11] The Kōnoike family carried out a major reclamation project in the vicinity of Osaka, amounting also to
120 cho.[12] The draining of swampy river land in Osaka
itself added 68 cho of paddyland to the arable area during
the second half of the seventeenth century and the first
decades of the eighteenth.[13]

A writer of the Tempō era (1830–1844) tells of vast land
reclamations which indicate the tremendous wealth of the
new landlords.[14] He laments the fact that, at a time when
retainers of feudal lords received a bare 10 koku of rice as
sustenance, merchants amassed huge profits from newly
reclaimed lands. Then he cites a few examples: In Shonai
(Tsuruoka) of Dewa province, a merchant received 140,000
koku of rice as rents from land while the officially assessed
gross total product of the same area amounted to only
150,000 koku. In Kaga province two merchants paid
80,000 koku as feudal taxes and received 160,000 koku as
rents from their reclaimed land. In Hokuriku there were
frequent instances of new landlords receiving anywhere
from 1,000 to 10,000 koku in rents from new land. In Shikoku, too, such new landlords were numerous, among them

a merchant in Iyo han who received 10,000 koku in rent in a fief totaling 10,000 koku of the gross total product. In Kyushu, he comments, the number of owners of large areas of newly reclaimed land was smaller, but many received 500 to 1,000 koku as rents, and receivers of 100 to 200 koku were very numerous. In Kyushu some feudal lords themselves undertook land reclamations. The writer goes on to explain that, wherever the feudal tax rates were high, land reclamations were few, but low tax rates and general prosperity induced new reclamations. High taxes sometimes made peasants desert their plots and emigrate to other areas.

Even if we allow for the obvious gross exaggerations of this account, the fact that merchants engaged frequently and quite successfully in the reclamation of wasteland seems to be well established. The land reclamations raised total productivity, but at the same time drove a wedge into the agricultural system. The new landlords were the first to siphon off the added surplus away from the feudal class, effectively setting a ceiling on feudal taxation. But there were other entrepreneurial, and therefore disrupting, elements on the rural scene.

The merchants from Omi region along the shores of Lake Biwa had been known as peddlers and long-distance traders, even before the Tokugawa period. They were traveling salesmen who crisscrossed the countryside, down to the last village, offering their local products, buying up new goods and selling them elsewhere. Prior to the closing of the country they had gone abroad; their ventures made them somewhat comparable to the Hanse merchants of the Baltic countries. The Omi merchants controlled the trade along Japan's coasts, sailing from the Ryukyus up to Hokkaido.

The exploration of Hokkaido made the Omi merchants

famous. At the beginning of the Tokugawa period, Hokkaido was still underdeveloped: rice was not grown and many articles of daily use were lacking. Samurai who settled in Hokkaido were assigned areas to exploit by the feudal lords, and it was here that the Omi merchants came in. They received commissions and monopoly rights in these backward areas to establish fisheries and trading services; they supplied the samurai with rice, wheat, salt, swords, and textiles. Groups of Omi merchants acquired extended rights in connection with fisheries, and they invested in fishing fleets, developed fishing villages, and started a lucrative monopoly trade in fishery products, notably herring, herring roe, and seaweed.[15]

Dried herring and dried sardines, along with nightsoil and dry leaves, became fertilizers throughout Japan. With their tradition of long-distance trade, the Omi merchants naturally became the promoters and traders of fertilizers, especially of the kinds produced from fish. The use of fertilizer increased, thanks to the activity of the Omi merchants, and contributed much to the increase in agricultural productivity. Thomas Smith mentions that in 1714 the third largest item among all of Osaka harbor's shipments was imports of fertilizer.[16] The use of fertilizer, despite its immediate economic advantages, was for many a marginal farmer the beginning of his undoing. The Omi merchant willingly gave credit at high interest and thus took the first step that would eventually lead to the acquisition of peasant land. There were frequent cases of landlords who had started as peddling merchants from Omi and had bought up large areas of land through the fertilizer trade and moneylending.

Once the Omi merchant had secured a foothold in the village through land ownership, he usually continued to combine moneylending and trade, and added to these occupations some kind of manufacturing. Special favorites of the Omi merchant-manufacturers were vegetable-oil production, the brewing of sake, and miso and soy-sauce making. The area of Hino in Omi became known as the headquarters of sake brewers and soy-sauce producers; such merchant landowners also dominated the sake brewing of the Kanto area. A survey of sake and soy-sauce manufacturing lists 59 establishments of Hino merchants, all started between 1688 and the last years of the bakufu. They were spread all over the country but centered especially in the Kanto area.[17]

A good example of an enterprising Omi merchant house is the Uchiike family in Fukushima prefecture. Between 1763 and 1848 this family had succeeded in moving from peddling to landownership and manufacturing, doing a lucrative business in sake, drygoods, oil, and silk yarn; their large farm was cultivated by hired laborers. As a sign of wealth and progress, the family collected books and employed a samurai as a teacher for its children.[18]

Cash Crops and Concentration of Landholdings

The feudal economy had originally been based on the growing of staple crops and taxes in kind, with a maximum avoidance of luxury consumption and commercialization. There had, of course, been some specialization in commercial crops all along, depending upon conditions of soil and climate. There had been sugar growing in Kyushu and the Ryukyus, cotton in Kinki, and mulberries in the highlands north of Edo. But Tokugawa policy was to discourage further specialization in favor of a maximum production of rice and grains.

Large-scale commercialization of agricultural produce became a necessity, however, with the concentration of samurai in the castle towns. Rice and the other tax commodities had to be transported to the consumer centers, and so they passed through the hands of the commissioned merchants. Part of the feudal tax had to be paid in money, and this forced the peasants to sell their farm products to the local merchant to get the tax money. In this fashion rice and other agricultural products became commercial commodities, and the natural economy increasingly gave way to a money economy.

Records from Sendai han in the 1820s show that agricultural tax deliveries in kind amounted to only 51 percent of total han income; another 21 percent were paid in money, while 28 percent were profits from han-managed enterprises. In the same han, the farmers marketed over half of their total produce left over after payment of taxes in kind, in order to pay the money tax and make their own purchases of fertilizer, clothing, and home utensils.[19]

Once the farmers became this much involved in the market economy, there was little to prevent them from taking full advantage of specialization in accordance with soil conditions and distance to the cities. In the north, rice growing became predominant. Akita han became the main exporter of rice and cereals and imported chiefly textiles. At the end of the Tokugawa period, 45 percent of Akita han's total imports were textiles, while 90.7 percent of its exports consisted of rice and other grains; of this latter sum, one third was exported from the daimyo warehouses and two thirds were shipped by merchants, who apparently had bought directly from peasants.[20] On the whole, however, the cash crops most favored were those connected with textiles, luxury items, and special foods. If the soil was favorable to cash crops, the peasants would sometimes go so far as to purchase the rice for their own use.[21]

The areas with the heaviest concentration of specialized cash crops were those close to the great consumer centers,

the Kinki and the Kanto areas. Naturally cash cropping
and manufacturing of the home-employment type usually
went together and were concentrated in the same areas.
By 1874, commercialization of agriculture was most pronounced in Kinki, followed by Shikoku and Kanto (if we
take into account the size and population density of these
areas — otherwise Kanto comes ahead of Shikoku), while
Kyushu, Sanin, and Tohoku had the lowest percentage of
agricultural commercialization. These ratings are based
on the following products, which were the main items of
trade: cotton and cotton textiles, silkworms and silk, tea,
vegetable oil, wax, tobacco, sake, soy sauce, sugar, paper,
tatami.[22] By 1877, the five Kinai provinces were producing
34.4 percent of all Japanese cotton.[23] Silkworm rearing and
silk reeling were most heavily concentrated in Fukushima,
Yamanashi, and Gumma prefectures. Osaka became the
trading center for commercial produce: 7 percent of
Japan's rice output was shipped to Osaka and 21 percent
of total textiles and raw cotton were concentrated there
as early as 1736.[24]

Although the degree of agricultural commercialization
varied greatly according to soil conditions, climate, and,
most of all, demand and the possibility of transporting the
product to the consumer centers, it is probably reasonable
to assume that by the time of the Restoration half or more
of all agricultural products were put on the market in
one form or another. This would include sales of rice to
meet tax obligations in cash, as well as the sale and purchase of specialized products and converted foodstuffs like
miso, sake, soy sauce, and textiles, along with ceramics and
diverse household goods.

The response of the daimyo and the bakufu to this
commercialization was varied. They feared the undermin-
ing of feudal agriculture and sensed that too much of their

potential tax was being absorbed by merchants. But, at the same time, they urged peasants to resort to cash cropping and home employment so that they could pay higher taxes in money.

A number of daimyo with initiative began to make use of special crops and local industry by establishing their own trading monopolies. A well-known instance occurred in Satsuma han.[25] This han had been almost bankrupt at the beginning of the nineteenth century, with a total debt of 5 million ryo against a yearly han revenue of only 140,000 ryo. An energetic reform program centered on monopoly trade in sugar; sugar had been traditionally a special crop of the Ryukyu islands, which were under Satsuma jurisdiction. These islands were put on a barter-trade basis with Satsuma, delivering the raw sugar to Kagoshima. There it was refined, packed, and shipped to the Osaka market; 60 ships were built for this sugar trade. In Osaka the Satsuma sugar sold very well and provided large revenues for the han's tottering economy. By 1869 sugar accounted for 49 per cent of the total han exports; 54 percent of its imports were textiles.[26]

Other han specialized in porcelain, lacquer, wax, paper, or silk. The peasants had to sell the products at stipulated prices to the han monopoly-trade companies. Rich peasants and local merchants were strongly opposed to these han practices and often became ringleaders in uprisings against the heavy tax burdens.

One of the side effects of agricultural commercialization was an increasing indebtedness among the marginal peasants and the eventual loss of their land to the merchants or rural usurers and rich peasants. The merchants introduced new consumer goods to the villages, and peasants became used to a rice diet, to tea and sake, to better clothing and traveling, all things that were prohibited in the frequent rulings issued by the bakufu and daimyo. Village life became subject to disruptive external influences. The old *oyabun–kobun* relationship and cooperation within the *gonin gumi* gave way to individual ambition and competition. The strong ones could now move ahead of the others. The idea of an immutable rural status quo disappeared; land that had been considered unsalable was sold, and no amount of bakufu prohibition could change this.

From the middle of the Tokugawa period, the number of tenants increased: the wealthy peasants amassed more land, and the marginal peasants became landless laborers or tenants. Landowners of the new type came mainly from the ranks of village samurai, village headmen, merchants, and rural manufacturers. By the 1830s, of the landowners with 50 or more cho of land in the Kinki area, 48 percent were merchants and 24 percent village samurai and village headmen; in Tohoku, 30 percent were merchants and 19 percent samurai and village headmen. In Kanto and Kyushu, the latter group, with 65 percent and 35 percent, was ahead of the merchants, who represented only 13 percent and 18 percent of the rich landowners.[27] In the Kinki region, with its heavy concentration of merchant capital and cotton growing, landownership became particularly skewed. In some places at the end of the Tokugawa period, landless peasants comprised as much as 70 percent of the total village population.[28] The Hirano area, close to Osaka, was most conspicuous for cotton growing and had numerous cotton merchants; by the mid-eighteenth century the merchant-landlords had as many as 2,000 tenant farmers under their control, and 8.2 percent of the population owned 46 percent of the cultivated area.[29]

I shall not follow up the social implications of this concentration of land ownership or comment on the role of the rich peasants and landlords in the Restoration movement. From the entrepreneurial vantage point, the most important function of the rural merchants, usurers, and rich peasants was their engagement in manufacturing.

The Putting-Out Masters and Rural Manufacturers

The men who became landlords through trading, usury, and cash cropping were often very imaginative and enterprising; not bound by tradition, they tried new ways of making money and of investing their capital. Cash crops usually provided an immediate opportunity for investment in some type of manufacturing, as by-employment for the tenant farmers or even as full-time employment for landless laborers. The field of activity was wide and varied according to local conditions and the availability of capital. Investments in such activities as sake brewing, usually combined with miso and soy-sauce making, required large capital, while cotton and silk spinning could be entered into with small initial investments. The sake brewers frequently had their tenants help them during the agricultural off-seasons of winter and early spring. Sake brewing was somewhat restricted by a bakufu license system, but the Hino merchants made sake brewing their favorite investment. The rural manufacturers in the field of silk and cotton textiles provided the tenants and landless laborers with raw materials and some working capital; they also bought looms and rented them out.

The two most famous centers of "putting-out," or domestic, manufacturing were the Kinki area (for cotton textiles) and Fukushima (for silk). In the first decades of the nineteenth century, the Fukushima silk industry had become nationally famous and the silk market drew buyers from far away. A record of 1818 mentions that several thousand producers sold their silk yarns and silk cloth there, worth 15,000 to 16,000 ryo.[30] In the Fukushima area specialization was carried down to the village level, some villages concentrating mainly on silkworm rearing, others on reeling, and still others on weaving.

On the whole, rural putting-out manufacturing did not reach the factory-production stage. There were a few exceptions: spinners in some cases were assembled in one place, and there were other types of large-scale and factory manufacturing that occurred under han management prior to the Restoration. But most of the putting-out masters remained farm landlords, becoming merchants and usurers at the same time.

Satō Gentabei of Kakeda village in Fukushima was a typical highly successful rich peasant, manufacturer, and trader. Records of 1727 from the Satō family indicate that he produced and traded sake in large quantities, and did a lucrative business in yarns, tea, rice, and soybeans. In a single day the ledger shows 279 koku of sake produced; another day records 356 koku of sake sold for over 591 ryo, and silk yarn sold to Fukushima for 184 ryo — yarn that had been spun by people he employed.[31] In this fashion the rich became richer and the poor villagers became ever more dependent upon these village capitalists. The case of the Satō family is of course an extreme one, but lesser capitalists of a similar type were to be found in almost every village. Sometimes a poor farmer could manage to climb the ladder to success, starting with some extra employment or moneylending on a small scale and, with luck and skill, becoming a rural entrepreneur. Smith mentions such a case — a landless peasant in Mino province who had started out in the Meiwa era (1764–1771) trading cotton, rice, and fertilizer and by 1819 had become a landowner of 190 koku, scattered over 15 villages.[32]

Putting-out manufacturing was a mixed blessing to the rural population. It made the majority of the villagers de-

pendent upon a few magnates, but at the same time it did
provide additional income and employment for wives and
daughters. Peasants and local authorities therefore often
welcomed new home-employment opportunities which
helped to alleviate economic pressures. An application of
four villagers in Settsu to be permitted to start weaving
was endorsed by the village headman and the leader of
the *gonin gumi*. Incidentally, of these four only one was
a landless peasant; the other three owned their land, one
earning 33 koku and the other 20 koku, the third an unknown amount. These men argued that it was impossible
to make a living by farming alone.[33] But with home employment even small tenant peasants and landless laborers
were often not badly off, and their wage rates rose with
the further spread of home employment and rural manufacturing.

As a consequence of the attractions of home employment,
rural wage workers became scarce. In the Tempō era
(1830–1844) there were complaints that domestics were
difficult to find because the girls were employed in spinning and weaving.[34] Because of rising wage rates it became
profitable to rent out land instead of operating large units
with hired help,[35] a practice that increasingly broke down
the large household units in the villages. The tenants, in
turn, cut loose from the large farming units and unable
to live on agriculture alone, were forced to seek extra
employment.

From various sides, then, the solidarity and cooperation
within the village were undermined, and the establishment
of small independent working units opened the way for
enterprising individuals. Smith cites a village in Shinshu
in which the size of the average family declined from 3.3
couples to 1.2 couples and from 12.3 members to 3.8
members between 1755 and 1830. The total number of
families in the village rose from 30 to 83 during the same

period.[36] This means, incidentally, a drop in population by about 15 percent. Small family units certainly helped greatly to bring mobility as well as progressive new attitudes to rural Japan. The commercialization of agriculture and putting-out manufacturing had a leavening influence on rural life and prepared the way for the Restoration and the success of the Meiji government's industrialization and modernization efforts.

Rural putting-out manufacturing prior to the Restoration, and the beginnings of factory work, offered a training ground for Japan's industrial labor force. Farmers were getting used to having their daughters work for wages at spinning and weaving: the only change that came later was that the daughters went to the city to do the same work in factories, sending their wages home to support the family. The first workers in Japan's industries did not sever all ties to the village, but the way had been prepared when the villagers were reduced to tenant position and were forced to work for wages on the side. The first steps toward severing the strong bond to the soil was one of the secondary effects of rural entrepreneurship during the Tokugawa period.

During the later part of the Tokugawa period, the most enterprising elements in Japan were to be found in the villages, not in the cities. In the villages the shackles of tradition were thrown off and a liberal and "bourgeois" ideology emerged among the new landlords, rich peasants, and putting-out masters. The guilds that hampered progress in the cities had no significance in the villages, and economic conditions succeeded in changing village attitudes. The rich peasants and putting-out masters took pride in displaying their break with the old restrictions that had been imposed on peasant life. They indulged in luxury consumption and took on political and literary interests. Social critics during the last decades of the Tokugawa frequently complained that rich peasants indulged in literary pursuits that were quite unsuited to their status. They paid more attention to collecting books and taking lessons from samurai tutors than to tilling their lands. They purchased samurai titles, traveled about the country, and took part in politics. Being close to the villagers, many of the rich peasants promoted general education. Many of the village schools were built and financed by landowners and putting-out masters. A survey of Fukushima area, which had many prosperous silk spinners and weavers, shows that at the end of the Tokugawa period 37 percent of all its village schools (terakoya) were sponsored by rich farmers and another 15 percent by village headmen.[37]

Of the leading entrepreneurs in the early Meiji era who were sons of rich peasants, landlords, or putting-out masters, most had come into contact with Western ideas and had participated actively in political life while still on the village farm. Shibusawa Eiichi, the greatest of all Meiji entrepreneurs, was a prime example. He was interested in literary pursuits and wanted to become a samurai. His father was a rich farmer, merchant, and moneylender in the village. Shibusawa received a literary education as well as practical business experience. His deep antagonism to the feudal system became a decisive factor in his later career.[38] Hara Rokurō, another famous Meiji entrepreneur, had a similar background as the son of a rich peasant and putting-out master. His father owned a farm of 67 koku and operated a silk-reeling factory prior to the Restoration; the tenants delivered the cocoons to this mill where their wives and daughters did the reeling. The Hara family, hereditary village headmen, was known for its broadmindedness and progressiveness and its lavish treatment of guests.[39]

In sum, we find that all the requirements for becoming modern industrialists existed among the rural entrepreneurs before the Restoration. Those who combined agriculture, trade, brokerage, and manufacturing succeeded in accumulating relatively large capital resources. They had basic experience in putting-out manufacturing and at times even in factory management. They were progressive and vitally interested in political and social changes that would allow greater scope to their entrepreneurial interests. The question that arises immediately, then, is whether these landlords, rich peasants, and merchant-manufacturers constituted the chief element among Japan's modern entrepreneurs — that is, whether there was a straight line of continuity from village manufacturing to city industry.

In the following section I shall examine rural entrepreneurship after the Restoration, in pursuit of an answer to this question of continuity. At this point it may be stated that, on the whole and with some qualifications there was no such evolution. Three basic factors were responsible for the failure of rural manufacturing to move in a continuous direction toward modern industrial enterprise. The first is that the gap of technological backwardness was too great for the rural manufacturers to overcome. The second factor is that their very success in rural areas prevented them from making a break with the country, and migration to the cities became an almost necessary condition for successful entrepreneurship in modern industry after the Restoration. The final factor is the lack of government promotion of rural industries. Government coaching and subsidies were concentrated on a small elite in a narrowly defined sector; the rural manufacturers did not belong to this elite, and their own capital was not sufficient for successful large-scale ventures of the modern type. After a while they found it more profitable to turn from manufacturing and to go back more or less exclusively to farming. The extent to which these three arguments hold will become clear as we proceed.

THE RURAL MANUFACTURERS AFTER THE RESTORATION

The reader may have been somewhat annoyed at the casual treatment given here to the various rural entrepreneurial activities during the Tokugawa period. I have cheerfully lumped together merchants, pawnbrokers, landowners, rich peasants, Omi merchants, and putting-out masters. They differed widely in their activities, of course, but more often than not they were one and the same person. On the whole, a division of labor had not taken place. In the field of rural manufacturing, too, it is possible to give the same treatment to textiles as to oil extraction and sake brewing, to sugar refining as to paper production. All these products faced a uniform market, increased as demand did, and were neither threatened by imports nor promoted by export possibilities.

This uniform situation changed after the opening of the ports. Foreign trade became a major, if not the most important, determinant of the further development of rural industry. Some were threatened by imports and had to struggle for their existence; others received a strong boost through exports and grew by leaps and bounds; still others remained unaffected until internal competition from modern industry made itself felt in the late 1890s. Since foreign trade strongly influenced the course of Japanese rural manufacturing, let us examine separately the development of these three different groups of rural industries.

Silk Reeling

It is sometimes maintained that Japan owed her continued independence, her avoidance of reduction to colonial status, to the poverty of her natural resources. This may have been one reason, though probably not a very important one. But the lack of natural resources would certainly have become a severe handicap to industrialization if Japan's agriculture had not provided an exportable surplus for financing capital-good imports. Most underdeveloped countries of today export primary products in which they have a comparative advantage owing to climatic conditions and natural resources. Japan had neither of these advantages over the Western countries.

There were two commodities that offered great promise for trade: tea and silk. Both had a long tradition in Japan and had been highly developed through rural entrepreneurship. Tea and raw silk were the chief export items that went to pay for the bulk of Japanese imports in the first fifteen years of the Meiji, and even later they occupied commanding places in the export lists, along with rice, copper, coal, camphor, and silk cloth. The main export commodities are shown below (five-year averages, units in million yen).

Years	Raw silk	Tea	Rice	Total exports
1868–1872	8.38	3.82	0	15.44
1873–1877	9.42	5.76	0.78	21.32
1878–1882	11.40	6.64	1.44	29.62
1883–1887	15.40	6.82	1.92	42.36
1888–1892	26.44	6.62	5.30	70.36
1893–1897	39.98	7.74	6.38	120.52
1898–1902	58.18	9.02	6.70	216.30
1903–1907	72.50	12.14	4.04	311.56

Computed from *Dai Nihon gaikoku bōeki* (The foreign trade of great Japan), ed. Nōshōmushō shōmukyoku (The Ministry of Agriculture and Trade, Department of Trade; Tokyo, 1911) , pp. 3, 7, 10.

The Japanese raw-silk export boom had actually started with the export of silkworm eggs. They were in high demand after the opening of the ports, because of a silkworm disease that had crippled French sericulture around 1860. The opening of the Suez Canal in 1869 also aided Japan, since the export trade in silkworm eggs catered to the European market. But a few years later the silkworm disease in Europe was eradicated, and the new breed imported from Japan had restocked the European supply. Silkworm-egg exports began to drop sharply after 1868. From 3.7 million yen in that year, their export value fell to 347,000 in 1877 and to almost nothing by 1887, with not quite 3,000 yen.⁴⁰

Japanese exporters had to switch to raw silk and compete on the European market with quality yarns. This raised new problems in silk reeling. The traditional hand reeling that had been practiced under the putting-out masters produced rough and uneven yarns; mechanization of the reeling process was called for. The House of Ono was among the first to initiate factory reeling using imported machinery; three mechanical mills had been built by 1873.⁴¹ Ono invested heavily in raw-silk production, especially in its Tsukiji reeling mill, which became the immediate reason for the house's bankruptcy in 1874.⁴² The government itself established two model mills, one in 1874 (Kankōryō) and the other in 1875 (Tomioka). All of these pioneering mills were either Italian- or French-oriented in machinery, management, and scale. Each of these grand beginnings ended in failure because the Japanese were not used to large-scale operations of this kind. The successful mechanization of silk reeling was effected through another approach — imported machinery was used, but on a small scale and adapted to rural conditions.

The success stories in raw silk are to be found among

the rural capitalists, the sake brewers and merchants and landlords who had some experience in the employment of rural hands. Two of the first mechanical reeling mills were established in 1869 by two sake brewers in Fukushima prefecture (at that time still Shirakawa han); they were well aware of the silk-export opportunities and had sufficient capital from their trading and brewing to purchase machinery and build reeling factories.[43] The man who had the greatest success in silk reeling was Katakura Kentarō. He was a landowner with literary interests who kept in close touch with events in Tokyo. He started a silk-reeling establishment on his farm, and after the collapse of the House of Ono he bought part of its machinery, sold his farm, and became exclusively a silk spinner. By 1894 his mill had a larger output than the government-built Tomioka mill. This progressive entrepreneur sent his son to the United States to study modern reeling techniques, thus assuring the further progress of his mill.[44]

Mechanical reeling did not take the lead over hand reeling, however, until after 1895, and even then the scale of operation was usually small. It is interesting that the degree of mechanization was by no means uniform in all areas of raw-silk production. Nagano prefecture was the most mechanized, while Gumma prefecture remained largely at the hand-reeling level. A survey of 1879 showed Nagano to be far in the lead with 358 mechanized mills, each with at least 10 employees; Gifu prefecture had 143, Yamanashi 80, and Gumma only 11. But generally the operation was a small one; the capital of most mills remained under 300 yen, and the mills did not operate for more than half a year on the average in the agricultural slack periods.[45]

Essentially, then, raw-silk production retained the character of rural small-scale manufacturing, financed by the former putting-out masters and silk spinners. This was a straight line of continuity. The sudden leaps into large-scale operation attempted by the government and by the house of Ono were not crowned with success; the rural entrepreneurs preferred a slower step-by-step advance. The large, fully mechanized reeling mills did not come until the second decade of the twentieth century.

One of the important groups to jump on the bandwagon of the silk-yarn export boom was the samurai. Many of them had spun silk earlier, before they were deprived of their status. When the government started to encourage the establishment of businesses by samurai, many samurai companies took up silkworm rearing or silk reeling, in almost all cases by hand. Of the fifteen samurai companies that started in Nagasaki prefecture between 1881 and 1888, eight were in silkworm rearing or silk reeling.[46] In Akita a large company of fifteen hundred samurai families engaged in raw-silk production.[47] Silk reeling was practiced in almost all parts of the country, and a large contingent of these new producers were samurai.

In the first decade after the Restoration when mechanization was still in its infancy, Gumma had by far the largest output of all the prefectures. It had an old tradition of silk manufacturing and was close to the export center of Yokohama. The silk-export boom brought prosperity to the villages, and rich farmers, merchants, and other moneyed men took up silk reeling on a putting-out basis or in small factory-like establishments. A collection of two hundred biographical sketches of prominent men in the Gumma silk industry during the Meiji era provides interesting information on the methods used and the general trends displayed by these rural entrepreneurs.[48]

The Gumma farmers enlarged the mulberry-growing area, organized local unions for the promotion of sericulture, and had their own marketing boards, which maintained close contacts with Yokohama. The well-to-do employers frequently went to Yokohama, not only to arrange their export deals but to gather the latest information and purchase machinery to raise standards of quality. Some sent their sons abroad to study the silk industry. Local training schools were established to teach people better reeling techniques and to raise the general level of education. The skyrocketing price of raw silk (it quadrupled between 1859 and 1867) brought a general air of prosperity and progress to the villages of Gumma prefecture.

But one thing is noteworthy: with only a few exceptions, these successful men in silk production and export did not consider moving to the city. The village enterprise, after all, had brought them prosperity and was the basis of their success. It was a direct and rather simple continuation of what they had done before, with the addition of a few new machines. They were not completely bypassed by the modernizing influence coming from Yokohama and even more from Tokyo, but they did not encounter the full impact of Western technology. Raw-silk production, even where it became mechanized, remained halfway traditional; and because profits were assured even with relative inefficiency, these rural putting-out masters were not forced by economic necessity to become modern industrialists, at least not for a few more decades. Silk production did not provide the avenue toward Western large-scale industry, and we find almost no successful silk reelers among the great entrepreneurs of the Meiji era.

Cotton Spinning

One of the great worries of the Meiji government was the balance-of-payments problem. Government officials did everything possible to institute a new era of progress and tried to demonstrate the advantages of Western technology. But as a side effect of their efforts there developed an ever-rising demand for Western imports, notably cotton yarns and cotton cloth, which constituted as much as 30–40 percent of Japan's total imports in the first Meiji decade. Inevitably, this had an adverse effect on Japanese cotton growers and spinners. In some rural areas people began to riot and demonstrate against the cotton imports, and campaigns were launched against all Western goods that were competing against the established rural manufactures. It was claimed that these imports would ruin rural Japan and with it the whole national economy. Calico cloth, lamps, railways, even the solar calendar and Western-style haircuts, became targets of criticism.[49] The government was probably little impressed by the rural riots and protest meetings, but the balance-of-payments problem caused serious concern, and some effective measures were called for.

The government established two model spinning mills and bought machinery for ten mills which it sold at discount rates to prospective founders. In order to stimulate interest in mechanical cotton spinning among the cotton merchants and putting-out masters, the government launched a propaganda drive. A series of exhibitions on cotton spinning was staged, and on these and similar occasions the speakers hammered away at the point that many more mills must be established to save Japan from the menace of imported yarns. Defense against this threat was presented as being rather simple, as though the application of Western technology to spinning would assure success and high profits.

Those who ventured first into the founding of spinning mills, those of the so-called two-thousand-spindles era, were typically men who readily responded to the govern-

ment's appeals and who were already imbued with a faith
in modern technology. Among the twenty founders of
mills prior to 1884 — the year that marked the transition
to the second stage of large-scale, profitable mills — ten
were samurai and ten were merchants or peasants. The
samurai were mostly officials of one kind or another, to
whom a concern with the "menace from imports" came
naturally and who could rely on public funds or pressure
moneyed men into contributing capital.

The mill founders who were either merchants or rich
peasants, most of them connected with the cotton trade,
showed traits and motivations surprisingly similar to those
of the samurai-officials. They belonged to the progressively
modern wing, had close connections with government officials, and were quite conscious of being among the avant-
garde of their time. But the vast majority of cotton merchants and putting-out spinners were still cautious and
did not invest in the new mills; they were too rational, in
the profit-maximization sense. They realized apparently
that, in spite of some monetary and a great deal of moral
support from the government, these mills would not be
able to compete effectively with the imported yarns. Indeed, until after 1885 the small-scale cotton mills were
barely managing to survive; profit rates were on the average not higher than 3–4 percent, but some mills stayed in
the red for years. So even the fervor of the enthusiasts was
in danger of cooling down in the struggle for survival.
Naturally, in the years of pioneering, it was the progressive,
politically inspired idealists who dominated the field.

Kashima Manpei, the first cotton merchant to switch to
mechanical spinning, is typical of the progressive pioneering group. He had urged the bakufu to introduce mechanical spinning as a solution to the high prices of cotton goods,
and he then established, with capital contributions from

a few of his fellow merchants and against formidable odds, the first private spinning mill in Japan, completed in 1872. Later Kashima insisted on having his spinning machines produced in Japan according to his own designs, in order to make Japanese cotton spinning "independent of imported machinery," although the machines made in Japan cost him much more than the imported ones.[50] The pioneers in cotton spinning, be they samurai or merchants, were all interested in innovations, and once they had ventured into the area of the untried, they fanned out over a broad range, promoting modern methods and technology. There was, for instance, Kurihara Nobuchika, the founder of Ishikawa Spinning Mill (established in 1882), the son of a broker and scholar. He had originally shown little interest in business but was a man of public affairs with a great esteem for the emperor. Once he started to innovate, he did not stick to one field. He promoted agriculture and trade in various ways and founded a bank, in addition to the spinning mill.[51]

Men of this kind were drawn into entrepreneurship partly through politics, through their close contacts with officials and with the new tide of events. If their start was politically inspired, this does not mean that they were entirely uninterested in maximizing their own profits. The point is that from the beginning they were far removed from the conservatism that still prevailed among the majority of the cotton capitalists of the Kinki area, the center of cotton growing and trade. It is said that the immediate reason for the founding of the Kuwahara Mill in 1882 was a strong appeal by Matsukata, who urged the building of spinning mills to provide competition against imports. A rural manufacturer and vegetable-oil producer, Kaneda Ichihei, responded by deciding there and then to build a mill with his capital.[52] The more hesitant men of the cotton trade and the rural putting-out masters stayed away from mechanical cotton spinning, by and large, until after the breakthrough achieved in this field by the Osaka Spinning Mill (1883). Shibusawa Eiichi had founded this large-scale mill after careful study of the technological problems involved; it had ample capital resources, the latest machinery, and an expert technician, none of which had been available to the other faltering mills. In 1884, the second year of its operation, the mill paid out an 18 percent dividend.

By this time the cotton merchants had come into severe economic straits. The imports of calicoes and yarns, as well as the competition from the mechanical mills, caused a serious depression in the trade: cotton growers and hand spinners found themselves hard hit and had to seek a new economic basis. With a profitable avenue of investment opened up by the breakthrough of the Osaka Mill and under ever-growing pressure for change, the conservative cotton merchants finally moved into mechanical spinning. They still had large capital resources to invest and needed neither government help nor political incentives.

Between 1886 and 1894, thirty-three new mills were founded, most of them large. Of these, ten were located in the vicinity of Osaka, the center of the cotton trade; by 1913 the Osaka area had nineteen spinning mills. Okayama came next, with nine.[53] The representative founders of this period were wealthy rural capitalists or merchants from Osaka. When five Omi merchants applied for permission to build the Kanakin Mill (1888), the government investigated their financial position in order to assure stability for the venture. It became apparent that one of them had assets totaling 9 million yen, three 500,000 yen apiece, and the last 100,000 yen.[54] Such men had kept back their capital until a sure investment project turned up. Pioneering in untried areas with new technology was not to their liking. As one of them, the founder of Kurashiki Mill (1886) put it, his theory was not to strive for the first place but to stay in the second or third, because that was more profitable.[55]

Among the mills founded in the late 1880s and the 1890s, some had too little capital and failed. The prolonged depression in cotton trade and spinning had impoverished many merchants and putting-out spinners, and founding a mill became their last hope. The Hirano Mill was a case in point. The eleven founders could muster just enough capital to buy the site and build a wall around it with their combined 25,000 yen. An Osaka financier rescued this venture with a large loan, so that the mill was completed and eventually became a success.[56]

Hand spinning was practically extinct by 1895. Handloom weaving, however, continued for some time longer, although here too the depression became severe. We find a few cases where spinning mills were established for the purpose of supplying cheaper yarns to local weavers and thus alleviating their plight. The Kurume Mill in northern Kyushu started this way. The Kurume area had been nationally famous for its rough cotton cloth. The weavers suffered because the imported yarns were not suitable for this cloth, and hand spinning had become disorganized. Some wealthy putting-out weavers and merchants established a mill in 1889 for spinning the required yarns.[57] The development of handloom weaving and its eventual decline need not be traced any further, but it is probably not wrong to assume that the phases of its changeover into factory weaving were similar to those of cotton spinning.

Silk reeling and cotton spinning were the first industries in Japan to achieve substantial success, but for different reasons and through different approaches. Silk reeling re-

mained rural and small-scale, changed only in part by the
introduction of some Western machinery. It was carried
out chiefly by the rural capitalists by way of a continuous
development from putting-out home employment. There
was no revolution and no crisis, but a gradual innovational
process. This type of development was aided by the export
boom, and its basis continued to be inherited local skills.
The initial capital requirements were not too large for
the individual rural capitalists; there was no need for joint
capital.

Cotton spinning emerged as a modern, efficient industry
through the crisis of import competition. Ultimately it
had the advantage of cheap labor, but in the short run the
technological problems and the necessity for joint-stock
enterprise, because of large capital requirements, made this
type of investment unattractive to rural capitalists. The
pioneering problems therefore had to be solved by men of
a different kind, those who had political connections and
a strong faith in technology. Such men were found chiefly
among samurai administrators and a small group of putting-out masters and merchants who had come far in absorbing Western influence and the new Meiji outlook.

Traditional Rural Industries

Despite the large imports of foreign cloth, Japanese
daily life and general consumption patterns were little
touched by the Western craze. The effect of innovations
like haircuts, beef eating, umbrellas, and many of the other
signs of "civilization" of the day was marginal and largely
confined to the cities. Japanese home life went on as it had
for centuries. People built their houses as they had before,
of wood with almost no furniture and no heating except
for the traditional hibachi or the kotatsu. They kept the
getas as their footgear and kimonos as their favorite gar-

ments. Eating habits proved to be most resistant to change. Beef, milk, butter, and bread, not to speak of beer and whiskey, had to wait until the next big Western "boom," after 1945, to become popular. The dogged adherence to traditional living and consumption patterns became an economic blessing to Japan. It prevented unnecessary capital outflows and the erosion of the economy by the so-called demonstration effect, the great problem for present-day underdeveloped countries.

Foremost among the traditional manufactured products that were not affected by foreign trade were sake, miso, and soy sauce. As general consumption levels began to rise, these foodstuffs enjoyed a period of prosperity. Sake, miso, and soy sauce were often manufactured by the same producers — merchants or rich peasants. They occupied the top position among all manufactured goods. According to a survey of all prefectures carried out in 1874, the value of the total sake production was 18.6 million yen; next in value came the weaving sector, with 17.1 million yen. All textiles combined, including raw silk, were worth 31 million yen, as against 30.1 million for sake, miso, and soy sauce alone.[58]

Since the three foodstuffs were articles of daily use (sake consumption had long since spread to the peasant level in spite of the bakufu's efforts to the contrary), their production was not concentrated in particular areas. Aichi prefecture led in sake and Gumma prefecture in miso production, though the degree of concentration in these areas was not too pronounced. In almost every village, one rich farmer had a brewery. Sake production had been restricted prior to the Restoration by a license system; when this system was abolished, new breweries sprang up everywhere. The number of Omi merchants from Hino area who operated breweries and produced soy sauce almost tripled between 1868 and 1906, the establishments going from 59 to about 150.[59]

The location of the sake breweries moved from the countryside over the next few decades, and the scale seems to have increased with rising demand. The sake brewers in the 1880s still typically combined trading, land-ownership, and moneylending. Specialization in large-scale sake brewing and miso and soy-sauce production in modern factories came gradually. By 1895 more than half of 137 surveyed sake breweries and miso and soy-sauce factories were located in cities; only 60 were rural establishments. Of the 137, 44 had over 10,000 yen and 60 over 20,000 yen of invested capital.[60] The gradual movement of the brewery industry toward the cities marked the beginning of the final stage of traditional rural manufacturing. The landowners, merchants, and putting-out masters began to specialize; some finally became industrialists, but most of them returned to agriculture and became landlords.

Vegetable-oil production had been another of the more important rural industries of the Tokugawa period. It did not remain entirely unaffected by imports. The introduction of petroleum lamps was a serious blow to vegetable-oil producers, who had been the principal suppliers of oil for the old-fashioned lamps. Prices of vegetable-oil declined and so did oil production. This process of decline, however, was slowed down by two new factors: the introduction of the hydraulic press, which greatly increased efficiency in extracting oil, and the use of vegetable oil as a machine lubricant. Since the new demand came mainly from the industries in the cities, oil production, whatever remained of it, also began to move there.[61]

Sugar production which had played a large role in the economic recovery of Satsuma, and had been produced in three varieties as black, red, and white sugar, suffered a

similar decline. Sugar-cane growing, which had been concentrated in Kagoshima prefecture and also in parts of
Shikoku and Shizuoka, vanished with the coming of imported refined sugar.

Import and export conditions, and the patterns of Japanese consumption, were not the sole determinants of the
course followed by rural manufacturing after the Restoration. Another, and highly important, factor was the changing situation in agriculture itself. After the Restoration it
became very profitable to go back to primary-food production.

The Landlords' Return to Agriculture

The return to primary-food production by those putting-
out masters who had not become cotton spinners or raw-
silk producers was induced by two factors: the steep rise of
primary food prices and the land-tax reform. Both together
greatly encouraged the abandonment of traditional industries that had once been very profitable but were now increasingly difficult to manage.

The prices of staple foods soared in the post-Restoration
years and were highest of all for basic foodstuffs, according to the Tokyo commodity-price index. The group of
five commodities consisting of rice, barley, wheat, soybeans,
and red beans moved from its base 100 in 1873 to 172 in
1893, with a peak of 192 reached in 1890. The next highest group, consisting of salt, soy sauce, miso, and fuel,
moved during the same period from 100 to 154. On the
other hand, lumber, coal, raw and refined copper, and iron
declined from 100 to 85.[62] It is evident, then, that the production of rice and other grains became more attractive
than the once lucrative production of miso and soy sauce.

As an inducement to a return to exclusive primary-food
production, the land-tax reform of 1873 was even more

important than the favorable price movements of agricultural products. This most important reform has been discussed frequently in Western literature and will be presented here only in bare outline form.

The three most important features of the land-tax law of 1873 were: (1) The tax was to be determined by the market value of the land, not by its yield, as had been the rule during the feudal era. In 1873 the tax level was set at 3 percent of the market value; this was lowered to 2.5 percent in 1877. (2) All taxes were to be paid to the central government, and in money, not in kind. (3) The owners and not the cultivators were taxed. The sale of land had already become legal in 1872. But this did not really constitute a practical change because the prohibition against land sale had long since lost its effectiveness.

In effect, about 30 percent of the gross agricultural produce was taxed away under the new land tax. This was no real change from the prior feudal rates. The nominal rates of the feudal tax (50 percent or even 60 percent) had been lowered in the course of the Tokugawa period through increases in productivity with which the upward revisions of the yield surveys had not caught up. Furthermore, the feudal tax had been substantially lower on reclaimed land. The initial 30 percent tax rate very soon became lighter because of the revision of the assessment from 3 percent to 2.5 percent of the market value of the land; but even more important, the inflationary price spiral reduced the real burden to as low a rate as 15.5 percent of the yield by 1888–1892. Nevertheless, agriculture had to bear the main tax load; the rest of the economy — that is, the secondary and teriary sectors — had tax rates on the average of only about 2.3 percent.[63]

In addition, in the wake of the land-tax reform, about half of all forests and wasteland became state property.[64]

This was a heavy blow to many marginal farmers who had supplied themselves with fertilizer and firewood from the common forests and wastelands.

Although the land-tax reform lowered the actual tax burden in comparison with the feudal rates, it must still be called high in absolute terms. If approximately 20 percent of the gross produce of agriculture could immediately become government revenue, this throws light on the solution sought by the Meiji government to its central problem of capital formation. The primary solution lay not in heavier burdens on agriculture and not in raising additional sources of income, but in channeling the samurai into productive processes. The savings of agriculture which had previously been consumed by that class were now made available for industrialization. Indeed, thus conceived, the cost of industrialization in a sense fell most heavily upon the abolished feudal class.

The government succeeded in financing its armament and industrialization program almost completely from land-tax revenues. Except for two major debt issues — the commutation bonds of 1876, with 173.9 million yen, and the adjustment debt to liquidate inflation and the inconvertible notes in 1886, with 175 million yen — no major borrowings were necessary, either internally or externally. The land tax provided 85.6 percent of all government revenues in 1888–1892, although in this same period agriculture produced only 50 percent of the national income. Business taxes furnished a bare 1.6 percent, income tax gave 2.4 percent, and 10.4 percent was provided by customs duties.[65]

In spite of the fact that agriculture financed industrialization, a considerable surplus over and above the tax was still left to the cultivator, if he happened to own his land. The sustenance of the cultivator and his family required about 40 percent of the yield; if we add approximately 20 percent or even less for the tax, a surplus of 40 percent remained. The landowners and rural capitalists saw in this exploitable surplus their great opportunity. Around 1887 the rents charged the tenants averaged, for the whole country, 58 percent of the yield for paddy land and 56 percent for dry lands.[66] The difference between the 58 percent or 56 percent and the land tax was the profit rate for the landowner.

The stimulus toward landownership is quite clear from these figures. The question that remains is why peasant proprietors lost land if the conditions for owners were so favorable. The answer is doubtless complicated, but one reason is certainly the erratic price movements of agricultural commodities and the fluctuations in the income level of the farmers. The price of rice fluctuated in wide arcs; for example, it rose from 5.82 yen per koku in 1878 to 10.07 yen in 1880 and fell again to 4.62 yen in 1883.[67] And it was not only the price of rice that was affected — one can argue that low rice prices were caused by bumper crops and that sales volume at least partly compensated for declining prices. Total agricultural income followed the same jerky movement: the gross value of agricultural produce rose from 254 million yen in 1878 to 534 million in 1880 and fell to 253 million in 1884.[68] These examples should suffice to show that, despite favorable average conditions for proprietor-peasants, the unwary and marginal ones could easily be thrown into debt and lose their land. It is easy to get used to higher levels of living in a series of two or three good years and then resort to borrowing in a year of sudden income loss. Those who did not have sufficient capital reserves, the marginal owner-farmers, were always in danger of being reduced to tenancy.

For the whole country, the percentage of tenant land continued to rise after the Restoration: from 31.1 percent in 1873, it rose to 36.8 percent in 1883, 40 percent in 1893, and 44.5 percent in 1903.[69] Landholdings were largest in the northern sections of Japan, notably the Niigata and Akita areas, which were the chief rice-producing regions. In the Kinki area the merchant-landlords succeeded at times in reducing almost entire villages to tenant status.

The village of Kuga near Kyoto illustrates this general trend. The percentage of large holdings increased steadily at the expense of the middle-sized farms, while the percentage of small farms stayed about the same. This indicates, of course, a sliding down the scale from middle-sized to small, and the exodus of the small farmers into tenancy. The number of landowners with over ten cho of land more than tripled, rising from 0.9 percent to 2.9 percent between 1875 and 1905, while the medium farmers of one to two cho declined from 14.1 percent to 7.8 percent in the same period.[70] A rich vegetable-oil producer and merchant in this village lent money at 10 percent interest to other growers, and demanded in addition that they sell their vegetables to him at 10 percent below the market price.[71] In this fashion, rural moneylenders and manufacturer-merchants used the economic weakness of small farmers to reduce them to tenant position. In the same village the rural capitalists had succeeded by 1893 in enlarging their landholdings to 82 percent of all village land.[72]

The movement of rural manufacturers and merchants into landlordism has elicited much criticism and comment from Japanese economic historians. Depending upon the writer's particular school of thought, both praise and blame are accorded these "parasitic" landlords.[73] My concern is not whether these landlords were good or bad, whether they were bourgeois or feudal. The important fact here is that the new landlordism constituted the terminus of

Tokugawa rural entrepreneurship, insofar as it had not moved into modern industry via raw silk or cotton spinning.

But the contribution of the new Meiji landlords to the astonishing increases in agricultural output throughout the Meiji era was by no means insignificant. These men occupied something like a middle position between the Prussian Junkers, who managed their own demesnes, employing land laborers, and the Western European absentee landlords, who left farming entirely to their tenants. In Japan rents were fixed neither by long tradition nor by law; therefore the landlord could raise rents if he succeeded in increasing the productivity of the land. Because the landlords ·did this, they contributed to agricultural progress. They tried out new seeds and techniques, regulated rivers and constructed dams to prevent natural calamities, in order to assure stable rent payments.[74] The use of fertilizer rose steeply owing to their initiative. Fertilizer use rose from its base 100 in the 1878–1882 period to 171 in 1888–1892 and eventually to a staggering 3,997 in 1913–1917.[75] During the same periods, the production of rice rose from 100 to 130 and then 185.[76]

All this time, however, Japanese agriculture remained labor-intensive and small-scale. Industry did not grow fast enough to absorb a large percentage of the rural population. Initially the jobless samurai were the main constituent of the industrial labor force; then population soon began to grow and to add to the labor supply. But owing to the steep rise of agricultural prices and the slowness with which the rural population migrated to the cities, land rents stayed high and provided a constant inducement to invest in further improvements. The rural labor force remained at approximately 15.5 million until the 1890s, when it began to decline gently.[77] The real income in agriculture continued to rise, although much more slowly than in industry.

The avoidance of a mass exodus from the villages into the cities was a characteristic of Japan's economic development. The landlords did not resort to extensive capital-using agriculture, but improved rice planting to yield higher productivity. Certainly this was important, since it made Japan a pioneer in high-grade rice cultivation, enabling the nation to achieve productivities several times greater than those of other Asian rice-growing areas. Today in some Southeast Asian countries, with their dense rural populations and still primitive rice-growing techniques, a more intensive agricultural effort may also be necessary and prove to be most advantageous, along with gradual industrialization.[78]

IV

THE INITIATIVE
FROM THE CENTER

The economic development and industrialization of Meiji Japan was a complex process resulting from the interaction of diverse forces, political, social, and economic; to dwell exclusively on economic variables invites serious misrepresentation of the entire process. A similar caution is necessary when we deal with the government and the private sector of the economy, for they were closely connected. Consequently, although my primary concern is with the emergence of entrepreneurs, and hence with the private sector, the paramount role of the government's initiative in the formation of a new entrepreneurial elite must be given due attention.

The word "government" will be used here in a broad sense. This is why I prefer to speak of the initiative from the center rather than of the role of government investments. Government investments were important, but not so much as one may be tempted to think. Probably a more far-reaching effect upon the whole course of Japan's modern industrialization came from the successful establishment and fostering of a new way of thinking. Initially the crucial task of the Meiji officials was to inculcate an unbending will to progress, to rouse the nation out of its long sleep and rally it behind the great program of advance. In a sense the Meiji government became for the people a symbol of what has been called the "post-Newtonian mentality." In communicating this newborn faith in modern technology and industrialization first to an entrepreneurial elite and then to the whole population, the Meiji officials performed brilliantly.

Alexander Gerschenkron stresses two important conditions that stimulate economic development in backward, tradition-bound countries.[1] One is the growth of internal tensions and dissatisfactions; some group or groups in the society come under economic pressure or rise economically while not receiving corresponding social recognition. If then the roadblocks that stood in the way of change are removed by external or internal events, a snowball reaction may set in and lead eventually to dynamic economic growth. My first three chapters have sufficiently indicated the rise of internal tensions in Tokugawa society, resulting from the economic plight of the samurai and the accumulation of wealth in the hands of city merchants and rural capitalists. The underlying discontents could not be mobilized as creative forces for change so long as the bakufu retained its iron grip on the country. When, after the opening of the ports, the bakufu rule started to show signs of weakness, general unrest and uprisings followed. Undoubtedly this gradual growth of tensions and discontent contributed much to the ease with which the Meiji government was able to initiate its new course.

But Gerschenkron mentions a second condition that is fundamental to the speed with which industrialization will take place. This is the amount of technological experience that the backward country can borrow from the advanced countries. The sudden realization of the vast gap of backwardness that separates the underdeveloped country from the industrialized nations can produce a psychological shock, as well as opportunities for cutting corners and for skipping intermediate stages. This shock can awaken a sluggish people to feverish activity and a firm determination to catch up as quickly as possible.

Like the castle community in the Sleeping Beauty tale, Japan not only awoke, but it came suddenly to realize how much the world had changed during its long sleep. This experience stunned the best men of the nation and propelled them to move at top speed in order to close the gap. Of course, there is always the possibility of a passive reaction, of adopting the bonanzas of modern industry by importing consumer goods from the West. In this fashion the contact with the West would have eroded the Japanese economy: the rich would have benefited, and the country as a whole would have remained backward and weak, subject to the exploitation of foreign interests.

It was at this crucial junction that the Meiji government demonstrated its strength and leadership. It made the best of the shock effect by harnessing all of the national virtues toward the great single goal of accepting the challenge and overtaking the most advanced Western countries. Natural ambition and national fervor, feudal virtues, and religion were appealed to and guided through conscious policies toward this one goal. Clearly, the establishment of a mentality of progress, and of a determination to compete rather than to accept passively, is of the greatest significance in the course of Japan's economic development. Therefore, despite the elusive character of this process, it will be discussed briefly in the following section. I shall then turn to the other problems associated with government initiative: the transfer of modern technology and government investments.

THE BUMMEI KAIKA

The rather sudden about-face of Japanese patriots, from deadly hostility toward the barbarians from the West to boundless admiration and acceptance of almost everything and anything Western, may seem like a total capitulation of the "Chrysanthemum and the Sword" before the steam engine and the cannon. But Japan exchanged the sword for guns and steam engines in order to preserve her most important treasure, the Chrysanthemum, that is, her national identity and self-respect. The shock of the realization of their national weakness did not make the Japanese subservient to the West but, in judo fashion, made them turn the best of that foreign strength to their own advantage.

At the very outset of the Meiji era, the emperor proclaimed a new era of "seeking knowledge from the whole world." Now was to come a glorious time of progress and civilization. *Bummei kaika* (civilization and enlightenment) became a catchword of the early years after the Restoration. In it was reflected not only an admiration of Western civilization, but the proud determination of the island nation to become equal to the West in every respect. The story of the drastic change from "hate the barbarians" to the *bummei kaika* mentality has often been told.[2] I shall concentrate here mainly on two aspects of that story. First we shall see that this apparently sudden shift in attitudes was not a freak of Japanese psychology but had its roots in a long development, and, second, we shall look at the economic consequences of the *bummei kaika* ideology.

When for the first time the West met the East on Japanese soil in the sixteenth century, the result was mutual admiration. The Japanese were awed by Western ships and culture and science, and the missionaries and merchants from the West became captivated by the natural grace and nobility of the people and their customs.[3] The course of Japanese history might have been very different if that early romance between the West and Japan had been given time to mature, and if Japan had adopted Western culture and Christianity as she had earlier accepted the Chinese influence.

For reasons that will not be elaborated upon here, this early romance deteriorated, step by step, until the country was closed completely to the West. First the European ships were limited to Hirado and Nagasaki in 1616; in 1641 all Western ships were banned except those of the Dutch. The latter were permitted to keep a trading post on Dejima, a tiny island connected with Nagasaki by a bridge. In one of the bloodiest persecutions history has known, Christianity was almost completely eradicated.[4] Information about the West was severely limited, but it did trickle into Japan through Dutch books, which were eagerly studied by the so-called Dutch scholars (rangakusha). All books that so much as mentioned the "wicked religion" were banned by the bakufu which made heroic efforts to build a self-contained, stable, and contented country. Any potential source of dissatisfaction and any wish for change were to be killed in the bud. Dutch learning was controlled; during most of the seventeenth and eighteenth centuries it remained limited to such practical matters as medicine and astronomy and was engaged in by the interpreters for the Dutch in Nagasaki and other lower samurai and commoners.

Dutch learning came to assume much greater importance in the field of science, and it was chiefly for this that the bakufu came to promote it by the beginning of the nineteenth century. The bakufu established a translation bureau in 1811, and in 1856 it opened a full-fledged school of Western learning, the Bansho shirabesho (place to study barbarian books), in Edo.[5] The bakufu's lead was followed by a number of daimyo, notably Mito but also Saga, Satsuma, Tosa, and a few others. During the first half of the nineteenth century, Dutch learning became increasingly a subject of political controversy. After Britain's victory over China in the Opium War, the Japanese wakened to the fact of Western military superiority and its potential threat to national independence. The bakufu and the han administrators fully aware of the inadequate state of the national defenses, established schools for military science and experimented with Western weapons.

Who were the scholars that carried on Dutch or, as it was later called, Western learning? They were more often than not Confucian philosophers with rigid ideas about the function of the state and the position of the individual in society, and with an unbounded belief in the superiority of Japan over the West. Western studies did not shake this basic belief but instead gave it a strongly patriotic force. No matter what their conclusions and policy recommendations were, these men thought in national rather than in individual and private terms. Even scholars like Fukuzawa Yukichi, who managed to stay out of political controversies and concentrated on the philosophical and scientific, rather than the military and political, aspects of Western studies, thought that national greatness, prosperity, and independence must be the ultimate end of Western studies.

It has been stressed that, although the Weltanschauungs underlying Confucianism and Western science are very different, Japanese scholars managed a synthesis of their own. Western learning was limited to practical aspects, while ethics and social philosophy remained thoroughly

Confucian and thus feudal. If anything, the acquaintance with Western technological superiority tended to bolster national pride in Japanese ethical superiority; all that Western learning could contribute was the means and weapons with which to keep the Western barbarians from the sacred soil of the nation of the gods.

But while Western learning thus fanned the fires of patriotism, it also caused clashes of opinion with respect to means. How far was Japan to go in using Western methods? The bakufu, with its insistence on the status quo, became extremely nervous whenever some scholar advocated social or economic change according to Western models. It then clamped down relentlessly on such "traitors."[6] On the other hand, when the bakufu was forced to open Japan to foreign trade, these scholar-patriots wrote and spoke against the bakufu and called its officials traitors. Yoshida Shōin was the outstanding example of this type of patriot; he became a leader of the sonnō jōi movement (revere the emperor, expel the barbarians) which at once fought against the bakufu because it had admitted foreigners to Japan and vowed to expel the Western powers from Japan. His great teacher, Sakuma Shōzan, had been much more judicious and moderate.[7] But Yoshida was a revolutionary, an indication that philosophers were tending increasingly to become embroiled in politics and that the study of Western science would become a vehicle for revolutionary tensions. Yoshida tried to smuggle himself onto Commodore Perry's flagship to be taken to America, but all the time he was full of hatred for foreigners and urged the samurai to study Western military science in order to drive out the barbarians.[8] Through his celebrated writings and the teaching at his private school in Choshu han, Yoshida exerted a great influence on the men who were to form the Meiji leadership. Among the most famous of his disciples were Itō Hirobumi,[9] Yamagata Aritomo,[10] Shinagawa Yajirō,[11] and the previously mentioned Inoue Kaoru.

The *sonnō jōi* movement was, of course, nothing but the Restoration movement. But while the slogan remained, many of its leaders changed their minds abruptly with respect to the *jōi*. A single experience was sometimes sufficient to convince them once and for all that Japan lacked the means to expel the Western powers —something the bakufu had realized before — and that it was not in her interest to do so. By the time the Restoration was achieved and the bakufu replaced by the *sonnō jōi* leaders, the *jōi* had changed beyond recognition. One of the first measures of the new Meiji government was to throw the country wide open to Western influence. Yet the basic goal remained constant in spite of the sharp change: Japan had to come onto an even keel with the Western powers, had to gain respectability, *and thus* would she retain her independence and integrity and demonstrate her ethical superiority. This theme recurs frequently in the speeches and writings of the Meiji period and was publicized time and again by the leading entrepreneurs as the ultimate rationale for their private empire building.

In order to achieve this new type of *jōi* — that is, the equality of Japan with the West — the *sonnō* became a primary force. The emperor moved from his centuries-long obscurity in Kyoto into the seat of attention and actual power; he came to Edo, which was renamed Tokyo ("eastern capital"). The nation itself became rejuvenated with the young emperor, and it looked with religious faith to the throne for guidance in a time of apparent contradiction and hectic change. From the imperial throne came the word, clear and strong, dispelling any doubt about the new direction. In the Charter Oath of the Five Articles, the emperor proclaimed in April 1868: "All absurd usages shall be abandoned; justice and righteousness shall regulate all actions. Knowledge shall be sought for all over the world and thus be [sic] strengthened the foundation of the Imperial Polity. In this way Japan break [sic] the shell of national isolation and tread the road of national reopening." [12]

The importance of the emperor as the symbol of national unity and purpose in the Meiji period cannot be overstated. The original Japanese Shinto faith, in which the emperor occupies the central place, was restored as the national religion in 1868, separated from its long amalgamation with Buddhism. The measure was followed by a wave of violence and vandalism against Buddhist monks and temples.[13] Although the establishment of Shintoism as a state religion met with only qualified success, the people as a whole, and government officials, became imbued with a strong faith in the descendant of the Sun Goddess, and they responded to his call with unquestioning loyalty. At times the very name of the emperor would break down resistance to the industrialization and modernization efforts. This is well illustrated by an episode connected with the building of the railways. Ōkuma Shigenobu [14] and his planning group were strongly opposed by conservatives who could not be swayed by rational arguments in favor of the building program. At this point Ōki Tamihira, the governor of Tokyo and later Minister of Railways, played his trump card by saying that the emperor would henceforth have to make occasional trips to Kyoto. Who would dare impose upon him the hardships of traditional travel if railways could make possible speedy and comfortable transportation? This argument is said to have silenced the opponents.[15]

From the very beginning the *bummei kaika* was asso-

ciated with the purpose of national greatness and had its
strongest symbol in the imperial throne. This strategic
combination of the most progressive ideology and the
oldest national faith and self-respect not only preserved
the Chrysanthemum at a time when the Sword had become
outdated, but it frustrated the dissatisfied conservatives
and prevented them from effectively splitting the country
into two opposing factions. The people as a whole were
willing to follow into the new era of progress.

Meiji officials and the men close to them expended great
efforts to popularize the new era.[16] In 1873 a group of intellectuals founded an association, the Meirokusha (sixth-
year-of-Meiji association) with the purpose of studying and
propagating Western civilization. Most of the prominent
members of the Meirokusha were members of the government or were closely associated with them.[17] The publica-
tions of the association were on such topics as modern
education, business methods, democracy, equality of classes,
and modern dress. Fukuzawa Yukichi, a prominent Meirokusha member, played a key role in the *bummei kaika*
efforts through his prolific writings on Western conditions.
These concerted efforts to establish progressive thinking
among the mass of the people ranged from learned treatises
and public discussions, to magnificent Western-style mansions for government officials, all the way down to songs
for children. In 1878 a play song was composed for children which made them "count the bounces of the ball re-
citing the names of ten objects deemed to be most worthy
of adoption — namely, gas lamps, steam engines, horse car-
riages, cameras, telegrams, lightning conductors, newspapers, schools, letterpost, steam boats." [18]

As much as the Meiji officials were preoccupied with
economic and military problems, they were certainly not
completely convinced that the building of an "infra-
structure" by direct investments would suffice to set the

process of modernization in motion. They apparently felt that economic development depended as much on cultural and ideological as on material premises, and that capital supply and investment programs could by themselves achieve little unless the changes were accepted and a dynamic will for development was born out of them. One might think that the government ought to have had worries larger than the popularizing of Western haircuts and dress, but it seems to have understood well the value of symbols, and these seemingly little things did serve as effective symbols of the new era.

It would appear that even measures of vast economic consequence were governed by cultural and ideological considerations. A case in point was the drive against infanticide, which had become such a deep-rooted habit during the Tokugawa period. Official pamphlets and decrees, it is said, stressed primarily the immorality of infanticide and its contradiction to the *bummei kaika*. Infanticide would put Japan to shame in the eyes of the world. Severe punishments were decreed for abortions; investigation offices were established; midwives and pregnant women were registered; societies were established to rear foundlings; and monetary rewards were given for births and for raising a third and fourth child.[19] At the time of the Meiji Restoration, the officials had no need to worry about a short labor supply. On the contrary, the government's biggest problem was how to employ the many jobless samurai; Malthusian thinking ought, on purely economic grounds, to have suggested rather a further encouragement of infanticide. But the government sensed that economic development depended a good deal upon the healthy vitality of the population rather than on the limitation of numbers that is born of a defeatist distrust in the future.

Among the variety of measures adopted to break down

traditionalism and to establish new and vigorous attitudes as a basis for development, two need special mention. One was the travel program and the other the introduction of compulsory education.

If merely reading about conditions in the West had been able to inspire many Japanese scholars and patriots, travel to a Western country would certainly be a complete eye-opener in revealing the gap of backwardness that separated Japan from the advanced countries. The traveler would then return to Japan as a champion of all-out modernization. Government officials who had seen the functioning of modern industry at first hand wanted others to share the same experience, and so they promoted foreign travel. Godai Tomoatsu of Satsuma han had sailed to England prior to the Restoration, and he had been so much impressed that he urged his daimyo to send others to Europe. Of those Satsuma samurai who were sent later, some became important government officials.[20] Itō Hirobumi and Inoue Kaoru of Choshu han had completely changed their political outlook during their stay in England and, after their return, fought the violent antiforeignism in Choshu at the risk of their lives.[21]

Itō considered foreign travel so important that in 1870 he originated a broad travel program. Generous subsidies were provided for studying in foreign countries and were granted to commoners as well as samurai.[22] Japanese students by the score sailed to the West in subsequent years and swarmed through European and American universities and factories. By 1872 the number of Japanese students abroad had reached 380.[23] Government officials also made frequent visits to the West. In 1871 almost the entire Meiji government sailed abroad under the leadership of Iwakura Tomomi, covering all of the important European countries as well as the United States. Their explicit purpose was to study "the laws and regulations concerning fiscal matters, taxation, public debt, paper money, public and private stock exchanges; also the establishment of insurance companies for fire, maritime disaster, and theft; furthermore the types of companies in trade and manufacturing, companies for steam engines, electric cables, and postal service. They ought further to study the establishment of gold and silver mints, various kinds of factories, and finally the laws and regulations covering those factories, and the real and apparent overall conditions. The objective of all this is to see how all these things can be applied and implemented in our own country." [24]

While government officials and students constituted the majority of the pilgrims to the West, progressive businessmen also joined in. The head clerk of Mitsui, who was close to the government, sent five of the Mitsui sons to study in the United States as early as 1872.[25] Sons of successful silk reelers and cotton spinners also crossed the ocean in order to learn. Some of the most influential entrepreneurs, like Shibusawa, Hara, and Ōkura, were decisively influenced in the conduct of their careers while in the West. The most efficient way to cure an obstinate conservative was to send him to the West. Kuroda Kiyotaka, the president of the House of Councilors, had been a leading opponent of Ōkuma's railway program. He denounced Ōkuma as an enemy of the state who would end by selling out his country to the foreigners. After his return from a journey to the West, he apologized publicly to Ōkuma and asked to be permitted to serve him loyally in the important task of building the nation's railway system.[26]

In spite of the heavy stress put on firsthand experience by travel abroad, most people could be influenced only by education in schools. The Meiji government moved quickly to establish a system of general compulsory education in 1872. The Japanese people at that time could by no means be called illiterate. Not only the samurai and most of the merchants, but even large segments of the peasantry were receiving some schooling. Some elementary instruction in han schools and *terakoya* (temple schools) and other private schools may have been given to as much as 30 to 40 percent of the young people. For most it did not go far beyond the fundamentals of reading, writing, and arithmetic; but many others received some instruction in Confucian ethics. The decisive turn in the Meiji education program was the reorientation of the goals of learning. Compulsory education was not only to assure that people learned how to read, write, and count; education was to be a chief instrument in spreading the *bummei kaika* ideology.

The Ministry of Education had the textbooks compiled exclusively after Western models; they were based largely on the teaching experiences of Fukuzawa Yukichi, who had been teaching Western subjects according to modern methods since 1864. Progress in implementing compulsory education was comparatively rapid. At the start, in 1873, a bare 4.24 percent of the eligible children attended. The others either continued to attend the *terakoya* or were left out for other reasons, such as lack of teachers and schoolrooms. By 1891 half of all eligible children were already receiving an elementary education, and in 1906 the figure was 95 percent.[27]

These few remarks on the progress of general education may suffice to indicate the determination of the government to spread a new outlook among the people. Next I shall turn to the more specific problem of technical education and the transfer of Western technology to Japan. This task could not be accomplished by the government alone, but required a combination of government and private initiative. Yet even here the impetus came very much from the center.

THE TRANSFER OF TECHNOLOGY

The Government's Efforts

The Industrial Revolution in England spanned a long period during which one step could be taken at a time. A gradual rise in the level of technical knowledge and experience prepared the way for the next step forward. It is true, of course, that inventions and innovations came in rapid succession at the end of the eighteenth century: the great breakthroughs by Crompton and Arkwright in cotton spinning and by Cartwright in weaving, Watt's fundamental improvement of the steam engine, and Wedgewood's innovations in pottery all came within twenty years. But the men responsible for these inventions, as well as those who put them to industrial use, could build upon knowledge and experience gained in previous stages of technology. It was therefore possible for inventors and innovators with little book learning to be wizards in practical matters. The general level of technical understanding was also high in other European countries and the United States. Moreover, the transfer of technology from England to the rest of the West was greatly eased through the bond of a common civilization and the relative unimportance of language barriers.

For Japan things were different. She had to absorb a technology coming from a completely alien culture; it had to be transmitted in Western languages that of themselves posed a formidable barrier; finally, it came at a very advanced stage to an unprepared people. The Japanese governmental officials who were so much awed by the marvels of European and American factories were not expert technicians. But they realized that there were few others in Japan who knew more than they. They understood, then, that their ambitious program of industrialization hinged decisively on effective technical training and on the formation of a native elite of technicians and scientists.

Foreign technology had not, of course, been completely unknown even in Tokugawa Japan. A considerable number of samurai had studied technical treatises and had made experiments in physics and chemistry in the 1840s and 1850s. They were even able to construct weapons and furnaces by following carefully the descriptions found in Dutch or English books. The building of Japan's first reverberatory furnace is a case in point. The daimyo of Saga han decided to have a furnace built to make cannons and put seven "experts" in charge of the project. A student of Dutch was to translate passages from Dutch books pertaining to reverberatory furnaces; another student of Western science was to give advice on the overall plan; a mathematician was to draw up the blueprint; and the other four experts, in metallurgy, gunnery, sword making, and administration, were given charge of the construction work itself.[28] These "seven wise men of Saga han," as they were called by the people, eventually succeeded, after repeated failures and immense difficulties.

The bakufu in its last years followed a more rational course by employing foreign experts; and the Meiji government did everything possible to enlist the help of Western technicians and teachers. It did not intend to rely on book knowledge alone or to waste time and resources on experiments of the Saga type. In almost all major government projects, foreign experts were given the double task of technical supervision and on-the-spot training of Japanese engineers. The Ministry of Industry, which was established in 1870 and was one of the most important branches of the Meiji government, sponsored this technical program. Between 1870 and 1885 the ministry employed over 500 foreign engineers and technical instructors; of these 393 were British, 71 French, 19 German, and 9 American.[29] This indicates, incidentally, Japan's heavy reliance on British industry in the early phase. Railway building received the largest contingent of foreigners (256), followed by machine shops with 81 and mining with 78.[30] The total expenditure for all foreign experts is not known; but the cost of 130 foreign technicians and instructors at the Technical University in Tokyo in the year 1879 was 341,000 yen, more than half of the ministry's 518,600-yen budget in that year.[31]

As important as foreign instructors and engineers were, their cost was felt to be disproportionately high. Their salaries, which were far above those of the highest-paid officials, hurt not only the government's finances but the feelings of the people.[32] The most important function of the foreigners, therefore, was to make themselves superfluous as quickly as possible. The government expended all efforts to build up native technical personnel and to promote technical education in order to dispense with direct foreign technical assistance. Technical education was introduced at the university and middle-school levels, and it covered a broad range of theoretical science and practical instruction in agriculture, trade, banking, and, above all, industrial technology.

Three agricultural schools were established by the government. The first was started in 1872 as an experimental station in Shinjuku. There foreign seeds were introduced and farming tools were modeled and manufactured. Another school was established in 1874 in Shiba, Tokyo, with an American, Horace, Capron, as instructor. He brought from America many sample seeds and tools and advised on new types of crops and on animal husbandry. From the whole of Japan students were called to this school, which was intended to pioneer the agricultural development of Hokkaido. In 1875 the school was transferred to Sapporo and became the forerunner of the University of Hokkaido. A third agricultural school was opened in 1876 in Kyoto.[33] Prior to 1880, thirty-four foreign experts on agriculture were employed by the government, and many Japanese were sent abroad to study.[34] The benefits of their studies and experiments were spread among the peasant population by information bulletins, seed-exchange societies, and discussion clubs in the villages. From 1874 on, in many rural districts farmers' organizations were set up for the purpose of disseminating technical information, better seeds, and improved cultivating methods. "Veteran farmers" traveled far and wide to teach other farmers. In Fukuoka prefecture, a private school of farming was established in 1883 which systematically sent its staff members and graduates on rural lecture tours.

Commercial and financial training also received the attention of the central government, because it had realized how inadequate the methods of the Osaka merchants were in dealing with foreign companies. In 1874 the Ministry of Finance established its own school with a four-year course in banking, finance, and bookkeeping. This school continued until 1893 and graduated six hundred students. In 1875 the Minister of Education, Mori Arinori, established a business school of the American type; in 1881 it had nine foreign instructors on its teaching staff. By 1883 Japan had seven commercial colleges, all but one of which were either private or prefectural.[35] Commercial training was promoted more by private entrepreneurs than by the central government, probably because the officials felt that trade was really not difficult to learn and that instruction in it could be left in private hands.

The training of engineers received top priority within the government's program of special education. Two technical schools at the university level were sponsored by the government. One of them, the Kōgakuryō, was established in 1871 with departments in civil engineering, machinery, construction, telegraphy, chemistry, finance, and mining. It had a six-year curriculum. In 1877 the name of the school was changed to Kōbu Daigakkō, and it eventually became the engineering department of the Imperial University. The other school was a continuation of the technical school (Kaiseikan) of the bakufu; it was established as an engineering school in 1873 with two departments, industry and mining, and a curriculum lasting six years.[36] The Ministry of Industry also had special training programs connected with certain of its offices, such as the telegraph office and the lighthouse office.

The top-level training of engineers was to be supplemented by a broad program of technical instruction on the secondary-school level. Middle schools specializing in foreign arts, industry, and mining were to be established, and each of these was to have foreign instructors. This ambitious training program did not materialize, however, because it was too far ahead of demand. The first middle school under the plan was started in Tokyo in 1874 with a four-year curriculum. Fifty-one students applied, and the staff included a German instructor. But in the following years applications dropped so low that the school had to be closed in 1877. A few other schools of the same type fared no better. The system was changed in favor of a practical apprentice training along narrowly defined technological lines. Such a school was the Tokyo *shokkō gakkō*, founded in 1881, in which engineering assistants and foremen were trained for jobs.[37]

In view of the high cost of foreign instructors and the strained finances of the Meiji government, these efforts to establish a system of technical education were certainly remarkable. We do not know the exact number of foreign instructors involved in this process of training Japanese engineers and middle-school students. There were quite a few private schools in which foreigners taught, and these are apparently not included in official government lists. The lists give the names of 151 foreign instructors employed by the government prior to 1900, but this does not include engineers, who often were also engaged in training and teaching on the spot. It is interesting that while British engineers outnumbered those of other nationalities, among the instructors in all fields, including mathematics, medicine, and the natural sciences, the Germans led with 60, followed by 39 Americans, 28 Britons, 20 Dutch, and 4 French.[38] And yet the educational system as a whole had been set up mainly on the French model.

In its effort to seek knowledge from the whole world, the government was the chief employer of foreign teachers, engineers, and other experts. Besides teaching, the foreigners served as technicians, particularly in railway building and other great government enterprises. The private enterprises were by far less well supplied with foreign experts, obviously because of the high salaries. Commercial shipping stands out as an exception in the private sector with many foreigners among the navigation officers. But in this field there was little choice, since few Japanese had any experience with modern ships and safety had to come first. Furthermore, commercial shipping was almost a complete monopoly of the Mitsubishi Company, which received enormous subsidies from the government and thus had the resources to pay handsome salaries to its foreign officers. In 1874 there were only 4 Japanese among 74 captains and navigation and technical officers. The Japanese learned fast, and by 1893 with a greatly increased fleet of ships there were 3,878 Japanese shipping officers and 722 foreigners.[39]

Entrepreneurs and the Problem of Technology

The government went to enormous pains to employ many foreigners in privileged positions, but there often seems to have been public resentment against foreign engineers. One complaint was that they received high salaries while apparently doing little work. Further, the presence of foreign experts was too strong a reminder of Japanese technical backwardness, and this reminder was hard to swallow at the time of the *bummei kaika* boom. Public antagonism toward the privileged foreign engineers was well illustrated in the construction of the Kyoto-Otsu railway line: Inoue Masaru, a British-trained engineer and chief of the railway-construction program, had by that time acquired sufficient experience to supervise the construction of the whole line except for necessary tunnels and bridges, for which foreigners were still employed.[40] This Japanese engineering achievement was given much publicity. The *Tokyo akebono shinbun* wrote on November 12, 1879, that the Kyoto-Otsu line had been advanced 78 miles in one year without foreign help and at only half the usual cost, although its course ran through mountains and rivers. No problem should henceforth be beyond the capabilities of Japanese engineers. The foreigners only wasted time and money because of their language problems and their inexperience with Japanese conditions. It ought to be possible from now on to dispense entirely with their services.[41]

Opinions may differ as to just when and to what extent

the Japanese should have sought to eliminate all direct foreign services. A certain amount of blundering by new and inexperienced native engineers, and the cost of mal-functionings and breakdowns, had to be weighed against the advantages of low salaries and the acquisition of early independence and self-assurance. But in those sectors of private industry where the government had shown less interest than in railway building and shipping, the attempt at independence from foreign help undoubtedly came too early. In many cases foreign expert advice was dispensed with completely or much too soon with disastrous conse-quences.

Cotton spinning in its early phase suffered particularly from a lack of expert engineers. At the Kagoshima Spin-ning Mill, the first on Japanese soil, British engineers were employed for one year; after that the samurai ad-ministrators took over, with considerable bungling and re-sultant prolonged losses. The mills that were established afterward relied almost completely on native personnel. Many of the enthusiastic founders of the two thousand-spindle mills in the pioneering period before 1885 con-sidered themselves experts if they had read a book on cot-ton spinning and had visited an operating mill. In some mills no engineer was available even to set up the machin-ery, and it had to be done by trial and error. Experts of sorts went from one mill to another, serving as engineers in two or even three mills at the same time.[42] The greater the enthusiasm and the louder the patriotic slogans that accompanied the founding of these mills, the smaller was the amount of practical knowledge, as a rule. It was thought that the new technology would by itself perform miracles.

It was Shibusawa himself who eventually broke the technological impasse in cotton spinning. He not only gathered capital for a large-scale mill but saw to it that the engineering problem was solved. He advised Yamabe Takeo, who was studying engineering in London, to receive practical training at the best English mills. Yamabe came back in 1883 and took over the technical management of the new Osaka Spinning Mill. He thus achieved the engineering breakthrough in cotton spinning and remained the expert in that field for many years.[43]

Other industries repeated these experiences. Paper manufacturing was plagued for years with technical difficulties and apparently had no foreign engineers in charge. Again Shibusawa broke the spell. He sent his nephew Ōkawa abroad to study paper manufacturing, and after his return Ōkawa became the great expert in paper manufacturing, as Yamabe had in cotton spinning.[44] In cement, glass, fertilizer manufacturing, and electricity, the picture of technological incompetence was quite similar, as were the losses for long periods.

Even Shibusawa, who usually planned very effectively, could be trapped by the technological problem. For instance, he had built a fertilizer factory on the advice of a Japanese engineer; but this expert left shortly, sailing abroad before the production began. Shibusawa was then left to his own devices, with no other expert available. He did not know enough either about the technology of production or about the use of the fertilizer. When the product was finally produced after a few years of wasteful experimenting, the peasants were given no instructions on its use and often achieved negative results. It took another few years to overcome this practical market problem.[45]

The next chapter will furnish more examples of technical difficulties in the sector of private industry. Usually, the few large industrial zaibatsu (lit., "financial clique," used for the giant trusts combining industry, trade, and banking) were able to overcome the technology problem either by enlisting foreign expert help or by their ability to hold out over the period of initial difficulty. But many of the lesser enterprises stumbled over the hurdle of technology. To the entrepreneurs with small capital resources, the salaries of foreign engineers appeared forbiddingly high, and they tried to save by following the brave example of the "seven wise men of Saga han." In this fashion the little knowledge picked up from a book or during a hurried visit abroad became a dangerous thing. It created an unwarranted enthusiasm and encouraged bold ventures without a thorough weighing of the practical difficulties involved. In the atmosphere of the *bummei kaika* and the government's strong encouragement and propaganda for modern industry, this hasty approach to new ventures is understandable. For the general success of the initial spurt toward modern industry, it was probably not altogether bad. True, the men who incurred the losses had to pay heavily for their bungling, at times being forced into bankruptcy. But other men picked up the pieces and somehow carried on the work. The boldness of approach and the overconfidence in Western technology greatly helped to break the initial timidity within the private sector. A more rational weighing of the detailed problems might have made for more caution and fewer losses, but might also have reduced the urge to invest at a time when it was most needed.

A certain bookish approach to practical engineering problems characterized the pioneering period of Japanese private industry. The entrepreneurs seemed to view independence of foreign help as an absolute ideal, as had the early samurai administrators of the progressive han. At a later stage of development, in the 1890s, the graduates from the universities, notably Keio and Waseda, moved into top managerial positions; they, too, stressed book learning as a prerequisite for industrial success. From the very outset, then, Japanese entrepreneurship noticeably underestimated practical training. This trend seems to be continuing even today.

This difference in approach between Japan and the Western, especially European, countries was decried by men who were in a position to make comparisons. Hara Rokurō, one of the top bankers and promoters of Meiji industry, complained about the neglect of technological training and the heavy stress on school records. According to him, many industrial failures in the Meiji era were caused by this onesided approach.[46] Industrialization had come to Europe as a gradual process with a continuous carryover of skills and experiences from the handicraft stages. There was no such carryover in Japan, but rather a sharp break with traditional craftsmanship. The entrepreneurial group did need better education more than handicraft training, since the transmission of technology came through books and through travel to countries with different languages. The entrepreneurs looked on their high level of general education as a distinctive mark of status. This stress on education was probably unavoidable in view of historical conditions, but it did leave a lasting imprint on Japanese industry. If European technology excelled in its precision and reliability, it was largely because of the continuity from handicraft traditions, whereby the reputation of the master was at stake in every piece that left his shop. In Japan the tendency until recently has been to imitate foreign samples or blueprints, and pride was taken in the closeness of the imitation, rather than in originality or craftsmanship.

In the classic time of the great Meiji entrepreneurs, achievement had consisted in close adherence to Western models. If a Japanese technician could do just that, he would not only save money but would successfully "expel" foreign engineers by making them superfluous. Imitation was of course necessary, and it does not detract from Japan's total achievement of absorbing an alien technology with truly remarkable speed. But we can recognize in the copying and in the attempted early independence from foreign engineers a strong ambition to be equal to the West; in a way it was the *sonnō jōi* attitude in a new shape. Entrepreneurs repeatedly mentioned this *jōi* motive as important for their industrial ventures and technical experimentation. Asabuki Eiji, a prominent Mitsubishi manager, expressed this idea at the opening ceremony of Mitsui Bussan in 1880, saying that he had been a fanatic *jōi* partisan until about ten years before. Expulsion of the foreigners still remained his ideal, but the means had changed. Now the expulsion had to be accomplished by peaceful competition, not by force of arms.[47]

The Transportation System

The Railways

The construction of an efficient transportation system, particularly of a railway network, constitutes the classic case for government investment, or at least for government subsidy and planning. Railways are essential for successful industrialization, to open up the country and to create a unified national market. But the long gestation periods involved, and the large initial capital outlays required for railway construction, do not make it very attractive for private capital in the initial stage.

In Europe, all countries except Britain witnessed active government planning and investment in railway construction. The first instance was Belgium, which as a young state started its industrialization period with the building of a well-planned railway network, financed entirely by the government. In Germany, too, the industrial revolution gathered speed only after the full layout of a railway system. The German states — mainly the southern states — had either invested directly or, as in the case of Prussia, had at least planned and coordinated private investments. In Russia railway building had initially been left entirely to private initiative, but, as soon as the government started its industrialization drive under Witte in the 1890s, the government took over the construction of important trunk lines and supervised the building and operation of the others.

The Meiji government did not follow Belgium's example by establishing a state monopoly on railways; it intended to follow more closely the example of Prussia, by way of a mixed approach of direct investments and subsidies plus overall planning and control of private lines. Private capital was urged to participate in the building program, but the initiative came entirely from the government. General interest was completely lacking in the beginning, for the simple reason that very few people with capital resources had seen the railways in operation abroad; the attitude toward railway construction was hostile rather than friendly.

The officials who promoted the railway-construction program knew its importance for the economy. They realized that Japan, perhaps even more than the European countries, needed an efficient means of land transportation. The country had been unified politically by the abolition of the han and the establishment of prefectural administration. But the division of Japan into many han had never been an effective barrier to internal trade, as had been, for example, the division of Germany into many small principalities, each with its own tariff sovereignty. In Germany the abolition of those tariffs and the establishment of the Zollverein in 1834 had been a crucial step toward the formation of a unified market area. In Japan the han had never had a tariff monopoly, and the checking stations along the highways had been established by the bakufu for the sake of political security and not to interfere with trade. A much greater obstacle was Japan's natural trade barriers, consisting of mountains and rivers that made overland travel extremely arduous. Bulk goods had to be transported by ship or carried by men. Travelers went on foot or were carried along the highways; but the mountains and the many unbridged rivers, impassable during heavy rains or floods, made traveling a mixed pleasure.[48]

In the debates over the railway-construction program, one of the main arguments in favor of the rapid layout of a railway net was that the country could thus become economically united. The other arguments frequently advanced were that railways could develop the backward areas of the country and that railway transportation would serve both the convenience of the people and the military needs of the nation.[49]

From the very beginning, the officials realized that the financing of a broad construction program would far exceed the means of the government alone. Some advocated floating a large foreign railway loan, but eventually it was decided to let private Japanese capital participate. Mitsui was asked to raise capital for a company to construct a railway line between Osaka and Kyoto, while the government started its own line connecting Tokyo with Yokohama. Since the construction cost of the proposed Osaka-Kyoto line was estimated at 700,000 yen, at least that much capital subscription was required for the private company. The government was willing to guarantee a 7 percent dividend rate on invested capital while sharing half of the profits exceeding 7 percent. As an additional inducement to would-be investors, the government stressed the great honor of cooperating with the government in this national endeavor. In spite of considerable effort on the part of Mitsui, however, the company did not materialize for lack of subscribers.[50] For the time being, the government remained alone in the field and went ahead with the construction of its Tokyo-Yokohama line.

The Tokyo-Yokohama line was completed and opened to traffic in 1872, with 18 miles laid out. Total construction cost had been estimated at about 800,000 yen, plus the cost of locomotives and cars, which amounted to another 150,000 yen. This railway was a complete success from the start. It carried from 1872 to 1886 a yearly average of 1.5 million passengers and averaged annual profits of 234,000 yen; in 1886 profits were as high as 333,771 yen.[51] With a profit rate of about 20 percent on its capital investment, the government felt greatly encouraged and the opposition was silenced. Two years later the government began to operate 20 miles of a line between Kyoto and Kobe, and it completed the 47 miles between the two cities in 1877. Traffic density on that line even topped that of the Tokyo-Yokohama line, with 1.8 million passengers per year until 1886, with annual profits averaging 319,981 yen for the same period.[52] This already marks a considerable drop in the profit rate, from about 20 to some 10 percent. Still, prospects were good for further extensions of the railway network by the government.

In the years from 1870 to 1874, the government had its heyday of railway construction: total outlays for the program in these five years constituted 33 percent of total government investments. But in 1875 this suddenly stopped, and government funds were diverted from railway construction to a military buildup, in connection with the chastisement of Taiwan and the threatening conflict with China. Railway outlays dropped from 30.2 percent of government investments in 1874 to 7.1 percent in 1875 and were kept at an average of 4 percent between 1875 and 1882.[53]

If the railway program was not to bog down at this early stage, private capital had to come in. Fortunately, the immediate success of the two government lines that had been completed dispelled many of the previous misgivings. With a good deal of persuasion, especially from Iwakura Tomomi, a group of nobles joined together in the establishment of the first private railway company, in order to construct a line between Tokyo and Aomori. This Nippon Railway Company received tax exemption on all land that was needed, plus a guarantee of 8 percent dividends for ten years, starting from the time of commencement of traffic. Furthermore, the government itself took charge of the construction work; the shareholders had only to contribute their capital. The government never had to supplement the dividend rate; from the very start the Tokyo-Aomori line was a sound success. By 1885 the Nippon Railway Company had grown into the largest joint-stock company in Japan, with a total of 20 million yen capital. Iwasaki's Nippon Yusen Company came next, with 11 million yen.[54]

The private railway boom was on, but the success of the Nippon Railway Company was not repeated. On the contrary, profit rates began to drop sharply for the subsequent lines. After 1880 the government again increased somewhat its own outlays on railway building, but the mileage of private companies grew much faster. By 1892 Japan had laid out a total of 1,870 miles of railways, of which only 550 miles were government-owned; the other 1,320 miles had been built and were operated by private companies. The government lines had cost 35.4 million yen and in 1892 netted some 2.4 million yen in profits. The cost of constructing the 1,320 miles of private lines had been 47.5 million yen, which means that the government lines had cost almost twice as much as the private ones. But profits rates for the private lines (2.7 million yen in 1892) were even lower than those on the government lines.[55]

In the years 1883 to 1892 private companies received government subsidies in various forms, notably tax exemptions. The government's direct investments in railway construction picked up in the 1890s, averaging in that decade 8.1 percent of total government investments, and in the first decade of the new century the figure rose to 18.8 percent.[56] At the same time, private lines were bought up by the government in a program to nationalize the railway network. But it is of great significance that at the point when the government was harrassed financially, private capital had taken up the task and, in spite of mounting difficulties owing to low profit rates, had continued to expand the country's railways.

Shipping

As a country of islands, Japan naturally was dependent on shipping as a means of transportation, quite irrespective of her foreign trade. Until the coming of the railways, bulky cargo could not easily be carried overland since vehicles could not be used on the bad roads. Prior to the closing of the country, shipping must have been fairly well developed, with large ships used for foreign trade, as the records on the Omi merchants suggest. But in 1636 the bakufu prohibited the construction of ships exceeding eighty gross tons (five hundred koku), and this prohibition was officially maintained until Japan's seclusion was ended.

But after 1853, and even before then, the bakufu and the daimyo of the major han that faced the Pacific Ocean moved energetically to build or purchase large modern ships, in view of the military danger from foreign vessels.

Modern shipping in Japan was thus from the beginning strongly stimulated by military considerations. The defense of the country dictated the creation of a modern fleet, and to a large extent this military approach continued to characterize the shipping and shipbuilding efforts in the first decades of the Meiji period. Large sums were expended by the daimyo and the bakufu for modern ships, cannons, and coastal-defense installations. And in order to acquire the needed capital for this program, the large southwestern han began their well-known reform programs, which eventually put them ahead of the rest of Japan economically and militarily and enabled them to overthrow the bakufu.[57]

Satsuma, Choshu, Mito, Saga, and Tosa had their own military and economic reform programs in which naval construction, or the purchase of modern ships, was one of the most important items. The economic reform program of Tosa han was closely linked to the objective of building a strong naval-defense force. A large economic-planning and administration center contained departments of fishing, mining, medicine, translation, finance, and production encouragement. Connected with the center were a naval and a merchant-marine school. A han monopoly trading company with branch offices in Osaka and Nagasaki provided the main financial backing for the purchases of arms and ships. Iwasaki Yatarō was chief of the Nagasaki branch, which handled the foreign imports and exports. Within one year, 1866–67, the company purchased ships, guns, and machinery from abroad worth 426,851 ryo, and it ran a deficit of 100,000 ryo.[58] Because of the heavy deficit operations, the company came under fire from han officials and was then turned over to Iwasaki as a private enterprise; in this way it became the nucleus of Mitsubishi, Japan's most powerful shipping company.

The double objective of *fukoku kyōhei* (wealthy nation, strong army), had been stressed in the han reform programs, and during the last years of the Tokugawa and the early Meiji it was largely biased in favor of the military objective — the *fukoku* was made subservient to the *kyōhei*. Spinning mills were founded, mines modernized, and reverberatory furnaces built for the sake of defense, to build cannons and to acquire modern ships.

By 1868 Japan had 138 modern ships, of which 44 were owned by the bakufu and 94 by various han; the total capacity was 150,000 tons. Most of the ships had been purchased; only one steamer and twenty sailing vessels had been constructed in Japan.[59] Of the four shipyards inherited by the Meiji government, one, the Ishikawajima yard, had been built in 1856 and operated since then by Mito han; in it the first Western-style ship, the *Asahi Maru*, had been constructed. This yard was soon abandoned by the Meiji government, and its machinery was transferred to the Tsukiji machine shop. In 1876 a private entrepreneur, Hirano Tomiji, took over the dilapidated shipyard and struggled for many years before he finally made it a success in the late 1880s. Two other yards, one established in Nagasaki in 1861 and the other in Kobe in 1864, were small and could only handle repair work on larger ships; they remained small and inefficient under government management, until they were transferred to private entrepreneurs in 1884 and 1886.

It was on the Yokosuka shipyard that both the bakufu and the Meiji government concentrated their efforts in modern shipbuilding. Yokosuka had been modeled after

the Toulon shipyard and was two thirds of its size. It had
been planned under the aegis of the French consul, and
its staff included French engineers. Connected with the
Yokosuka yard was an iron-construction plant in Yokohama. Within four years the bakufu had invested in Yokosuka over 4 million yen. The Meiji government expanded
its facilities further and turned it over to the navy for
the construction of military vessels. In view of the great
military importance of shipping it is somewhat surprising
that the Meiji government did not invest more heavily in
shipbuilding from the very start. Shipbuilding, in the first
decade of the Meiji era, had to take a back seat to railway
construction.

The Meiji policies in the first years were dominated by
the goal of economic reconstruction, particularly between
1871 and 1874. But beginning with 1874 military build-up
received more attention because of the Taiwan expedition,
growing hostility toward Korea, and internal unrest that
reached its climax in the Satsuma Rebellion of 1877. As
soon as military needs dictated a change of policy, the
priority in outlays on the transportation system turned
from railways to shipping.

Between 1868 and 1874, total government investments
in railway construction (which had actually started only
in 1870) amounted to 8.71 million yen, while investments
in shipbuilding and the purchase of ships, both merchant
and naval, ran only to 1.57 million yen. But between 1875
and 1879, expenditures for railway construction dropped
to 1.44 million yen, and government outlays for the construction of naval vessels rose to 5.95 million yen. Merchant shipping also received top priority in these years
in spite of the low figure of 103,300 yen of direct government investments in that field.[60] The fact is that commercial shipping was a private monopoly enterprise of

Iwasaki; it received huge indirect subsidies and privileges that are not included in these government figures.

The turn from purely economic considerations, with railways occupying a central place, to military investments, closely connected with shipping, is highlighted by a comparison of the percentages of total government investments: from 1870 to 1882 railways sank from 33 to 4 percent and military investments rose from 2 to 40 percent of government investment outlays.[61] Thus it is quite obvious that shipping maintained its military focus, while railways kept their primarily economic significance.[62] The build-up of a strong naval force became quite naturally a very important, but also costly, concern of the government. Naval construction took 60 percent of all military investments between 1875 and 1893; in 1894, on the eve of the conflict with China, naval-construction costs rose almost ten times over the average of the 1875–1893 period.[63]

Iwasaki's merchant fleet also retained a strongly military character, as did Iwasaki himself. The Tosa samurai regarded his work as a fight for Japan's equality with the Western countries on the high seas, true to the tradition of *fukoku kyōhei*. During the Taiwan expedition and the Satsuma Rebellion, Iwasaki's shipping company was of strategic importance in transporting troops to the battlefields. It was therefore in the economic and military interest of the country that the government should accord heavy subsidies to Iwasaki. A few examples of the types and sizes of these subsidies to the champion of Japanese shipping will show the intense concern of the Meiji government for commercial shipping, something that is easily lost sight of in the statistical figures on the government's direct investments.

In 1874 the government bought 13 ships abroad worth $1.56 million (over 2 million yen at the prevailing ex-

change rate) and handed them over to Mitsubishi, together with 18 other ships that had been inherited from
the bakufu. During the Satsuma Rebellion 10 more large
steamers were purchased for $700,000 and turned over to
Mitsubishi with additional large subsidies for their operation. By the end of 1878 the total of subsidies for the operation of this shipping company had reached 2.7 million
yen. Sixty percent of the budget of the Ministry of Trade
and Agriculture for 1881 consisted of subsidies to Mitsubishi.[64] Finally, the government turned the Nagasaki shipyard over to Iwasaki at a bargain price; Iwasaki transformed the small inefficient yard, through huge investments in new equipment, into one of the most modern
shipyards in the Far East.

By 1880 the shipping company of Iwasaki operated a
stately fleet of 56 modern ships, of which 37 were steamers.[65]
We shall see in Chapter Six that Iwasaki's ruthless practices made him enemies inside and outside the government.
A powerful rival shipping company was set up in 1882
with large government support. Both Mitsubishi and the
rival Kyōdō Unyu Company were almost ruined by the
ensuing cutthroat competition and came close to collapse
in 1885. But after their amalgamation into one company
under Iwasaki's control, progress in shipping was rapid.
In 1895 Japan had, all told, a total shipping capacity of
350,000 tons, with 701 ships, of which 528 were steamers.
By the end of the Meiji era, in 1912, Japan ranked sixth
in the world in total shipping capacity and could boast of
1.635 million tons. This put her close on the heels of
France, with 1.638 million, and far ahead of Italy, with
only 1.1 million tons.[66]

The building of Japanese transportation, both railways
and shipping, had resulted from a close cooperation between the government in the form of direct investments,

subsidies, and general encouragement to would-be investors, and private industry. But while the railways were more closely connected with purely economic considerations, shipping, true to the tradition of the southwestern han, retained a distinctly military coloring. This was so not only because of the government's heavy investments in naval construction, but also because of the role that commercial shipping played in military engagements and in Japan's struggle with the West on the high seas. It was both typical and providential that a militant Tosa samurai became the leading exponent of Japanese commercial shipping.

Other Government Enterprises

From the viewpoint of classical international-trade theory, Japan ought to have specialized from the start in labor-using industries because of her scarcity of capital and her abundant labor resources. The capital accumulated during the Tokugawa period by the city merchants and rural putting-out masters had in part been dissipated in the turbulent years of change, and it could certainly not be considered as adequate to finance a large-scale capital-using investment program. The surplus rural population and the many jobless samurai could supply abundant labor for highly labor-intensive industrial employment.

But the Meiji government did not follow the classical prescription of specializing according to relative factor endowments. It did not accord top priority to light industries, but from the very beginning invested primarily in heavy, capital-using enterprises. The construction of a railway network and a modern shipping system was very costly, but the two areas were highly important as suppliers of overhead capital for the ensuing development program. The government also invested a good deal in mining and chemical factories, while textiles were soon left, after some initial help and guidance, to the initiative of private capital.

The stress on capital-intensive investments on the part of the government was wise development policy, in spite of the extreme scarcity of capital. This is not only true for railways and shipping, since the establishment of an efficient transportation system is a prerequisite for industrialization; the statement also applies to the capital-using manufacturing and mining enterprises. For one thing, the latest Western machinery and production methods made it quite clear to the Japanese that they could no longer rely on their own past experience and that trial and error would not do. Whenever trial-and-error methods were used, they usually failed badly. This forced them to adopt and master the new advanced technology.

Another, and in my view extremely important, aspect of this concentration on heavy industry has to do with the self-confidence of the Japanese people. Modern enterprises were eloquent symbols of the new era, of progress and national achievement. They helped to harness for industrialization at least part of the strong patriotic emotions so characteristic of the Meiji era. It was in the government enterprises that, with the aid of foreign technicians, the most staggering technological problems could be and were overcome; these large endeavors became monuments of the nation's progress. It is true that there was much waste of capital involved in the prolonged losses and inefficiencies of the first factories and mines, but this was compensated for by these other, indirect, effects. For a nucleus was formed from which the most enterprising men of the period could make a start into modern industrial ventures.

The Meiji officials were by no means unanimously in

favor of government involvement in industrial investments. Some had been opposed from the beginning to
any type of government intervention, while others insisted
that the government ought to assume full responsibility
for building the nation's industries. Until 1878 economic
policy was by and large determined by the Minister of the
Interior and strongman Ōkubo who, together with Ōkuma,
the Minister of Finance, went as far as possible in com-
mitting the government. They were of the opinion that
the private sector was still too immature and that the
government ought to occupy the central position in economic life. The government investments that coincided
with the costly liquidation of the feudal system and the
samurai-employment program caused strong inflationary
pressures. Ōkubo was assassinated in 1878, and Ōkuma
resigned as Minister of Finance in 1881, making room for
the other economic policy group, represented by Matsukata, the new minister.[67]

Matsukata's policies represented a significant step toward
laissez faire and private enterprise and a transition from
direct government investment in industry. But the blessing to the private sector came in a harsh disguise indeed:
in 1881 Matsukata initiated a long-overdue deflation policy which for a few years played havoc with private industry. The large amounts of government paper money
had caused not only rapid price inflation but also a dangerous balance-of-payments deficit. Matsukata curtailed government expenditures drastically and initiated the sale of
government enterprises, which were one of the main
drains on the treasury. The Bank of Japan was established
in 1882 to regulate the money supply, and a large amount
of paper money was withdrawn from circulation in order
to achieve convertibility at par of paper money against
specie.

By the end of the deflation period in 1884, a positive

balance of payments had been achieved. But the typhoon of deflation had also left in its wake the wreckage of numerous trading and industrial enterprises; many of them had started under the favorable conditions of inflation and were unsound to begin with. After 1884 private industry made a new start. Solid monetary conditions had been established; the government enterprises which had been sold out at bargain prices, as well as many of the wrecked enterprises, had been cemented into this new foundation. It was a heavy but perhaps necessary price to pay during a transitional period.

It is not necessary to go into the details of the government enterprises, which have been well described and analyzed elsewhere.[68] In absolute terms, these investments were not overwhelming and should not be exaggerated. Mining was the main field of concentration. The government operated nine modern mines, chief among them the Takashima and Miike coal mines, the two most profitable mines in Japan. But the government also paid a heavy penalty for inefficiencies and technical incompetence: for example, a total of 2.5 million yen was invested in the Kamaishi iron mines; smelting was finally started there in 1880, but the smelting operations lasted no longer than 198 days. Owing to a combination of disasters and technical difficulties, the project was abandoned. The mines with all the installed machines lay unused for a few years, until finally Tanaka Chōbei, a private entrepreneur, was persuaded to continue the work.[69]

Besides the already mentioned Yokosuka shipyard, and two arsenals in Tokyo and Osaka, the government operated a large-scale construction plant in Akabane. From that plant came most of the durable equipment and machinery that was produced in Japan: steam engines, boilers, machinery for cotton spinning and silk reeling. In 1881 the machine shop employed 537 workers, a large-scale operation for the time. Akabane served also as a training center for the engineering department of the Ministry of Industry.[70]

There were also the chemical factories: Fukagawa cement, Fukagawa white bricks, and Shinagawa glass. Finally, in the field of textiles the government briefly operated two cotton-spinning mills, the large-scale Tomioka filature, a mechanical thread-plying mill, and a weaving factory. None of the government textile factories was economically successful; they operated at losses or very low profits prior to 1884 while under government management, and they were the first to be sold.[71]

If measured solely in terms of profit rates, the government factories were complete failures and a constant drain on the state finances. This was one of the main reasons why they were sold out as part of Matsukata's deflation and retrenchment program. Between 1868 and 1884 the total investments in these enterprises amounted to something over 32 million yen, while total profits for the entire seventeen-year period were no more than 17.173 million yen.[72] When these model factories and mines came up for sale, it was sometimes very difficult to find purchasers, in spite of the giveaway prices that were asked. The sale of the government factories, shipyards, and mines represented of course a substantial subsidy to private industry. But without it, private enterprise would have had little chance even to start in these fields, since the government had failed to demonstrate the one most important thing, the possibility of making profits. With so much done by the government in technical experiments and machinery investments, the purchasers of the enterprises, with some additional investments, could overcome the critical stage rather quickly and make these factories and mines the foundations of their own industrial empires.

Two rather extreme examples may suffice as illustrations of the favorable rates of the sales. The Shinagawa Glass Factory was sold for 79,950 yen to be paid in installments over a period of fifty-five years, beginning ten years after the sale. Total government investments in that factory had been 350,000 yen. The Ani Copper Mine had cost the government 1.6 million yen in investments and was sold for 250,000 yen, of which 10,000 yen were paid immediately and the rest spread over twenty-four years, starting five years after the sale.[73]

It would be interesting to know the relative position of government enterprises within the whole of the economy and of the modern industrial sector. But private modern enterprise was not well surveyed at that time. The data on manufacturing that do exist lump together the traditional and the modern sectors; and even within the modern sector most establishments were still small-scale. Within the totals of output figures, the model factories do not occupy a prominent place. Figures on factory employment indicate a rather steady ratio of 10 to 1 between the private and the government sectors throughout the 1880s and 1890s.[74] But if we concentrate attention on mining and heavy and chemical industries, the government enterprises are seen to be highly significant, because of their scale of operation and their advanced technology. Whether intended or not, Ōkubo's early insistence on government leadership and dominance in modern industry paid handsome dividends to the private sector after 1884.

INDIRECT SUBSIDIES TO PRIVATE INDUSTRY

It has been indicated that the sale of government enterprises to private entrepreneurs marked a turn in the direction of laissez faire. The direction was clear, but nobody at the time within the government thought that the private sector could altogether dispense with help from the center. The sales in themselves were a form of subsidy; other encouragements and subsidies followed, some of them planned, some of them unwittingly extended to the emerging leaders of modern Japanese industry.

I shall not go into detail on the varieties of direct and indirect subsidies and of monopoly rights granted to industrialists. Instead, I shall concentrate on one aspect that was of considerable importance: the way in which the government subsidized private industry by becoming its chief customer. The Japanese market could easily absorb the traditional products, and it was also open to cotton textiles, if the cotton industry could overcome foreign competition. But the situation was altogether different with regard to electrical industries and to chemicals, such as cement, bricks, paper, glass, and leather. There the private entrepreneurs faced their greatest difficulty. People were hesitant to buy the things they did not know, and their demand was usually much too small for large-scale production. Government orders saved many enterprises from bankruptcy in the critical years prior to about 1895. This was the case with leather manufacturing, where the main demand came from the army; with paper manufacturing, where government offices bought large amounts; and also with cement and bricks. The woolen industry depended almost entirely on the military demand for uniforms and blankets.

Asano Sōichirō, who had purchased the government cement factory, succeeded in increasing the efficiency of production and solved some technical problems magnificently. But this would not have saved him from bankruptcy if government orders had not come in to solve his market problem. The government bought up most of

Asano's cement for its railway program, and for the building of the Imperial Palace and the Ueno Museum.[75]

The Meiji government seems to have followed the bakufu's tradition of doing its business with monopoly contractors. There was no competitive public bidding, and consequently business with the government invariably became a source of handsome profits for the suppliers. This method could and sometimes did support inefficiency, but the general impression is that the officials did not mind monopoly profits, so long as it was certain that these profits would be reinvested in modern enterprises. The chief government suppliers were usually also the most daring entrepreneurs.

During the Satsuma Rebellion, all army provisions were supplied by Mitsui Bussan (Mitsui Trading Co.), and the Ōkura and Fujita companies. Mitsui Bussan received 60 percent of total contracts, and the other two 20 percent each. Mitsui, which started its operations in 1878 with 100,000 yen in capital, earned a net profit of 500,000 yen in that one year. Ōkura and Fujita made similar gains. Mitsubishi, which was in charge of all troop transports, netted in that year over 1.2 million yen.[76] But these same companies were in the forefront of Meiji industry, and the huge profits were used to expand their enterprises, which grew eventually into the zaibatsu.

Light and labor-using industries, in contrast with the capital-intensive industries, received more verbal than financial encouragement. Direct help for cotton spinning and silk reeling was confined to the years prior to 1884, and even then was not too large in absolute terms. The government apparently made the correct forecast that textiles would take care of themselves if sufficiently encouraged by a promotion program. Capital requirements were relatively small even in cotton spinning during the two-thousand-spindle-mill era (something like 50,000 yen per mill on the average), and for silk reeling the figures were much lower. The field of textiles was also under direct stimulus from foreign competition and, with proper handling, could be stimulated to respond to the challenge. The government's promotion program consisted consequently in spreading technical knowledge and in drumming up patriotic sentiments against the importation of cotton yarns.

Fairs and exhibitions served this purpose. The first fair for the promotion of exports and of import-competing cotton spinning was held in Kyoto in 1872 and attracted over 31,000 Japanese and 770 foreign visitors. After this encouraging start, the fair was repeated annually until 1888. Local fairs and exhibitions across the country had the same purpose. By 1887 the number of local fairs had reached 317, with over 2 million visitors.[77] One point that always received strong emphasis in the speeches and writings on these occasions was the need to expand and improve the production of raw silk and to build mills. A report from an exhibition held in Osaka in 1880 stated that Japan was producing no more than 3 percent of its total cotton-yarn consumption in its mechanical mills. Another 241 mills would have to be built in order to stop the importation of foreign yarns.[78]

We have seen in Chapter Three that this general encouragement of the textile industry, both silk reeling and mechanical cotton spinning, had its positive effects. In spite of the heavy competition from the imports and the continued losses prior to 1885, the cotton-spinning industry weathered the difficulties and eventually became Japan's number-one industry and her first industry to move into the world market. Thus the sector that had received comparatively little direct help in fact grew fastest and became the mainstay of Japan's modern industry. The pioneering problems in cotton spinning were overcome with great speed because of the positive response to the general encouragement offered by the government. Later, Japan's natural advantages in the area made themselves felt: the availability of cheap labor, a ready home market, a comparatively simple and labor-using technology, and the readiness of the cotton merchants and cotton spinners to invest in a field that was close to their former business. Where these advantages were not present, as in the chemical and heavy industries, continued indirect support by the government was a practical necessity.

JAPANESE INDUSTRY IN THE MID-MEIJI YEARS

Before turning our attention to the private sector and its entrepreneurs, we may take a brief glance at the state of Japanese industry relative to the whole economy in the late 1880s and early 1890s. It is important to keep in mind that my period of investigation, 1868–1895, marks the very beginnings of industrialization. But the pioneering phase during the eighties and early nineties is of particular interest because during this time many of the most crucial problems were solved and obstacles to industrial growth removed. Notably this came about through the energetic initiative from the center and the efforts of a small entrepreneurial elite.

During this period the primary sector, in particular agriculture, retained its strongly dominant position in quantitative terms of output and employment. But its relative position began to decline noticeably, which in itself is a sure sign of industrial growth.

Field	Production	1878–82	1893–97
Employment	Primary	82.3%	73.1%
	Secondary	5.6%	10.4%
Real income	Primary	64.0%	51.0%
(percent)	Secondary	10.0%	18.0%
Real income	Primary	909	1,467
(totals in	Secondary	147	528
million yen)			

Adapted from Ohkawa Kazushi et al., *The Growth Rate of the Japanese Economy since 1878* (Tokyo, 1937), p. 17, 27.

The decline of employment in primary production was accounted for mainly by the increase of total employment in the secondary sector; there was actually very little decrease in total agricultural employment. Agriculture remained highly labor-intensive and small-scale, but all the time its productivity kept rising per capita. Over the fifteen-year span, as indicated in the table above, it achieved a productivity increase of 4 percent per annum, mainly owing to better seeds and techniques and the increased use of fertilizer. But if brought into relation to the secondary sector, incomes fell by 20 percent in the primary sector while employment totals diminished by only 11 percent. In secondary production during these fifteen years, there was a threefold increase in total real income produced; this indicates the magnitude of relative industrial growth. The secondary sector in the above table does, however, include domestic manufacturing, and this obscures the evidence concerning industrial growth. Although both the domestic and the industrial sectors were moving upward, their rates of growth were different.

A comparison between the secondary and the tertiary sectors would not serve my purpose of illustrating the speed of industrialization and modernization, because both sectors presented a mixture of traditional and modern establishments. I take instead, as another indicator of the modernization process, the authorized joint-stock capital of all limited companies. We may safely assume that shifts toward the company form of enterprise and increases in totals of joint-stock capital in any field reflect rather closely the growth of that particular sector as well as its modernization.

	Authorized joint-stock capital			
	End of 1883		*End of 1893*	
Field	*Totals (thousand yen)*	*Percent*	*Totals (thousand yen)*	*Percent*
Agriculture	1,053	0.76	2,542	0.85
Trading	35,904	25.80	57,616	19.33
Manufacturing	14,725	10.59	68,259	22.91
Railways	12,080	8.68	57,945	19.45
Banking	75,375	54.17	111,635	37.46
Totals	139,137	100.00	297,997	100.00

S. Uyehara, *The Industry and Trade of Japan*, rev. ed. (London, 1936), p. 271. Percentages computed.

Agriculture played a negligible role as an investment possibility for joint-stock capital. But of the four other fields in the table, banking and trading were far in the lead in 1884, the point at which the government was preparing to sell its own enterprises and to promote private industry by direct and indirect subsidies. We have seen in Chapter Two that modern banking had achieved a breakthrough after 1876, with many samurai becoming founders of national banks. Banking capital, though still growing absolutely and still occupying first place, had within ten years fallen from 54.17 percent to 37.46 percent of total joint-stock capital. Manufacturing and railways had by that time already overtaken trading, which ten years earlier had had three times as much joint-stock capital as railways, and more than twice as much as manufacturing. Only railways showed gains similar to those of manufacturing, moving from 8.68 percent of the total in 1883 to 19.45 percent in 1893, and in absolute terms increasing five-fold. This sharp increase in manufacturing and railways, each to outstrip even trading capital, is an eloquent sign of the dynamic growth of modern industry in Japan in the decade that began with the liquidation of government enterprises and ended just before the Sino-Japanese War.

Within the field of manufacturing, the trend was increasingly toward factory production. But prior to the turn of the century, domestic and factory manufacturing grew side by side in absolute terms. During the period from 1878 to 1895, the gross-value product of domestic manufacturing rose from 37 to 199 million yen, and factory production registered during the same time a rise from 40 to 323 million yen; [79] while factory production increased 8 times, domestic production nevertheless registered an increase of 5.4 times. These average figures of domestic and factory gross-value products do not, however, reveal the very erratic movements that took place in domestic manufacturing — movements that not only caused hardship but helped to hasten the eventual decline of domestic manufacturing in absolute terms. From a 79-million-yen gross-value product in 1885, domestic manufacturing rose suddenly to 114 million in the next year, and then fell from 196 million yen in 1888 to a calamitous 71 million yen two years later.[80]

Employment figures within the secondary sector indicate a wide discrepancy in productivity per worker between traditional domestic manufacturing and modern factory industry. During the 1893–1897 period the total employment in the secondary sector registered an average of 2.468 million workers, but only 418,140 were factory employees, and of these 60 percent were women.[81] This last fact, incidentally, reflects the heavy preponderance of textiles within the modern industrial sector. But while around 1895 the labor force in factories constituted only one sixth of total secondary employment, the total gross-value product of factory industry had by that time already surpassed that of dometsic manufacturing with 323 versus 199 million yen, as shown above. The low productivity per worker in domestic manufacturing, which was often nothing but a by-employment for tenant farmers, was the main cause of the inevitable decline after the turn of the century.

In 1884, at the beginning of the decade of energetic growth, Japanese industry still showed predominantly rural characteristics. Not only because of the domestic manufacturing sector, but because factories also were frequently rural, especially in the fields of textiles, ceramics, food processing, and iron. A survey of factory production in 1884, which comprises a total of 1,981 establishments employing 5 or more workers, gives the following picture: of chemical industries like paper, matches, and cement, 56 percent were located in cities, 26.4 percent were rural, locations of the rest were unspecified.[82] Shipbuilding and weaving were also typically city industries. Machinery construction was a "city" industry to the extent of 47.4 percent of its total; only 15.8 percent was rural, and the location of 36.8 percent was unspecified. On the other hand, food-processing industries, ceramics, and iron casting and refining, as well as silk reeling, remained typically rural industries.

In 1884 the division between city and rural factories corresponded closely to a grouping by size.[83] The typically large establishments tended to be city-located. In terms of workers employed, the largest factories were found in the chemical industry, followed by machine and machine-tool plants and then by textiles. In the chemical industry 31.9 percent of all establishments employed 50 or more workers, machine and machine-tool factories followed with 23.6 percent, and textiles with 9.7 percent.

If we were to take cotton spinning alone, it would perhaps rank even above the chemical industries in the size of its establishments; the large number of silk-reeling factories that the survey includes in the textile group overshadows the spinning mills and unduly pulls down the arithmetical average of the size of all textile establishments. Of all 1,981 factories in the survey, no less than 1,043 belonged to silk reeling, and of these 69.5 percent had less than 20 workers per factory. We see here also that in the mid-1880s, when factory production was emerging, it was still dominated by silk reeling, with typically small-scale operations. At this time, textiles — and this means mainly silk reeling — accounted for over 60 percent of all factories, followed by the traditional ceramics and food-processing industries with 21.3 percent.

In textiles Japan achieved her first industrial success. Silk spinning had been stimulated by early export opportunities and cotton spinning by competition from imports. But, apart from textiles, other modern large-scale industries began to multiply and to make vigorous inroads into traditional putting-out manufacturing. This movement was supported by direct and indirect government subsidies and by the building of a broad transportation system. The government's efforts in stimulating and subsidizing the nascent modern industrial sector were crowned with remarkable success.

V

THE SPIRIT OF ENTERPRISE
IN THE PRIVATE SECTOR

The Meiji Restoration brought about a new evaluation of the government and its role in the life of the nation. During the feudal era, the bakufu officials were feared but hardly admired, and few talented and ambitious men were attracted into official service. The Restoration carried the government from the margin of attention into the center of everyone's interest. Everything that was great and exciting in these years, the restoration of the emperor, the unification of the country, the abolition of feudal privileges, the beginnings of modern industry, all had been wrought by the Meiji officials. The light radiated again from the imperial precincts, and those who wanted to stay in the light had to move to the center and become officials, or at least associate with them. By way of contrast, the rest of the population appeared to be all the more backward. There is small wonder that the officials were idolized and the common man counted for little at this time. This *kanson minpi* attitude (awe for the official, contempt for the crowd) was but the other side of the coin of the astounding Meiji achievements.

Few people expected any initiative or contributions to

progress from the private business sector, which still seemed so backward and which had disappointed hopes so often during the first Meiji years. The great industrial enterprises, the large and centrally located factories, had been established by officials; now the private sector was expected to accept guidance gratefully and humbly. Indeed, the bowed head and passive obedience to government officials had been the chief traits of the *shōnin* all through the Tokugawa period. The populace had no other image of a businessman than the one represented by the former merchant class, and that class, during the first decade of the Meiji era, was not only leaning nostalgically backward, but had become disorganized, unreliable, and prone to pursue profits in total disregard of the public interest.

In the early years of the Meiji, two new types of businessmen emerged in the private sector: the *seishō* (political merchants), who rode on the crest of government favors and used every opportunity to amass fortunes for themselves, glorying meanwhile in official titles and patriotic slogans; and the many second-rate businessmen or industrialists who had neither experience nor capital but only enthusiasm. We find the latter chiefly among the founders of national banks and also in cotton spinning in its first period. But neither of these two types could be counted upon to build a viable and independent sector of the modern economy. The private sector needed a progressive business group that would develop its own initiative with less reliance upon government coaching and government subsidies.

The Entrepreneur, A New Status

In the last decades of the Tokugawa period, the merchants had, through the back door of daimyo lending, purchase of samurai titles, and land reclamations, managed to break down at least part of the social prejudice against their lowly status. The Meiji Restoration had practically wiped out those gains. Business needed a complete rehabilitation of its status if it was to succeed in the establishment of a strong private sector. The public as well as would-be entrepreneurs had to be impressed with the fact that modern business was not only beneficial to the country, but was as vital as the work of the Meiji government itself. Only by restoring the social status of private business, or rather by establishing it for the first time, could a healthy growth of private industry be guaranteed.

The need to create a new image of business, and to make the businessman confident of his own worth, was clearly perceived, and the task was taken on by a small group inside and outside of the business sector. A conspicuous contribution to the eventual rehabilitation of business pursuits and the creation of new status for the entrepreneur was made by two men: Fukuzawa and Shibusawa, the one an educator, the other an entrepreneur.

Fukuzawa Yukichi (1835–1905), the founder of Japan's first modern college, the Keiō Gijuku, had been for a few years following the Restoration closely associated with the government: he was a close friend of Ōkuma Shigenobu, one of the leading government officials. He had been one of the brain trust that promoted the *bummei kaika* and had been chiefly responsible for shaping the new educational policy; the graduates of his school entered government service. But when Ōkuma was ousted from the government in 1881, Fukuzawa also severed his ties to the regime and became one of the most outspoken enemies of government control over economic and cultural life. Although he had stressed modern business rationality in the education of his students, he now steered his graduates almost exclusively into the private business sector. Thus Fukuzawa's Keiō Gijuku and the Imperial University came to deviate widely in their educational policies: the former represented Western liberal thought and stressed individualism, in the tradition of John Stuart Mill; the latter was a state institution, working for the state, educating officials, and maintaining more of the feudal Confucian mentality.

Mori Arinori,[1] the Minister of Education, shared with Fukuzawa an admiration for Western ideas and methods, but he wanted college education to serve primarily the purposes of bureaucracy. Officials, not businessmen, were to be educated in the state universities, in pursuit not of the English but of the Prussian example.[2] Fukuzawa often gave expression to his aversion to the prevailing *kanson minpi* mentality and insisted that his graduates ought to stand on their own feet and spurn government connections. The prevailing bureaucratism became an object of his scorn, as the following shows: "The schools are officially licensed, sermons and moral preachings are licensed, cattle raising, sericulture, and indeed, eight out of every ten enterprises are connected with the government . . . the flattering of the official, the awe and idolization of the official, is ugly and unbearable." [3]

The Keiō students were trained for private enterprise, while the graduates of the Imperial University regarded private business as degrading. When Shibusawa on one occasion asked a few graduates of the Imperial University to join the Tokyo Gas Company, they answered typically that they did not intend to "descend to the level of the common people." [4] Fukuzawa taught his students to respect business pursuits, and he himself presented an example: he insisted that he taught "for money" and demanded that the tuition fees be paid into his hands, something unheard of for a samurai-teacher. By tradition, teaching was an honorable occupation and teachers were given presents, wrapped in special paper.[5] Since almost all of Fukuzawa's students were samurai, he had to fight their deep-rooted contempt for business.

A frequently recurring theme in his writings was the stress on a new business rationality. His "merchants of the *bummei kaika*" were to take pride in their occupation if it was "for profit and for Japan." In his opinion, only educated and independent businessmen could build up the economy of the country. Fukuzawa insisted on education as a prerequisite for modern business because without learning a merchant could neither understand the problems inherent in the new business activities nor find social respectability.[6] Fukuzawa urged his students to enter business and not the government because, at a time when everybody was rushing into administrative positions, pioneers were needed in industry and trade.

Fukuzawa's influence was by no means confined to his Keiō Gijuku; it reached the entire population through his numerous writings. His most successful book was *Gakumon no susume* (An exhortation to learning), which in the five years between 1872 and 1876 reached the record sale of 3.4 million copies in 17 editions. In this book Fukuzawa forcefully propounded a new pragmatism and assailed the traditional views on learning, business, and status. Learning was to be emancipated from its theoretical bias and put into the service of daily life, notably of business; it was to open the way to social and economic success. Self-respect ought not to depend on status but on learning and business achievement. Other of his books contained similar views. In *Seiyō jijō* (Conditions in the West) he described life in Western societies, with its stress on the respectability and rationality of business. At a time when newspapers and books were still scarce, Fukuzawa's books with their many editions must have exercised a tremendous influence on the public mind. By 1897 the total sales of his books and pamphlets had reached about 10 million.[7]

The immediate effects of Fukuzawa's pragmatic approach were, of course, most evident in the Keiō Gijuku. The school became the chief supplier of the leading Meiji business managers and entrepreneurs. The Mitsubishi and Mitsui zaibatsu in particular drew heavily on Fukuzawa's graduates to fill top positions in their enterprises. Fukuzawa's connections with Mitsubishi were particularly close, and people used to say the Mitsubishi Company was run by Iwasaki's money and Fukuzawa's men.[8]

Shibusawa Eiichi (1840–1931), perhaps the outstanding entrepreneur of Japanese modern history, through his knowledge and moral leadership most decisively influenced the course of private industry in the crucial stage of its development.[9] Like Fukuzawa, Shibusawa insisted upon joint-stock enterprises and upon independence from the government. He himself resigned his respected position in the Ministry of Finance in order to work as a leader in establishing a viable private sector.

The son of a rich farmer in Musashino province, Shibusawa acquired some early experience in business dealings, but had leisure enough to become an ardent *sonnō jōi* partisan; he even entered into a plan with a few others to overthrow the bakufu. After the failure of this scheme he entered the service of the Tokugawa and gained the confidence of the last shogun. He was chosen to accompany the shogun's younger brother, as his financial manager, to the World Exhibition in Paris in 1867. In France Shibusawa absorbed his new experiences with intelligence and zeal. Three things in particular made a lasting impression on him. First, he saw the ease and liberty with which businessmen moved in the highest social circles and were accepted as equals. Second, he realized that large industrial ventures and other vast projects could only be realized on the basis of joint-stock operations. Finally, he was introduced by a friend, the banker Flury-Herald, to the technicalities of the modern banking system.

After his return to Japan in 1869, Shibusawa was called by Ōkuma to serve in the Ministry of Finance; he accepted on condition that he might resign at any time to work as a private businessman. During his four years in the Ministry of Finance, Shibusawa is said to have been the man chiefly responsible for the tax reform and the monetary reorganization. Although at the age of thirty-four he had become second in command in the Ministry of Finance, he resigned his post in 1873.

Shibusawa had not yet left the ministry when he was elected general superintendent of the newly established First National Bank (later the Dai Ichi), a joint enterprise with capital mainly from Mitsui and Ono. In 1875, after the downfall of Ono, he was unanimously elected president of the bank, which became the headquarters from which he coordinated and directed many of the newly emerging business and industrial enterprises. Shibusawa had not only spurned a career in the Ministry of Finance. He also refused extremely tempting offers from the private sector: Minomura Rizaemon wanted him as his own successor as manager of the entire Mitsui combine, the largest enterprise in Japan; and Iwasaki invited him to become a partner in the powerful Mitsubishi zaibatsu. Shibusawa firmly declined both offers in order to remain free for the work of promoting modern industry in general.

One of Shibusawa's chief concerns was the spread of the joint-stock form of enterprise. The traditional merchants shunned the pooling of capital for a common purpose, and the new strongmen of industry and finance, such as Iwasaki, sought their own aggrandizement and built up private empires. Shibusawa was strongly opposed to both types; he chided the old-fashioned merchants, and he fought Iwasaki's dictatorial monopoly tooth and nail by organizing a powerful rival shipping company. For Shibusawa the common good, the progress of the country's economy, was more important than personal gain and power, and he demonstrated this unselfish attitude time and again in organizing new joint enterprises from which he could expect little or no gain. He felt that the company form of enterprise was necessary not only in order to gather sufficient capital for large-scale ventures, but also because the capital owners were still too uneducated and immature for modern business management. The company form of enterprise made it possible to entrust direction and management to capable and progressive men, whether or not they had capital of their own. Shibusawa himself had become president of the Dai Ichi Bank because of his capabilities alone, and he in turn chose the managers for his own numerous enterprises on the same basis.

Shibusawa, like Fukuzawa, was most emphatic about the need for education in the conduct of large-scale enterprises, and in this he wanted his businessmen to be radically different from the Tokugawa merchants. According to Shibusawa, a modern businessman had to be able to evaluate trends and to understand the consequences of his plans and actions, for his own enterprise and also for the whole country; this could only be accomplished by means of a thorough education. He was so insistent upon learning as a prerequisite for his type of entrepreneur that he refused assistance and cooperation to those who failed to qualify. Suzuki Tōsaburō, the pioneer in sugar refining, recalled with bitterness that he had been refused a loan by Shibusawa on grounds of insufficient education.[10]

In 1874 Shibusawa, together with Mori Arinori, planned

the establishment of the first business school in Japan, which developed into Hitotsubashi University. Under his presidency, the Jitsugyō no Nihonsha (Japanese association of enterprise) published a periodical to bring business knowledge and ideas to those who could not attend a school. As president of the Tokyo Chamber of Commerce and of the Bankers' Association, both of which he founded in 1878, he exercised his leadership to form the new business attitudes. The ever-recurring theme in his many speeches was the necessity for the modern entrepreneur to be different from the old merchant in terms of education, standards of honesty, and dedication to the public good, while at the same time maintaining his independence from the government.[11]

Shibusawa was not content to be the recognized leader in the top echelons of the Meiji industrial, banking, and business communities. He also wanted to extend his influence over the younger generation. In his own house he gathered a group of business students who became known by the name Ryūmonsha (lit., "dragon door club"). They published a periodical, the *Ryūmon zasshi* (Ryūmon periodical), one of the first in Japan to be dedicated to economic matters. In it were propagated the basic tenets of Shibusawa's business ideology, which was essentially the same as Fukuzawa's. In one article Shibusawa was compared to the famous warlord of the eleventh century, Minamoto Yoshiie.[12] "Just as the samurai gathered behind Minamoto to follow him into the battle of war, so now the younger generation gathers around Shibusawa to follow him into the battle of enterprise, as merchants of the modern kind." [13]

Shibusawa's leadership in raising educational standards, and consequently the efficiency and the self-respect of the new business community, was imitated by many of the pioneering entrepreneurs of his time. Among the fifty entrepreneurs selected for discussion in Chapter Seven, nine built schools at their own expense. Godai Tomoatsu established a private school in Osaka for the education of the children of merchants in order to break down their conservative business attitudes. The first three subjects taught there were accounting, economics, and arithmetic. The rapidly increasing number of students made enlargement of the school necessary within a few years.[14] Iwasaki, who was probably the most successful of all Meiji entrepreneurs, acted differently from Shibusawa in many ways, especially insofar as government connections and political machinations were concerned, but he agreed with him completely with respect to a thorough education. And Toyokawa Ryōhei, himself a Keiō man, made his most valuable contribution to Iwasaki's Mitsubishi company by scouting for talented college graduates and bringing them into that zaibatsu.[15]

Independence from the government and freedom from bureaucratism were very difficult to achieve in reality. As much as Fukuzawa insisted that private enterprise should be built "for profit and for the sake of Japan," the first thirty years posed such tremendous problems in terms of technology, organization, and, especially, capital supply that the ideal so much admired in Britain and the United States was almost unattainable. Shibusawa, however, took energetic steps in the direction of independence. He frequently scored the group of political merchants who made hay from government contracts and boasted of their titles and privileges, and he asserted that his basic motive in giving up his own government post was his desire to fill the vacuum of leadership in private enterprise.

Godai Tomoatsu also exchanged a government post for an entrepreneurial career in Osaka, although in his case political opposition was behind the move. He later received large favors from the Meiji government. Yet when he handed in his resignation, he told his friend Ōkubo: "There is no lack of able men in the imperial government; therefore I may now resign and descend to the level of the common people. I intend to promote henceforth the general state of business and industry, and to work for the prosperity of the people's enterprise. In this way I shall also be contributing to the prosperity and strength of the country and the nation." [16] This statement at least reveals the sorely felt need to boost private initiative, even if actions would not or could not always be in step with such pronouncements. For the time being, the private entrepreneur was not only a scarce commodity, but he enjoyed neither adequate capital backing nor social prestige. As Shibusawa once put it, he was like the tools in the kitchen, very useful but earning little attention as compared to the showpieces in the living room — meaning the officials.[17]

At the bottom of the widespread contempt for private business was the persistence of popular opinion concerning low business ethics and standards of honesty. The disorder in the business world since the opening of the ports aggravated the situation and brought the merchants' reputation to an all-time low. Shibusawa and his associates had to prove to the public that they were totally different from the speculators in the port cities or the monopoly traders of old. In order to stress this difference, Shibusawa went so far as to coin a new word for his type of businessman: the name *shōnin* (merchant) was to be replaced by *jitsugyōka* (entrepreneur, lit., "a man who undertakes a real task"). He defined a *jitsugyōka* as "someone who works with honesty for the establishment of industry." [18] In his mind honesty and industrial enterprise were linked. When

he once heard a graduate of the Imperial University remark at a banquet that in business matters "a lie must
sometimes also be considered as a way," he scolded the
man in public and insisted that a businessman should go
so far as to "vow to the Gods and to Buddha never to tell
a lie." [19] Other men followed Shibusawa's lead in fighting
for the honor of the businessman. Ōtani Kahei, a tea exporter of Yokohama, is probably best known for his untiring efforts to stamp out cheating and unreliability
within the trade association.

Indeed, Shibusawa did succeed in creating a new self-
respect among the entrepreneurs of the Meiji period; they
used the new word *jitsugyōka* with pride and eventually
came to be highly respected by the people. A large part of
his achievement must undoubtedly be attributed to the
bummei kaika mentality and to effective support by the
government. But the leadership of Fukuzawa and Shibusawa and of a few similarly minded men was most crucial
to the formation of the new status for private entrepreneurs.

As much as Shibusawa planned and founded new industrial undertakings, as generously as he encouraged and
supported the closely knit group of pioneering Meiji entrepreneurs in any work that would promote industrial
progress, he seemed little interested in building an industrial and financial empire of his own. Although he could
unquestionably have become a zaibatsu builder much like
Iwasaki, Ōkura, or Yasuda, he did not strive for this type
of power. The man who was connected with over six
hundred enterprises by way of presidential or advisory
positions often left control to others as soon as the enterprise was firmly established. Although he was president
of the Dai Ichi Bank from 1875 to his retirement in 1916,
his family owned no more than 4 percent of the bank's

stock by 1926.[20] Shibusawa was a man of cooperation; he wanted to serve the common cause, the cause of the country and of the business world.

Shibusawa's dedication was molded by his Confucian background. He used to carry the Analects of Confucius in his pocket and knew large parts of it by heart, quoting Confucius frequently in his speeches. In his Confucian outlook he differed from Fukuzawa whose thinking was molded by the English liberal school. Confucian ethics during the Tokugawa period had been an instrument to preserve the status quo. Shibusawa set out, in his own words, "to manage business enterprise using the Analects of Confucius." [21] It may be that it was precisely this fusion of the best of Japanese tradition with the most progressive ideas and methods of the West that gave Shibusawa his influence on the Japanese business world. But in a sense Shibusawa was a cross between a businessman and a government official. He never tired of proclaiming the need for self-respect in business for profit, but he acted half of the time like a Meiji government official, worrying and working on problems of economic and educational policy, of domestic and international politics. His thousands of speeches and addresses do not sound at all like those of a private businessman.

Perhaps Shibusawa's influence during his lifetime, and the great admiration he is accorded in Japan even today, can be explained by the fact that he was a transitional type, a businessman who was both a samurai and a Meiji official. This was an image that the samurai could imitate without lowering their idea of personal status. Shibusawa alone, of course, could not effect a change in the traditional valuation of business activity. Others donned the same robe of respectability and voiced the same kind of phrases; there is no need to investigate the sincerity of all these patriotic claims. They were intended for public consumption. When a class image is in the process of being transformed, one must not look too closely at actual performance; the image, once made creditable, can stand a good many factual discrepancies and contradictions.

In other countries, Germany for example, entrepreneurs also found it necessary to paint a new class image by claiming that they were working for the sake of the country. Some symbolic action or success itself in modern enterprise may then suffice to justify the claim of selfless dedication vis-à-vis the public. In this context, the situation in Russia in the second half of the nineteenth century deserves notice. The bourgeoisie, which was thriving at the expense of other groups, was despised and labeled base, greedy, and vulgar by the gentry, the intelligentsia and the peasants alike. Thus far the Russian situation can be seen as parallel to that of Tokugawa Japan. But in Russia the rehabilitation of the image of the merchant came very late, under the influence of the Marxian intellectuals, and even then the transformation was not complete. Entrepreneurial activity remained handicaped in Russia under the burden of the low esteem in which the business class was held.[22] In Japan entrepreneurial activity was stimulated by an early achievement of social respectability.

THE LOW PROFIT RATES

Even a *jitsugyōka* in Meiji Japan was in business primarily for money. The profit he earned was the yardstick of his success. One might take exception to the idea that money is the ultimate goal in all business activity. Most people, in Japan or elsewhere, are probably motivated ultimately by a desire for prestige, power, or success as such; but if they are in business, the achievement of the ultimate goal will depend on and be measured by the monetary returns they can earn. A man may operate a shop or a factory for charity and give away all his profits, but if he fails to earn them in the first place he is probably a bad businessman.

It is understood that entrepreneurial activity, especially in a pioneering period such as the industrialization of Meiji Japan, is beset with risks and uncertainties. But a rationally calculating entrepreneur has cognizance of the chances involved and does not let himself be carried away by undue optimism, like a gambler. Therefore, on the average and in the long run, we expect entrepreneurs as a group actually to earn the going rates for routine business activity, plus an extra reward for their innovations. In Schumpeter's view, the innovator is the one agent in the economy who earns profits in the strict sense; the returns on capital in the noninnovating enterprises occur as interest, rents, and wages. We should therefore expect the *jitsugyōka* of modern Japanese industry to have been rewarded for their risk-taking efforts by high profit rates, certainly higher than those in the traditional business sectors. A persistence of low profit rates in the private sector of modern industry, on the other hand, would present us with a problem in assigning motives to these entrepreneurs.

In order to answer the question of entrepreneurial motivation, it is important to ascertain comparative returns in the various sectors of the Japanese economy during the time when modern private industry was struggling for its existence and when it was making its first efforts toward independence of the government. Returns within the government enterprises pose no problem, since the government is not supposed to be in business for profit. But it is extremely difficult to draw the dividing line

between government and nongovernment operations because of the extent to which large-scale modern enterprise
was tied to the government by direct and indirect subsidies. We need to know the rates of return on private capital only, and on private capital that was invested by free
choice. Clearly, alternative investment opportunities do
not enter into the decision process if they are not open to
a particular entrepreneur, either because of lack of knowledge or because of outside interference. It can be seen
that to find and use comparative profit rates in various
investment sectors as indicators of entrepreneurial motivation encounters a host of snags.

As a first step I shall try to establish the comparative
rates of return on as broad a basis as possible, taking first
the going interest rates and profits on nonindustrial investments in the 1880s. Then I shall investigate profit
rates in private industry, with particular attention to those
sectors and those specific cases where government initiative
and subsidies were small or completely absent. Because
there are no general statistics, it will be necessary to try the
patience of the reader by detailing many individual cases.
But from these descriptions he may glean a partial answer
to the motivation problem and thus be compensated for
the lack of succinctness in what is basically a matter of
statistics.

The Alternatives to Industrial Investments

Interest rates during the mid 1880s must serve as a basis
for our comparison of rates of return on capital. Anyone
who invests his money into some enterprise can, as an alternative, either lend out his money or at least put it into
a bank for safekeeping. Rates charged by banks on loans
during the period from 1875 to 1884 averaged 15.09 percent,
with the lowest at 10.80 percent in 1883. Interest rates on

time deposits varied around 4–5 percent.[23] Of prime importance, of course, are the rates charged on bank loans. We have to assume theoretically that an entrepreneur borrows capital and pays interest on it, his profit being the difference between the interest on his loan and the total net return. If he uses his own capital, he forgoes the opportunity of lending it out against interest. Therefore profit rates in industry should be above the rates charged on bank loans. The rates on time deposits paid by banks are the absolute floor; a man who has money can at least put it into the bank.

Banking profits constitute another important item of comparison because we may assume that an investor in an industrial enterprise could as an alternative buy stock in a bank or perhaps establish a bank of his own. The profit rates of national banks during the 1876–1894 period averaged 16.29 percent on paid-up capital, ranging from 19.32 percent in 1876 down to 13.59 percent in 1886.[24] A statistical survey of all Japanese banks shows approximately the same picture for the same period, with only two years, 1877 and 1878, under 14 percent, and an average of 15.6 percent.[25] Surveys of Tokyo banks in 1881 and 1883, with 25 (leaving out 2 with over 100 percent profits) and 31 banks reporting, similarly showed averages of 19.80 percent and 12.10 percent on paid-up capital.[26] These figures should suffice to indicate that the banks were making somewhat higher profits than the going rates charged on loans. The general figures, of course, obscure the variations of individual banks, but we have seen earlier that few banks closed during this period and that the overall picture in banking was one of stability.

Trading enterprises are not as easy to handle as banks because, for one thing, they differ widely in character and type of operation and, for another, statistical evidence for these years is not easy to find. In fact I could find nothing that may represent a general picture of profits in trading, except for two surveys from Tokyo for the years 1881 and 1883. They have many deficiencies; we do not know how the profits were calculated or how such things as stocks, depreciation, and good will were handled. But it seemed desirable to take figures for as early a time in the 1880s as possible because my argument is based on the opportunity-cost principle. The entrepreneur who invested in industry, say during 1885 or 1888, had to base his calculations on returns in trading in the preceding years because investment there could be considered an alternative possibility. So statistics from after 1890, even if more reliable, would not do for my purposes.

In 1881, 22 trading establishments reported their total profit and loss figures.[27] The average profit rate was 14.4 percent, with the highest at 96.1 percent and the lowest at 0.3 percent. The average capital invested in these businesses was 48,305 yen, with the highest at 600,000 yen and the lowest at 313 yen. Eleven businesses had over 10,000 yen capital and averaged 10.6 percent profits, less than the overall average. It is anybody's guess whether and by how much these rates would have to be revised upward or downward if they were made to correspond to modern bookkeeping rules.

The 1883 survey presents profit rates of 24 establishments of the same type as in the 1881 survey.[28] If again we leave out two nonrepresentative businesses with over 100 percent profits, the other 22 have an average profit rate of 15.2 percent. Their breakdown according to capital shows that 6 businesses with under 10,000 yen capital averaged 18.6 percent; another 8 with capital between 10,000 and 49,999 yen earned 11.1 percent; and the last 8, with 50,000 yen capital or more, averaged 16.7 percent in profits.

Transportation enterprises are listed in the 1883 survey with 9 establishments; their profit rates reach the average of 11.2 percent with only one enterprise left out as non-representative. Two of those included, however, the Nippon Railway Company and the Kyōdō Unyu Company, each with over one million yen capital, had as low profits for that year as 3.4 percent and 1.3 percent, respectively. It is here for the first time that we encounter the phenomenon of very low profit rates in large-scale modern enterprises; more will be said about this later.

Manufacturing companies listed in the same two surveys from Tokyo include a large variety of types, with both old and new technologies. Furthermore there are no clues as to the structure of capital and ratios between total paid-up capital and fixed investments, and no way of determining how depreciation was handled. Direct or indirect government subsidies (cheap sales, special procurements, and such) may also be involved to make simple profit and loss statements all but valueless. To make matters worse, we must remember once more that the years 1881 and 1883 marked the beginning and the worst period of the Matsukata deflation. This deflation, though necessary and on the whole salutary in its effects, was the worst storm that the young Meiji industries had to weather.

Yet when all this has been said, there simply are no other data. Consequently I shall use these as very rough indicators of general direction rather than as exact statistics. Because of the importance of finding indications of profit trends in manufacturing, particularly of the modern type, as compared with alternative return possibilities, I shall then probe further into various industries and individual enterprises.

The Tokyo survey of 1881 lists a total of 90 manufacturing establishments.[29] If we leave out again those with profit rates of over 100 percent and less than 1 percent as non-representative, the remaining 84 averaged 18.8 percent in net returns on paid-up capital. The breakdown according to capital reads as follows: 28 firms with 10,000 yen and more capital averaged 14.3; 43 firms with capital between 1,000 and 9,999 yen averaged 17.1 percent; and 17 firms with under 1,000 yen capital averaged 21.6. We notice here a marked tendency for the smaller establishments to have higher profits than the larger ones.

The 1883 survey mirrors the severe effects of the Matsukata deflation: of the 80 reporting firms, 14 operated at a loss, while 19 showed profit rates exceeding 100 percent. If we lump all of them together and average the profit rates, we get 51.9 percent, obviously a meaningless figure. We would expect to find a lower-than-normal average, of course. Could it be that the superprofits in some cases were nothing but returns on sellouts prior to liquidation? I must leave the explanation to the imagination of the reader. It is perhaps worthy of note that of the 20 weaving establishments, all rather small-scale with on the average not more than 2,500 yen capital, half operated at a loss and the other half earned superprofits that pulled their combined average profits up to 52 percent. The years 1883 and 1884 saw the ruin of many such small-scale enterprises.

Taken as they stand, the two surveys indicate something about the general conditions of the traditional, rather small-scale manufacturing enterprises. The year 1881 provides us with a meaningful and not unexpected set of profit rates; the year 1883 has too many erratic data and the average is meaningless. With due reservations about the significance of these figures on capital returns in the 1880s, the picture in summary looks as follows:

Interest rates, 1875–1884	15.09%
Profit rates of banks	
National banks, 1876–1894	16.29%
All banks, 1876–1894	15.60%
Tokyo banks, 1881	19.8%
Tokyo banks, 1883	12.1%
Profit rates of trading enterprises	
Tokyo, 1881	14.4%
Tokyo, 1883	15.2%
Profit rates of transportation enterprises	
Tokyo, 1883	11.2%
Profit rates of manufacturing enterprises	
Tokyo, 1881	18.8%
(Tokyo, 1883	51.9%)

In spite of the weakness of the Tokyo survey data, we can probably assume with a high degree of confidence that the prevailing rates of return in all the well-established lines of business stayed at an average of 10 percent or higher. With this much ascertained, let us now take a close look at the modern large-scale enterprises that should be considered as alternative investment opportunities for private capital.

Profit Rates in Industrial Enterprises

The railways are here included in my "industry" concept; cotton spinning and railways were the beneficiaries of a private-investment boom. The initial public aversion and even hostility to railway building rapidly changed to great enthusiasm after the completion of the first government lines and the private Tokyo-Aomori line. The Tokyo-Aomori line was founded in 1881, and two years later dividends of 10 percent were paid to stockholders. Probably as a consequence of this success, no fewer than ten railway companies had been founded by 1887, with 42 million yen in paid-up capital and 1,000 miles of lines laid.[30] The steepest growth occurred in the years between 1887 and

1890, as indicated by the increase of capital in the regional railway companies, from 12,130 million to 52,390 million yen. In 1887 a Private Railway Regulation Act was passed which set up standards for the foundation and operation of private companies. Among the outstanding entrepreneurs of the early Meiji era, we find many who founded or actively stimulated the founding of several such railway companies.

If the first railway company was a success, how did the others fare in terms of profit rates? This question can easily be answered from statistics on capital, fixed investments, and returns on capital, as well as on fixed investments, over the period from 1883 to 1893.

Year	Paid-up capital (million yen)	Fixed investments (million yen)	Profits on fixed investments	Profits on paid-up capital (computed)
1883	5,966	905	21.00%	3.18%
1884	11,830	2,062	12.80%	2.24%
1885	11,830	3,106	10.20%	2.68%
1886	12,080	5,493	8.90%	4.03%
1887	12,130	6,703	11.80%	6.51%
1888	31,870	11,834	9.50%	3.53%
1889	45,390	20,366	7.00%	3.14%
1890	52,390	33,816	4.80%	3.11%
1891	52,960	44,062	4.80%	4.00%
1892	56,235	47,508	5.60%	4.73%
1893	63,145	52,050	6.70%	5.49%

Nihon keizai tōkei sōkan (Survey of Japanese economic statistics), ed. Asahi shinbunsha (Asahi Newspaper Co.; Tokyo, 1930), p. 820.

The table indicates that these private regional railways averaged, over 11 years, a bare 7.65 percent on their fixed investments and 3.88 percent on the paid-up capital. With the increasing ratio of fixed investments to paid-up capital —that is, with the extension of the mileage — these two rates moved closer together, to around 5 percent. The government-operated lines did not fare much better. Their returns on fixed investments moved gradually upward, from 3.90 percent in 1886 to as high as 10.40 percent in 1896, the average over these 11 years being 7.32 percent.[31]

With such poor results in the railway companies over at least one decade, we cannot very well attribute the investment fever solely to the effect of the 10 percent dividend rate of the Tokyo-Aomori Railroad. Even the most ardent optimists would soon have learned better. There must have been strong noneconomic stimuli in operation which supported a dogged optimism in the face of prolonged low returns.

It cannot be claimed that the investors, if they were samurai, remained unaware of the opportunity-cost principle. We have an interesting example of samurai calculation in the case of the Maruya Company, now known as Maruzen, which was established in 1869. The samurai founders first made a thorough inquiry into the going profit rates in Tokyo and then decided that their trading establishment must yield at least 15 percent; they set up a very interesting and elaborate system of rewards and punishments for workers and managers to assure that they would actually receive their 15 percent dividend payments.[32] Undoubtedly the men who rushed into railways had the same opportunity to investigate the returns of existing companies and to find out that returns were on the whole very low. Nor were the railways the only instance of this apparently irrational enthusiasm for modern industry, as we shall see.

The full impact of foreign competition was felt in the import-competing industries; they were not shielded by any protective tariffs to speak of and had to grapple internally with the two basic problems of technology and lack of demand. Lack of demand may sound paradoxical at a time of large imports, but the market for imported goods was not automatically ready to absorb the competing products "made in Japan," which were often of poorer quality. It was felt all the more that import-competing industries had to be given special attention and that their promotion was a national task of great urgency. While by their very nature the import-competing industries were mainly modern enterprises, we may expect to find here also both prolonged low returns on capital and a marked display of motives other than that of private profit maximization.

The following table lists the most important import-competing industries and indicates their position toward the end of our period of investigation, in 1892.

Industry	Number of companies	Paid-up capital (1,000 yen)	Number of employees	Power (horsepower)
Textiles	47	11,224	29,103	8,334
Paper	37	1,575	2,744	2,466
Shipbuilding	13	522	3,072	1,023
Machines	18	45	1,041	206
Cement	14	775	919	694
Bricks	39	538	2,122	145
Glass	19	192	555	8
Matches	73	452	15,264	32
Soap	16	97	337	6
Electrical equipment	12	1,710	135	1,021
Type printing	95	556	4,299	28
Total	383	17,686	59,591	13,983

Takahashi Kamekichi, *Meiji Taishō sangyō hattatsu shi* (The history of manufacturing during the Meiji and Taishō eras; Tokyo, 1929), p. 240.

I again call attention to the fact that the Matsukata deflation from 1881 to 1884 had a shattering impact on the young industries. The impact of the deflation is reflected in the fall of interest rates from 14.05 percent in 1881 to 9.10 percent in 1886; between 1882 and 1887, about 7 million yen of export surplus was accumulated annually; the general price index fell from 162 in 1881 to 110 in 1884.[33] By 1885, the inconvertible government notes had been absorbed, and the ensuing years marked the establishment of numerous companies in cotton spinning and in a number of other import-competing industries. The losses incurred during the Matsukata deflation must be attributed largely to the extraordinary external conditions and cannot be of much use to us in substantiating the case for noneconomic motivations. It is the whole picture over this period, with external disturbances and internal difficulties taken together, that will serve as an illustration of the odds that faced the entrepreneurs.

Cotton spinning, which had been so much stressed and promoted as being in the national interest, was severely hit by the deflation. The president of the Ichikawa Mill said in a speech that during the years of the depression many mills had to sell almost at raw-material cost; prices dropped by 20–30 percent and stocks of unsold yarns piled up.[34] The mills, which had all been enthusiastically established with strong government encouragement, were in severe trouble by 1883–84.

The Hiroshima Spinning Mill had been built by the government as a model enterprise, for 49,000 yen, and was sold to 5,860 samurai shareholders for 12,000 yen. After seventeen months of operation under the samurai, in 1883 a total operating deficit of 23,000 yen had been reached. The government then placed the mill under prefectural supervision, and regular reports had to be filed with the Ministry of Agriculture and Trade. From 1884 on, operating losses were avoided, but a considerable debt load remained for a number of years.[35]

One author gives figures of total profits and losses for twelve mills, covering sporadically the period from 1882 to 1888.[36] If we take the initial capital investments and calculate an average from twenty-six profit-and-loss statements on these twelve mills, we arrive at a 6.17 percent profit per mill; this figure should, if anything, be revised downward because of additional unspecified capital investments that were made after the foundation of the mills. Another author gives 6 percent as the average dividend rate for cotton spinning in 1883.[37] This dividend rate reflects closely the profit rates, since in that year only 2,000 yen of undistributed profits were retained against 280,000 yen capital in that industry.

The depressed state of mechanical cotton spinning caused concern in official circles. At a time when cotton cloth and cotton yarns made up some 30 percent of total imports, the success and expansion of spinning was of vital importance to the national economy. But verbal encouragement would fail to find a response unless the underlying problems were solved. The large capital suppliers still avoided investments in cotton spinning.

Capital scarcity and technical difficulties were the basic reasons for the failure of the two-thousand-spindle mills. The ratio of overhead to productive capacity was much too high, and low labor efficiency and underutilization of machinery because of exclusively day-time operation added to the problem. The use of water power necessitated stoppages when the rivers were flooded or dried up. A dire lack of trained technicians caused breakdowns and rapid depreciation of costly machinery. And on top of all this came the poor quality of the Japanese yarns, which were no match for the imported quality yarns.

Shibusawa, who as president of the Dai Ichi Bank was well aware of the foreign-exchange problem, decided to make a supreme effort to break the impasse in cotton spinning. He succeeded in interesting a few top entrepreneurs and a number of nobles in founding a large spinning mill. In 1883 the Osaka Mill was established by this group with 280,000 yen capital; the mills then in existence usually had no more than 30,000–70,000 yen. Under the expert technician and manager Yamabe Takeo, a Keiō graduate, the mill became a resounding success. Yamabe used steam power and introduced night-shift work for this 10,500-spindle mill; in the year after operations started, 18 percent in dividends were already being paid. In 1886 the mill was enlarged to 31,000 spindles, and in 1887 the dividend rate was up to 30 percent.[38]

The phenomenal success of the Osaka Mill broke the caution and timidity of the wealthy Osaka men, especially of the cotton merchants. Between 1886 and 1894, 33 new mills were established: the average capacity per mill rose to 10,000 spindles and the profit rates now compared favorably with those in traditional investment industries.[39] Most of the founders and capital suppliers in this period were rich merchants; they needed no patriotic enthusiasm and did not claim to work "for the national economy" or to "stop the imports." They invested for profits and received them.

Paper manufacturing received almost no help from the government. The first mill on Japanese soil was built by the economic reformer of Tosa han, Gotō Shōjirō. When paper production encountered many unforeseen difficulties, the mill was sold to its engineer in 1876. He in turn sold it after a short time to Sumitomo, and it was shortly sold again. It changed hands so often because it could not be made into a profitable enterprise; losses alternated with very low returns.[40] The daimyo of Hiroshima also had a paper mill built, which piled up losses for three years and sold no paper. It was only when the government ordered paper for title deeds from this mill that final ruin was avoided: nevertheless, low returns continued for several more years.[41]

The Ōji Paper Mill, founded in 1875 by Shibusawa with capital mainly from Mitsui and Shimada, was the largest and most famous paper mill of the early Meiji era. Shibusawa established it because of his belief that paper and printing were prerequisites for the progress of learning and of civilization in general. He regretted the amount of attention being paid to armaments and heavy industries.[42] After five years the mill was considered quite successful, achieving a profit rate of 10 percent. But the young apprentice Ōkawa, Shibusawa's nephew, wrote a memorandum to his uncle explaining that a 10 percent rate could by no means be regarded as satisfactory when, at the same time, the interest rate charged by banks was as high as 12–13 percent. Considering the risks and the initial waiting period involved, the profits should rise to at least 20 percent. Ōkawa, under the influence of the English economists, was thinking in terms of economic rationality. His memorandum contained the sentence: "The famous economist Smith determines the average rate of profits on capital from the general rate of interest." [43] Ōkawa was sent abroad to study paper production and after his return eventually made the Ōji Paper Mill a great success. All told, by 1878 Japan had four paper mills, and their number did not rise above five until 1889, although the quantity and quality of the paper produced did improve throughout the whole period.

The pioneering attitudes and the courage that the entrepreneurs displayed in founding of modern industrial enterprises at this time are brought out by the example of Sakuma Sadaichi. He had gone to great pains to build a

printing establishment and then, when he was ordered to
do a book with cardboard covers, he decided not to import
the cardboard but to set up a factory to produce it. He
succeeded in his drive to raise 170,000 yen share capital
and established a cardboard factory in 1885, but it operated so inefficiently that the shares very soon fell from
50 yen to 6 yen. Sakuma handed control of the enterprise
over to the "industrial troubleshooter," Asano Sōichirō.
Still, the enterprise remained in the red for eleven years.[44]
Depressed conditions in paper manufacturing were mainly
traceable to technical difficulties, which resulted in poor
quality and high prices, and to lack of general market demand. Shibusawa and Sakuma Sadaicha seem to have had
some definite ideas about the necessity for paper and cardboard manufacturing, assigning the factor of profitability
to second place.

Cement production was started by the government in its
Fukagawa works in 1874. In 1884 the enterprise was first
rented and later sold to Asano. At the time when Asano
was to take over, the prospects were so bleak that Shibusawa felt it necessary to warn him and to suggest that he
might better invest in cotton spinning. Asano is on record
as having replied that the raw material for cotton spinning
had to be imported in part from China, while all raw
materials for cement production were available at no cost
in Japan.[45] Asano succeeded, owing to the combination of
his own entrepreneurial genius, the technical skill of his
engineer, Utsunomiya Saburō,[46] and the large government
orders he received. Profit figures, however, are not available
from the company records.

By 1890 a total of ten cement mills were in existence in
Japan, with total capital of over one million yen. The
records stress the fact that profit rates were very low in
almost all of these establishments.[47] The Aichi Cement

Mill, for example, constructed four furnaces in 1887, bought two fret machines, and was to set out on a large scale, but remained in the red for some years and was then sold.[48] Onoda Cement, which was the most successful of all after Asano Cement, reported its first real success in 1890, ten years after its establishment, when it could distribute 10 percent in dividends. Before that year, the rate of dividend payments was considerably lower, and in some years no dividends were paid, owing to operating losses.[49] Dividends, of course, do not necessarily reflect profit rates, but in those years they were usually quoted to describe the profitability of an enterprise. In cement production the basic problems were the same as in paper manufacturing — namely, technical difficulties that resulted in high unit costs in spite of low wage levels and the lack of market demand. But the optimism and courage of the entrepreneurs were undaunted because they were struck with the idea of producing cement from "dirt at home" and thus preventing the outflow of gold to pay for imported cement.

Glass manufacturing, like cement production, had been started by the central government. The Shinagawa glass factory was established in 1876, but it was run by the Ministry of Industry at continued losses that totaled 15,000 yen.[50] In 1884 Nishimura Katsuzō, a very patriotic and dogged entrepreneur, rented the glass factory from the ministry jointly with a partner. He lost 13,000 yen in that one year, and his partner wanted no more of it. Nishimura bought the factory in 1885 for 79,950 yen, to be paid in installments over fifty-five years with payments starting in 1890. He lost no time in trying to modernize the plant; he made a trip to Europe to study production techniques and introduced a few improvements. In 1888 he joined with Shibusawa Eiichi and Masuda Takashi and made the enterprise a joint-stock company, with 150,000 yen capital. But the factory remained uncompetitive; [51] it was closed in 1892 because of continued losses. In 1887 another glass factory was built, by the Iwaki Glass Company with Shibusawa, Asano, and Masuda as its main shareholders. Shibusawa pushed the plan because he was worried about the rising imports of glass. This company lasted only three years and had to labor under the same difficulties as the Nishimura Company.[52]

Iron mining must also be regarded as an import-competing industry because a considerable amount of iron and steel were imported into Japan. The government decided to modernize and enlarge some of the existing small-scale iron mines in the Kamaishi area. In 1874 the government investments in these mines began; among other things, machines were imported and a ship for the transportation of pig iron was procured. Smelting did not start until 1880 but by that time a total of 2.5 million yen had been used up. Technical difficulties, insufficient supply of charcoal, and destruction of buildings by fire caused a stoppage of work after only 196 days of actual operation. The total pig iron produced during government management was worth 175,126 yen.[53]

This truly spectacular failure of one of the largest government investments turned even the most optimistic officials against any further government commitment in iron mining. It was argued that Japan should continue importing iron from abroad because mining still presented too many difficulties to Japanese technology, and Japanese iron ore was too poor in quality to warrant large investments.[54] The Kamaishi mines were for sale, but nobody was interested in purchasing them. Tanaka Chōbei, a political merchant, bought initially only the residue of iron ore that had already been mined. In this deal he lost

30,000 yen.[55] But Tanaka was convinced by his head clerk, Yokoyama Hisatarō, to purchase the mines and all the equipment and to continue the work of the government. Yokoyama's arguments are interesting and reflect not only his own attitudes but also those of many entrepreneurs of the period.

Yokoyama argued that a few million yen in government investments and eight years of effort must not be permitted to go to waste. Somebody must continue the operation of the mines or all the machines would rot and enormous amounts of ore would be lost to Japan. He further stressed that a defeat at this stage would discourage for a long time any further attempts in iron mining. His final argument was that the government would certainly not fail to lend assistance to someone who undertook to continue its own frustrated efforts.[56] His confidence in government assistance follows from his first two arguments: if an entrepreneur acted with a view to general economic necessity he could rightly expect official assistance; public and private enterprises were not strictly separated, but were viewed as integral parts of one great effort in Meiji Japan.

The import-competing industries reviewed here owed their staggering difficulties both to competition from imports and to internal technical problems. But the persistence of low returns over long periods was not unusual in other modern enterprises; there, too, it took courage and perseverance to carry on to final success. For instance, the famous Tomioka filature, which was sold by the government for 130,000 yen after five years of operation, totaled in the next five years losses of 159,800 yen.[57] The shipyards fared quite similarly. The pioneers in leather-good manufacturing and sugar refining also had to overcome long periods of losses and low returns. It is significant that these were all ventures with large capital investments, usually over 100,000 yen, as contrasted to the average capital of the Tokyo manufacturing firms, in 1881, of 13,790 yen.

This survey of import-competing industries and other modern enterprises has often lacked exact figures, because they are not available. But the descriptive approach thus necessitated should also have conveyed an impression of the prevailing attitudes, above all of the stubborn determination, of the first entrepreneurs. Persistence and continued pioneering in spite of low returns over long periods is one of the characteristics of all the leading Meiji entrepreneurs. I may add here two more cases in which this typical trait was displayed by Shibusawa.

A brick factory was founded by Shibusawa and Masuda, with 200,000 yen in capital.[58] Unexpectedly, various technical troubles developed and the anticipated government demand did not materialize. Consequently the brick factory operated for five years at a loss. The stockholders insisted that the project be abandoned, but Shibusawa remained adamant and himself invested more capital in it. Only after the Sino-Japanese War, ten years after the start of the factory, were satisfactory dividends of 10 percent paid.

The Tokyo Gas Company was started by a government official in 1871, but was managed so poorly that Shibusawa was asked to take charge of it.[59] By 1876 a total of 171,536 yen had been invested, with the total receipts during the five years amounting to only 6,310 yen. It took the Tokyo Gas Company thirteen years to achieve the first small gains. Again, lack of demand was the most important difficulty: people did not trust the new lighting system. Shibusawa distributed pamphlets on the use of gas light and gave parties for shopkeepers, but he was still unable to change the prevailing attitudes. After a while even the city council voted to abolish the enterprise, and here, as in many other cases, the personal courage and prestige of Shibusawa prevailed. The company continued and, after years of operating losses, success was finally achieved. Even then success for a few years meant no more than a bare 5–10 percent profit rate.

The obvious questions that arise in view of these persistent low profits and the technological problems pertain to capital supply and to the motivations for investment. How was it possible that such large losses could be absorbed? From what source did the entrepreneurs gather the capital to afford these typically long waiting periods? What motivated them to keep on innovating in spite of the complex problems?

The question about capital supply for these private ventures cannot be answered easily, for the methods of securing capital were involved and by no means uniform. We shall see in Chapter Six how the most successful entrepreneurs — those who built empires of industry and finance — gathered their capital. Government subsidies played an important part, but while some received much, others got almost nothing. Direct subsidies in the form of grants, low-interest loans, and cheap sales of government enterprises were perhaps not so important as the opportunities created for the political merchants to amass fortunes as official army suppliers during military operations, and in other types of official and semiofficial trading and banking transactions. And in the frequent cases where future entrepreneurs accumulated huge gains as supply merchants or as foreign traders and merchants of fortune in the turbulent years around the Restoration, we still need an explanation for why these same men began to invest in modern industry in spite of the obvious risks involved. There must have been pressures and inducements in operation that do not become apparent in profit and loss figures, and to these I now turn.

THE QUESTION OF ECONOMIC RATIONALITY

There is risk in attempting to specify the motives for investment decisions. A man himself often does not know precisely why he makes one decision as against another; it is all the less likely that someone else should know the reason. The records that we have were not written from the viewpoint of psychological or historical accuracy; are lavish in praise of their heroes and stress lofty motivations in order to add to their stature. The patriotic angle in particular is often strongly emphasized, because these times were zealous ones. But such post-factum biographical idolizations must be discounted as sources for serious research on motivation.

I am not concerned here with the motivations of individual men, but rather with the trends and prevailing public valuations that demanded at least outward conformity. There is little doubt that the average Meiji entrepreneur was largely guided by the same motivations that prevail in other times and circumstances. But a part of his actions was determined by quite special forces, and it was this that often tipped the scale in favor of decisions that may puzzle the pure-bred profit maximizer.

The particular way in which modern technology entered Japan certainly had much to do with the kind of response offered by the pioneers of industry. The task was felt to be a challenge, not only personally but socially and nationally. Enough has been said on this point in Chapter Four in dealing with the *bummei kaika* and *fukoku kyōhei* attitudes. Cases were not few in which entrepreneurs stubbornly carried on because they hated to concede defeat — they considered themselves representatives of Japan, as do athletes in the modern Olympic Games. Or an entrepreneur could become completely absorbed in his task after he had achieved some initial success. This is of course a rather common phenomenon, found frequently among artists and scholars, but also among industrialists. Asano Sōichirō, the pioneer in cement production is an example. He used to spend all day in his factory until he finally became ill and threw up blood; yet he could not be persuaded to take a rest. Asked whether he loved money more than his life, he replied that more than money, and more than his own life, he loved his work. If his work so required, he did not mind giving everything to it.[60]

If we leave out the more common motivations that were not specific to the Meiji era, and those which of themselves cannot explain the persistence of a dynamic innovational drive in spite of high risks and low profits, we have to seek out a strong supplementary motivating force elsewhere. There is much circumstantial evidence: we know the general patterns of thought of the period; a clear picture can be gained of the ideology of Shibusawa and a few other business leaders. From this material we can form a hypothesis about prevailing motivations among entrepreneurs; the hypothesis can be made plausible, but it will be open to challenge. Although the attitudes of the entrepreneurs must be viewed in their complex entirety, we can perhaps best examine them under three headings, each throwing light on a particular facet of essentially the same phenomenon.

Optimism: Miscalculations and Time Horizons

Entrepreneurs are probably more often than not optimistic; otherwise they would not commit themselves to untried things. The early Japanese entrepreneurs were great optimists because of their unbounded faith in Western technology and because of their own ignorance of the practical difficulties involved. We can probably attribute much of their initiative to sanguine miscalculation. The steady encouragements offered by the government contributed to this state of mind.

We have seen that the rush to found national banks must be explained largely by the lack of other investment possibilities and by the strong government stress on the certainty of success. In cotton spinning, too, the same factors were operating. The enthusiasts of the first years did expect to reap high returns on their capital investments. Much of the railway boom, at least initially, was undoubtedly also the result of this kind of miscalculation.

Optimistic miscalculations also occur in advanced nations among seasoned entrepreneurs, but these entrepreneurs have the advantage of reliable standards of comparison, and are able and even forced to take a cool and rational look at the actual risks and uncertainties. In developed countries, where the innovations are carried out against a background of a known general technology and where experts are available, optimism will be kept in bounds by the facts. In Meiji Japan the harsh facts were often disclosed only after the investment decisions had been made. In Japan, however, there were frequent cases wherein optimism played a more active role. My impression is that the more important entrepreneurs were not so much victims of miscalculation as they were men who consciously viewed future returns according to a long time horizon and by applying unusually optimistic discounting factors. In order to understand this dynamic optimism, we must first examine briefly these methods of discounting.

The rational choice among various investment possibilities depends essentially on the discounting factor. Even if the Meiji entrepreneurs did not bother about the details of discounting procedures, they must have known the general rule that the present value of an income stream shrinks with a rise in the interest rate. High returns after a waiting period of five years look different if a 5 percent or a 10 percent rate prevails; the same investment may be desirable at 5 percent and may be completely irrational at 10 percent. This means simply that interest rates, which are but an expression of the relative scarcity of capital, dictate through the free play of the money market the types and gestation periods of investments. If capital is scarce, long-term investments with initially low returns will be "vetoed" by the high capital cost, no matter how important such investments may be in the long run and for the economy as a whole. The high discounting factor makes all future benefits shrink too much relative to the opportunity cost involved. The market mechanism directs funds through high interest rates toward present rather than future benefits, since the latter would require too much immediate sacrifice.

From all we have seen so far, the leading Meiji entrepreneurs did not discount rationally by the prevailing interest rates or by opportunity costs. They gave little weight to the sacrifices they imposed both on the public and on themselves. They had instead some absolute goal, some nondiscounted future value in mind. With their newly acquired faith in the modern era and all that went with it, they could not be shaken by intermediate losses; they knew that in the end they would succeed.

The conflict between the long view and the short became evident at the collapse of the Kyoto Pottery Company. This company was established in 1887 by the leading entrepreneur of Kyoto, Tanaka Gentarō, with 200,000

yen in capital from various sources. Tanaka's intention
was to combine Japanese traditional skill in pottery with
the latest production techniques of the West, and to
manufacture pottery on a large scale for export. A dele-
gation went abroad to study modern pottery, machines
worth 200,000 yen were imported, and the total of fixed
investments rose to 500,000 yen. But technical difficulties
and unexpectedly strong foreign competition caused losses.
The shareholders insisted on dividend payments, and when
they did not receive any for five years they demanded that
the enterprise be dissolved. A report on the collapse of
the company blamed the failure on the "stupid" and short-
sighted shareholders who wanted immediate results and
would not tighten their belts; with more time the pottery
factory could certainly have become a success.[61]

The leading entrepreneurs had firm faith in their final
success, and they were vindicated. While those who kept
investing in the traditional sectors gradually fell behind,
the returns of the new enterprises began to skyrocket. The
view of the top entrepreneurs was basically dynamic, not
static. They believed in the rise of a new order which they
themselves, by their innovations, would bring about. All
that was said previously about the *bummei kaika* ideology is relevant here. It did not make sense to the entrepreneurs to discount according to opportunity costs at a
time when things were changing so fast and when a flourishing business of today might be completely pushed to the
wall in a few years. It was important that, in a sense, present
values and present sacrifices be ignored. The abacus was of
no use in measuring future trends, which could only be
evaluated by men who did not nostalgically look back to
the past.

It was said of Asano, by his son, that he did not make
profit a necessary condition for the foundation of an en-

terprise. If the work was "in the interest of the public" and "economically reasonable," he would make a start no matter whether the profits earned would be 5 percent or 10 percent. In spite of this, however, he was sure of eventual success; in this respect he was a real *jitsugyōka* (entrepreneur) although he had started out to become a *shōnin* (merchant).[62]

The matter of the time horizon, of choosing the length of the investment and gestation periods, is of crucial importance in the process of economic development. Many a latecomer country of today faces this choice in determining its own perspective. Which types of investment should be given priority in view of the all-around scarcity of capital? The maximization of the present value of discounted future income may not be the best criterion for decisions. This approach does not take into account the dynamic chain reaction of large investments in key industries. The static application of the discounting principle may unduly permit scarce capital to be continuously siphoned into traditional lines of trade and manufacturing, or even into usurious moneylending, and thus forestall economic progress. Yet for the entrepreneur who intends to maximize nothing but his profit, the static approach appears as the optimum. Why should he bear the brunt of initial losses and low returns and set the economy into motion through his own sacrifice?

In today's underdeveloped countries the strategic pioneering investments are usually carried out by government planning agencies, which can impose the burden upon the whole population. Steel mills and irrigation dams will not only pay in the long run but, a very important point, they will change the structure of the economy; they will encourage a bold forward look by the people and kindle a sense of national purpose and achievement. This, ultimately, will far outweigh all the temporary hardships and losses that are unavoidable in the large new ventures of latecomer countries.

It was auspicious for Meiji Japan that, at a time when the government could not continue its initial building program, private entrepreneurs continued the task with almost the same bold perspective that is so characteristic of government planners. The long time horizon of the Meiji entrepreneurs is a fact, but it too calls for an explanation. One has been mentioned already: the entrepreneurs' faith in progress, their sense of being pioneers in a new era, and their optimism with respect to the new technology. However, I think that there were two more important, noneconomic, motives.

The Noncapitalist Mentality

Shibusawa wrote and spoke frequently about the ideal entrepreneur. He had to be, above all, a man with a keen sense of responsibility for the welfare of society. "While pursuing one's own advantage one should be also mindful of the opportunity for others. As one wishes to achieve one's own welfare and happiness, one has also the duty to exert oneself for the state and for society." [63] Shibusawa's business attitudes, while progressive in many ways, were hardly touched by the spirit of capitalism as it existed in the utilitarian and individualistic forms of the eighteenth-century philosophers and economists. Shibusawa's thinking was, of course, not identical with that of most of the other entrepreneurs. But, to a lesser degree, the whole status-conscious group of pioneering industrialists and foreign-trade merchants shared his outlook.

If we compare this keen sense of social responsibility with the spirit of capitalism in the West, we may say that the basic difference probably lies in divergent concepts of the relation between the individual and society. Capitalism in the West emerged through a gradual but fundamental shift in the value system. The individual, his worth and his welfare in worldly terms, moved into the central position so long reserved for the group, for society and the common good. This trend started as far back as Nominalism, which challenged the validity of universal concepts. The direction became clearer in the growth of the natural sciences, where men rejected all interference by the established religious authority with the individual's quest for objective truth. Humanism and the Renaissance were powerful movements forward toward this emancipation of the individual and of the establishment of a worldly value system. Protestantism sanctioned the supremacy of the individual by rejecting the mediation of a social authority — the Church — between God and the individual.

We need only translate this new concept of the individual into economic and purely secular terms, and we have "the economic man," who considers the achievement of material welfare as the ultimate rationale and reward for his work. "Man is dominated by the making of money, by acquisition as the ultimate purpose of life." [64] According to this capitalist creed, society and its welfare will be taken care of by automatic forces, by an invisible hand that will coordinate self-centered pursuits with the common good.

This evolution of the spirit of capitalism, as it appeared in much eighteenth-century thought, did not proceed in a smooth fashion. Rather, when the problem of man's relation to the world and to worldly activity was seen in a new light and given a new answer, that answer was at its best a religious one. The spirit of capitalism was for a time carried by a very strong religious movement which purposely set itself apart from the tradition of medieval

Christianity. Puritanism discovered its task in this world in terms of material pursuits and gave it a religious sanction. There is probably no contradiction between Max Weber's thesis that the spirit of capitalism owed its victory to the Puritans and the view that it had been prepared gradually by a shift toward the individual and toward secular values. Puritanism idealized what had previously been regarded as a lapse from spiritual concerns. Weber's term "worldly asceticism" pinpoints this mentality. What had been chided before as unworthy became now a calling by God: to do business, to accumulate, and to lose no time at it. This religiously conceived version of the spirit of capitalism, and not its selfish and materialistic basis, became the powerful urge that could drive men toward entrepreneurial endeavors in the face of great risk and sacrifice.

There seems to exist a parallel between this Western evolution and what happened to entrepreneurs in Meiji Japan. First there had been the well-established official contempt for business, maintained ostentatiously by the samurai and supported by Confucian ethics. Then came the breakdown of the Tokugawa political and economic system, and with it the disdain for material accumulation. But we do not find a smooth line of change toward a hedonistic and individualistic kind of capitalism. A new element appeared that resembled, in its function, the mentality of the Puritans. It was nothing religious, not a calling by God; it was rather a calling by the nation, by the emperor. The direction was that of service to the country in terms of business pursuits, and in the final analysis in terms of worldly success. But one's very success would be a sign of having fulfilled a noble duty. Iwasaki and Ōkura, in their quest for self-assertion, were singularly obsessed with the thought of fighting for an ideal and not just for private gains. Theirs was not a belief in the "invisible hand" that would take care of society — they were men for whom business was a sacred duty. There is a similarity between the Puritan drive to accumulate and that of the Meiji pioneers: the one was backed by a faith in God, the other by a faith in the Nation.[65] It is even possible to discover a certain parallel, however different the two men may be otherwise, between Benjamin Franklin, who preached thrift while quoting the Bible, and Shibusawa Eiichi, who preached business ethics while quoting the Analects of Confucius.

But a basic difference remains between the Puritan version of the capitalist and the type represented by Shibusawa and his school of thought. Western capitalism was ultimately individualistic; its religious sanction was individual perfection, a manifestation of one's own salvation, a problem of God and I. The Confucian version of Shibusawa stressed Society and I, the State and I, and thus demanded the subordination of the individual to the common good. This may account for a number of seeming contradictions in Japan's economic development. We encounter in Meiji Japan and later starvation wages, but not an anonymous employer-laborer relationship with hiring and firing according to the dictates of "economic rationality." We find that talented men were attracted to business, but only to those branches that were clearly recognized as in the service of the community; they had to be *jitsugyōka*, not *shōnin*. We find a ruthless drive for power and money, with a "survival of the fittest" as in Western capitalism, but then these same "fittest" assumed a role of service and worked for public objectives.

The community-centered thinking that was largely preserved by the union of Confucian traditions and Western influences can perhaps account in part for the extended

time horizons of many Meiji entrepreneurs. When these
men so obviously discounted present sacrifices in favor of
the future success of their enterprises, the enterprise assumed a function similar to that of the family, the community, or for that matter, the merchant store. The individual — entrepreneur as well as worker — was but a part
of and had to serve the higher unit, the enterprise, and
work for *its* success. This is quite similar to the attitude
displayed by the merchants with respect to their family
businesses. But the remarkable difference was this: the
merchants served their house traditions — with them the
time horizon was stretched to the past — while the modern
entrepreneurs applied the long view to the future. In any
case, the element of time lent a nonindividualistic character to economic pursuits.

It is open to question whether an unrestrained bourgeois
type of capitalism can work at all beneficially for economic
development in any latecomer country. The task does not
so much constitute a challenge for individuals as for society as a whole. It requires cooperation and sacrifices from
the community, and responsible leadership in both the
government and the private sector. In times of smooth and
continuous development, the pursuit of each individual's
welfare as the primary goal of activity may not reveal its
inherent dangers. But whenever crises and extraordinary
tasks appear, society cannot rely on an invisible hand, on
an "automatic harmony" between social and private benefits. A conscious coordination of the two, and even subordination of private advantage to society's needs, is then
called for. The swift and energetic modernization of the
Meiji economy owed a great deal to the continuance of
this kind of noncapitalist mentality among its best entrepreneurs; these men were characterized by a blend of Confucian ethics, patriotism, and faith in Western technology.

National Awakening

Nationalism unquestionably constitutes one of the most dynamic elements in the economic growth of many modern underdeveloped countries. Industrialization and a new sense of national purpose usually go together and thrive on patriotism as their common powerful motive. The determined leaders of a nation's elite, given the proper objectives, can mobilize immeasurable energies toward social and economic advance. A gradual process of development without these nationalist emotions may be less wasteful as far as capital resources are concerned; but it may evaporate without being able to overcome fast enough the great difficulties of the initial spurt. Nationalism is like a stallion; it may turn the cart upside down and create havoc, especially if the leaders are power-mad. But the same strong stallion, properly harnessed and controlled, may pull the cart of the economy all the way to the top of the hill, something a slow-moving plug horse may not accomplish. In the "new" countries, hostilities toward "oppressor countries" or toward their own former ruling classes are often only a means used to create passionate dedication to a national purpose which requires enormous sacrifices.

The Meiji was an era of national awakening. The cultural, social, and economic life that had been bottled up in the islands of Japan for over two centuries burst forth into a new spring of growth. Many events before and after the Meiji Restoration seem to the casual reader senseless and contradictory. But here was a people rushing forth with sudden energy, aware of both a new greatness and a new challenge. The greatness was epitomized in the restoration of imperial rule, accompanied by a sense of national unity and by the equality of all citizens who were to share the blessings of education and progress.

The challenge appeared first to be of a military nature. The daimyo built their cannons and the economic reformers revamped the han economies to provide capital for armaments. After the Meiji Restoration, the military aspect lost much of its importance, and the main task became economic. Attempts were made to keep up the appearance of a military challenge, in order to draw the attention of the dissatisfied samurai from their economic misery and to give their nationalism an easy outlet. The Taiwan expedition and the plan to subjugate Korea were instigated, it is said, primarily with this intention. But the militarists could not prevail; the men of the Iwakura Mission to Europe knew that the real challenge to Japan was one of economic development and industrialization. The unequal treaties left no doubt that unless full effort was made Japan, like China, could become an economic colony of the West.

It is from this vantage point and against this background that we must view the patriotic statements of the entrepreneurs. Iwasaki and Ōkura, two of the most successful zaibatsu builders, were certainly interested in personal power and money; but at the same time they were opponents of foreign competition, and they knew the importance of their work. I need not give concrete examples here: many have been mentioned already, and others will be supplied in the next two chapters when I discuss the entrepreneurs themselves. In any event, it would be wrong to deny the existence of patriotism as a most effective motive, even where other, almost contradictory, intentions appear along with it. Not all were idealists like Shibusawa, Morimura, and Kinbara, but all joined, more or less, in the acknowledged task of building a modern economy.

The feudal rulers had previously been looked upon as responsible for national affairs. The samurai were the defenders of the country. It almost seems as if the newly established *jitsugyōka* had inherited part of the former feudal responsibility for national economic affairs. The *jitsugyōka* were, it was often stated, to do business in the samurai spirit. The daimyo of Geishu is said to have proclaimed that "it is the duty of the nobility to serve the country by establishing enterprise." He ordered the building of a paper mill, the first in Japan, and used 100,000 yen of his own money for that purpose.[66] The public expected the top businessmen to display patriotic attitudes and to follow the lead of the government in modern investments. Public recognition, honor, and influence depended upon building factories and operating shipping lines to answer the threat of foreign competition. It was of secondary importance how much profit a man earned in the process of innovating; what mattered was that the chimneys begin to smoke and the machines begin to produce. The pressure of public opinion, the need to conform to an image of leadership that was largely of feudal origin, forced even those who may not have been genuine patriots to conform at least outwardly to that ideal.

There was a circular interaction between the public image of the "entrepreneur" and his duties toward Japanese economic progress, on the one hand, and the attitudes of the leading entrepreneurs, on the other. They had created their new status concept in the first place in order to gain esteem for private business. The most striking difference between the *shōnin* and the *jitsugyōka* was the latter's "mission" to build industries for the nation. If a small group suceeded in this rehabilitation effort, the larger group of important entrepreneurs had to conform to this esprit de corps. We frequently find the same men cooperating in a vast number of modern enterprises — it was all done in the single effort to build an industrial Japan.

This creation of an acceptable status image became a

very effective force in Japanese economic development. Nationalist sentiments were not channeled into battle cries and war hero worship, but into economic construction. There is a parallel case of the conscious steering of public acclaim and the creation of a status symbol for the sake of industrialization. The Saint-Simonian socialists knew that, in the tremendous effort of building their new economic order, they needed prestige and emotional support from the people. If these men called themselves "missionaries" and their institution a "bank to a higher power," they were doing essentially the same thing as the Japanese with their *jitsugyōka* status and their insistence on building factories for the sake of Japan. Gerschenkron remarks on the importance of new social values for economic development: "In a backward country the great and sudden industrialization effort calls for a New Deal in emotions. Those carrying out the great transformation as well as those on whom it imposes burdens must feel, in the words of Matthew Arnold, that 'Clearing a stage / Scattering the past about / Comes the new age.' " [67]

The challenge presented by external conditions and the dynamic leadership of the Meiji government resulted in a magnificent national revival. This was the "New Deal in emotions" that inspired the entrepreneurial elite, the men who created modern Japanese industry.

VI

THE ZAIBATSU BUILDERS

The zaibatsu, those giant combines that controlled large sectors of Japan's banking, trading, and industry until the end of the Second World War, had their origin in the early Meiji era. At a time when both capital and entrepreneurs were scarce, the emerging zaibatsu were able to seize a large share of both resources. Japan's modern industrial development, especially her drive into world markets, was spearheaded by these few combines. Their contribution to the successful breakthrough in modern industry, especially heavy industry, was of critical importance. But the fastest growth and concentration of economic power of the zaibatsu occurred after the turn of the century and up to the outbreak of the Second World War.

One of the major factors contributing to the rapid growth of the zaibatsu was their close cooperation with the government, whether in receiving subsidies or favors or in acting as government suppliers. The degree of favoritism varied, but it was never entirely absent. Another important factor was that the zaibatsu were characterized by a strategic combination of banking and industrial capital. The four largest zaibatsu — Mitsui, Mitsubishi, Sumi-

tomo, and Yasuda — were conspicuous for supplying the
capital needed for their industrial ventures from their own
banks. The zaibatsu banks had the fastest growth rates.
In 1936 the largest banks of Japan in order of magnitude
were: Sanwa, Sumitomo, Dai Ichi, Yasuda, Mitsui, and
Mitsubishi.[1] The trust companies ranked according to the
totals of funds were: Mitsui, Mitsubishi, Sumitomo, and
Yasuda.[2] Those who had, received more. Success in banking made possible successful investments in industry, and
the visible industrial achievements raised public confidence in the stability of the zaibatsu banks.

The fact to be noted is that these large financial resources were channeled into heavy industry and transportation. Shipping, railways, mining, chemicals, metallurgical
industries, and electricity were the preferred fields of
zaibatsu investment. Here they pioneered and came to
occupy monopoly positions because the general capital
market was still too weak for effective competition. Nonzaibatsu capital flowed largely into light and traditional
industries.

From the middle of the Meiji era on, the individual
zaibatsu were occupied partly in establishing their own
independent industrial or transportation empires — Mitsubishi in shipping, Sumitomo in copper, and Ōkura in
iron mining. More often they joined with other shareholders in particular projects in which they, however, held
the control. Sometimes two zaibatsu cooperated. In one
rather unusual case, the three-million-yen New Osaka Hotel,
we find four zaibatsu working together: Sumitomo, Ōkura,
Mitsui, and Mitsubishi.[3] Through a pyramiding of control, the zaibatsu empires expanded and absorbed ever
larger amounts of industrial and finance capital. At the
very beginning of their rapid growth period, around 1885,
we find that, with one exception, in all firms with over

half a million yen capital the zaibatsu were the leading
investors (here I am including the Fujita Company in the
zaibatsu group, to which it belonged at that time).[4]

Over and above the favorable external conditions that
promoted the zaibatsu, one must not forget the zaibatsu
builders. These combines by no means formed a homogeneous group. They differed widely with respect to their
origins; some had old merchant traditions, others started
from scratch. They differed also with respect to government connections and investment categories. But they did
resemble each other closely in the type of entrepreneurs
and managers they had. The following case studies of the
zaibatsu builders are intended to bring out this resemblance. The account of the zaibatsu growth process in
quantitative terms is kept to a minimum, serving only
as a background for the performance of the entrepreneurs.
This approach is intended to direct emphasis away from
an overly mechanistic stress on the obviously large subsidies and favors, to the remarkable achievements of personality.

The House of Mitsui and Minomura Rizaemon

The House of Mitsui was able to accumulate tremendous
wealth throughout the Tokugawa period. Its money exchanges and stores were among the most prosperous and
successful in the cities of Edo, Kyoto, and Osaka. Toward
the end of bakufu rule, Mitsui was close to collapse, as
were so many others of the financial magnates. A forced
loan of 350,000 ryo was imposed upon Mitsui when its fortunes were at an all-time low. This might well have spelled
ruin for that merchant house, but its head clerk, Minomura
Rizaemon, succeeded through personal connections with
a bakufu official in securing a remittance of 320,000 ryo of

the loan.[5] Mitsui then threw its lot in with the Restoration party before its victory, by making a substantial contribution and accepting the offer to act as the party's financial agent. With this political decision, Mitsui set out on
a road that led to many later favors and to a unique position as the official government banker. The advantages the
House of Mitsui was able to derive from its position were
staggering.

In 1874 alone Mitsui was holding no less than 3.8 million yen and 460,000 dollars of government money free of
interest, with no ruling imposed about reserves to be
held.[6] During the Satsuma Rebellion the Mitsui Trading
Company was commissioned to supply about two thirds of
the army provisions, and it increased its wealth within one
year from 100,000 yen to 500,000 yen.[7] Mitsui Hachirōemon, the senior member of the Mitsui Trust, occupied
no fewer than fifteen positions by government appoint-
ment in connection with enterprises that had been started
either through the initiative of the government or with
some special privileges granted by the government.

This tie-in with government finance and the large gains
that resulted from government contracts and later from
government sales can easily lead one to believe that the
ascendency of Japan's top zaibatsu resulted almost automatically from a combination of Tokugawa wealth and
Meiji government leadership. We must not forget, however, that Mitsui was not the only recipient of such privileges; Ono and Shimada shared them, yet they collapsed.
If, out of the whole group of rich Tokugawa merchant
families, only two, Mitsui and Sumitomo, became zaibatsu,
we have to look for some other explanation.

One of the conditions that underlay Mitsui's rise to
leadership in modern banking, trading, and industry was
its organizational structure. Although the Mitsui enter-

prises were nominally owned by several branches of the
Mitsui family, control was vested in the senior member
of the family group, who always received the name Hachirōemon.[8] But even he could not make decisions independently. The actual management of the enterprises was
put into the hands of a head clerk, who had near dictatorial power. A rule of the Mitsui family dating from the
seventeenth century stresses the strict subordination of
the family members to the decisions of the men in charge:
"Under a great general are no weak soldiers . . . you
must treat your own child like any other employee until
he comes of age." [9] The potentialities inherent in the
strong position of the Hachirōemon and of the head clerk
were not used in the later Tokugawa period, but they became crucial in the transition into the modern era. At the
time of greatest crisis, the "great general" for Mitsui was
found in the person of Minomura, who almost alone was
responsible for Mitsui's alignment with the new government and with the new era in general.

Minomura's first great achievement for Mitsui was the
aforementioned remittance of the forced loan. In appre-
ciation of his success he was given the post of head clerk,
and from then on he steered Mitsui's destinies. It is he who
is credited with the decision to side with the Restoration
government, in clear recognition of the trend of the times.
Minomura is said to have been the most active man outside of the government in the establishment of the exchange and trading companies, and later in the foundation of the first joint-stock banks. If in many records the
name of Mitsui Hachirōemon appears as the leader of
new ventures and as the president of various enterprises,
the man behind the scenes was Minomura. Recognizing
the need to be close to the center of administration and
of modern ideas, he urged that the headquarters of the

Mitsui family move to Tokyo from its centuries-old residence in Kyoto. He encountered stubborn resistance from both the Mitsui family and the Kyoto population, but eventually he succeeded, in 1873. Knowing that Mitsui could prosper only if it moved determinedly with the new trends, as early as 1872 Minomura sent five young members of the Mitsui family and two employees to the United States to study.[10] His close friendship with Inoue Kaoru became a great blessing to Mitsui; in fact, it saved Mitsui from the kind of catastrophe that befell Ono and Shimada.[11] This friendship with one of the most progressive planners of the Meiji government was based on a similarity of views and a congeniality of economic vision. If necessary, Minomura could cut resolutely through knotty managerial problems in complete disregard of traditions and sentimental attachments. He separated the old and famous Echigoya retail store in Tokyo from the rest of the Mitsui enterprises because it had been running at a loss. This separation became beneficial to the Echigoya, now the largest department-store chain in Japan, under the name of Mitsukoshi, and for Mitsui it was beneficial too.[12]

Minomura was a new man who came "from nowhere." He influenced and in the end ruled the greatest of all merchant houses, but he was not a typical merchant of the old tradition. Little is known about his early years except that he was born in poverty, probably in 1821, and that his father, a *rōnin,* died young. At the age of fourteen the orphaned Minomura came from Kyushu to Kyoto, then traveled widely throughout the country and settled in Edo at the age of nineteen to become a merchant's apprentice. His extraordinary abilities brought him into the Mitsui combine and eventually into the position of control. It can only be surmised that his extensive travels, his experience of poverty, and his unusual talents made him understand the signs of a new era sooner and more deeply than many others who had stayed at home in secure positions. As a man without allegiance to family and without prejudice of status, he fulfilled one of the conditions necessary to the new entrepreneurs: he could readily and thoroughly adapt to the new ideas and accept change. Despite Minomura's early death in 1877, his imprint on Mitsui was lasting. He took one of the oldest merchant houses and made it Japan's most powerful pioneering enterprise.

Masuda Takashi

Masuda Takashi (1848–1938), the founder of the Mitsui Trading Company (Mitsui Bussan), does not seem quite to have duplicated the strategic importance of Minomura, whom he succeeded as Mitsui's most important decision maker. On the whole, he continued the innovational policies of Minomura and furthered the modernization of Mitsui. Masuda's background differed greatly from Minomura's. Born the son of a samurai official with considerable means, he moved with his father at the age of twelve, in 1860, from the island of Sado to Edo. There he learned English at the American consulate and put his knowledge to good use after the Restoration by serving as interpreter to the foreign-trade merchants in Yokohama. During one year of employment in the Ministry of Finance, he became acquainted with Inoue Kaoru, who thought so highly of his abilities that in 1872 he made him vice-president of his own newly established Senshū Trading Company.[13] That company was dissolved after one year. Minomura then requested that the talented Masuda establish a foreign-trade company within the framework of the Mitsui combine. This man, who had gained an early acquaintance with foreign trade in Yokohama, had learned English, and had also been able to gain insight into the problems of the

import surplus during his employment in the Ministry
of Finance, was well prepared for his task. He was convinced that in competition with the foreign companies
only a large joint-stock venture could be successful.[14]

While the large gains of the Mitsui Trading Company
during the Satsuma Rebellion aided its rapid expansion,
Masuda's primary concern was the promotion of active
foreign trading. In order to bolster his position as an exporter in the Asian market, he decided to purchase the
Miike Coal Mine. He had a secret investigation made,
which convinced him that, despite the heavy losses the
government had incurred, he could make the mine profitable. Actually the mine became one of the greatest assets
of the entire Mitsui combine, but at the time Masuda had
to fight opposition to the purchase; the Mitsui Bank refused the necessary loan of a million yen, finally granting
it only after Masuda had thrown in all of his personal
assets. Masuda wrote that he had to make this decision
alone because the others could not understand his action.[15]
Like many of the leading entrepreneurs of that period he
was extremely eager to promote active foreign trade and
to invest in modern industry. We find him cooperating
frequently with Shibusawa, although it seems that he was
more of a supporter than an original planner. Masuda
claimed that in all his many ventures, inside and outside
of the Mitsui combine, he "did not want money but de-
sired to work for the progress of enterprise, and strained
all [his] energies to that end." [16]

NAKAMIGAWA HIKOJIRŌ

In spite of the efforts of Masuda, the House of Mitsui's
fortunes began to decline after Minomura's death. The
old merchant practices asserted themselves increasingly.
Around 1890 the total assets of Mitsui were at their lowest

point since the Restoration and caused serious anxiety.[17] The trouble spot was the Mitsui Bank, where the old clerks who had remained from the pre-Restoration period tried to gain favor with officials and large institutions by granting loans in spite of insufficient security. This was the pattern of daimyo lending of Tokugawa days, which had reaped social rewards. When the government called in its deposits from the Mitsui Bank, the bank came close to collapse; it was saved by the good offices of the old Mitsui friend, Inoue. He negotiated a loan to the Mitsui Bank from the Bank of Japan, but he also received permission from the Mitsui family to initiate a thorough reform of the bank and of the whole Mitsui combine.[18] Inoue's man was Nakamigawa Hikojirō (1854–1901), who entered Mitsui in 1890 as its chosen reformer. For the second time, the government official Inoue supplied Mitsui with an outstanding entrepreneur; in this respect, then, Mitsui "owed" its modernization to the government.

The choice of Nakamigawa may seem somewhat odd at first sight. Here was a man who went straight from a teacher's desk to prominence in Japan's industry — yet few were more successful than he. A samurai by birth and a nephew of Fukuzawa, he studied at the Keiō college. Then he spent three years in England and had a successful career as a teacher and newspaper editor. He wrote in the same vein as Fukuzawa, in favor of progress and economic rationality, and he made a point of scorning the prevalent samurai manner of citing lineage and past glories. He was made president of the Sanyō Railway Company but soon was at loggerheads with the shareholders, who acutely disliked his zeal for reform and innovation. But if the shareholders of Sanyō considered him too progressive, Inoue thought him the right man to modernize the Mitsui Bank.

Nakamigawa applied himself to the task with almost

ruthless courage. He dared to recall within one year a loan of one million yen from the powerful Higashi Honganji Temple in Kyoto, and the abbot was forced to initiate a nationwide collection to satisfy Nakamigawa, thus making him *persona non grata* among the Buddhist faithful of all Japan.[19] Although Nakamigawa had entered Mitsui through the influence of a government official, he wanted no part in any government favoritism that would interfere with business rationality. He went so far as to refuse a loan of 500 yen to a government official who could not offer sufficient security on the spot.[20] Nakamigawa's main achievement was the extension of Mitsui's industrial interests. He purchased the Tomioka filature and built two other silk-spinning mills because he foresaw a large increase in the demand for silk cloth. He secured control of the Ōji Paper Mill for Mitsui against the powerful Shibusawa-Ōkawa combination. He modernized the Shibaura Iron Works and insisted that they be kept open in spite of continued losses.[21] The man of cold economic rationality became here "irrational" in the same way that most of the other pioneering entrepreneurs did. Continued losses caused Mitsui to sever its ties with the Shibaura Iron Works after Nakamigawa's death.

In cotton spinning Nakamigawa achieved a major success, one that was crucial for the emergence of Japanese cotton spinning onto the world market. Mitsui had taken over the Kanegafuchi Spinning Mill from a group of Tokyo merchants who had invested a million yen but kept operating it at a loss. Under Mitsui management the same mill within four years lost 123,000 yen [22] and was nicknamed the "prodigal factory of Mitsui." In 1890 Nakamigawa took charge of the mill, poured another 700,000 yen into new investments, built an additional plant, and himself studied spinning from books, technicians, and workers. He then began production of fine yarns of over thirty counts, in spite of warnings from English specialists of the Platt Company and other advisers, all of whom predicted disaster. It became a do-or-die situation; yarns piled up unsold and cotton merchants called the Kanegafuchi yarns the "starved yarns." Nakamigawa later recalled that he was fully aware of the danger to the mill, but that he decided on this course for the sake of the future of Japanese cotton spinning. He succeeded in breaking down prejudices and solving technical difficulties, and he created a wedge with which Japan could effect an entry into the world market. Kanegafuchi became one of the most efficient mills in Japan.

Alongside his streamlining of the Mitsui administration and the building of a strong industrial branch went Nakamigawa's efforts to rejuvenate the company's staff of managers and clerks. He drew heavily on Fukuzawa's graduates for key positions within Mitsui and thus rid it of the remnants of Tokugawa merchant attitudes. At least seven men who later became well-known entrepreneuers were decisively influenced in their careers by Nakamigawa.[23] Thus Nakamigawa made it clear, through his own success and his employment of Fukuzawa-trained graduates, that his way to success in modern business, through books and study, was often shorter than the way from the accounting desk of the merchant stores. Nakamigawa also proved how little, in the long run, government favors could do for Mitsui, or for any other enterprise, if it was not vigorously led in the right direction by "a great general."

IWASAKI YATARŌ, THE BUILDER OF MITSUBISHI

The development of Mitsubishi from its small beginnings as a trading company in Tosa han to the powerful zaibatsu rival of Mitsui rested on two pillars: political connections and the genius of Iwasaki Yatarō (1834–1885). Iwasaki was daring in the extreme, but he was also shrewd in his use of men and especially in securing privileges. To this political merchant par excellence can be applied the criticism of a contemporay, who wrote: "These merchants with government connections pile up enormous profits because of their close ties with government officials. They know the laws before they are published, they receive the favorable deals in the sale of government enterprises." [24] But the same man wrote something else that is equally applicable to Iwasaki: "For business ventures Japan needs the spirit of the samurai who are ready to sacrifice their lives for the country. In competition with the foreigners only such a spirit can be successful; that is, a man must think not only of his private good but also of the benefit to the country." [25] In Iwasaki shrewdness and the spirit of the samurai were uniquely blended, and it is difficult to assess the relative strength of his two predominant motives, his drive for power and his patriotic idealism.

Iwasaki began his trading career within the framework of the Tosa han administration. There he learned very early the power of money. Although he belonged to the country samurai, who differed little from the peasants, he came into close contact with the great Tosa reformers and himself became an official. With his accumulated practical experience in trading, he did not find it difficult to exchange the samurai swords for the abacus. When after the Restoration Iwasaki acquired the official Tosa shipping company as his private property, he called it first the Ninety-Ninth Company and later changed the name to Mitsubishi. He assembled his samurai managers and told them to don the "apron of the merchants." They would fully acknowledge the power of money.[26] On the other hand, Iwasaki had been strongly influenced by Yoshida Shōin's patriotic ideas, and he remained essentially a fighter in the samurai fashion; his ambition was to make Japanese shipping competitive with the great foreign lines.

Iwasaki's close association with government officials, notably Ōkuma, made it easy for his enterprise to get huge subsidies and privileges such as no other zaibatsu got. He was considered the champion of Japan's competitive race with the foreign shipping companies. But Iwasaki was also ruthless in building a system of monopolies. In 1880 he started a documentary-bill company with over 3 million yen in capital. The customers of this company were obliged to ship their goods in Mitsubishi bottoms, to insure them with the Mitsubishi Maritime Insurance Company, and to store the freight in Mitsubishi godowns.[27]

Iwasaki's ruthless monopoly practices and his enormous profits created enemies in the government and also among leading businessmen. Shibusawa was one of them. He cooperated with others, notably with Mitsui's Masuda, to break the Mitsubishi monopoly in shipping; their endeavors culminated in the establishment of the Kyōdō Unyu Company in 1883. Ōkuma, Iwasaki's chief protector in the government, had been ousted in 1881, and Iwasaki's enemies among the officials succeeded in granting the Kyōdō Unyu Company a government subsidy — nominally a share subscription — of 2.6 million yen, thus raising the total of this powerful rival's capital to 6 million yen. In the fierce cut-throat competition, principles, personalities, and politics clashed. During the two years of war between the two giant companies, passenger fares between Kobe and Yokohama dropped from 3.50 yen to 0.25 yen.[28] Iwasaki conducted a rather unfair smear campaign against Shibusawa, charging him with working for foreign interests, while many labeled Iwasaki an enemy of the state.

This was in the last analysis a fight between two diametrically opposed principles: Shibusawa fought for an economic order ruled by cooperation, with joint-stock companies and fair competition. Iwasaki believed that the strong should rule and that monopoly was a good thing because private profits would eventually also benefit the nation: what was good for Mitsubishi was bound to be good for Japan. The war between the two companies ended in 1885. Iwasaki had secretly bought up the majority of the rival company's stock and had secured control in the new amalgamated Nihon Yūsen Company.

Although he concentrated on shipping and connected enterprises, Iwasaki and his associate managers branched out into other new ventures. In 1884 Iwasaki bought the Nagasaki shipyard from the government, which had not been able to make it a going concern. Iwasaki applied for the purchase by pointing out that Russia was just completing her large shipyard in Vladivostok while Nagasaki could barely handle minor repair work. He paid 539,000 yen for the yard; within a few years he had put into it another 6 million yen and had transformed this small repair yard into Japan's largest and most modern shipyard of the period.[29]

Iwasaki also bought the Takashima coal mine — actually not directly from the government — which had been operated at a continued loss, and transformed it into one of Mitsubishi's best assets.[30] He sent his close associate, Kondō Renpei, to Hokkaido to investigate new investment possibilities, especially in mining, and to exploit the untapped natural resources of that northern frontier area. In order to raise capital for this Hokkaido venture, he began his documentary-bill company. Shipping, mining, shipbuilding, and banking were the main branches of Iwasaki's activity, and within twenty years his entrepreneurial efforts had made Mitsubishi the second-ranking zaibatsu in Japan and a dangerous rival to Mitsui.

At the height of Mitsubishi's power, in 1936, the central Mitsubishi Company, which was totally owned by the Isawaki family, had a capital investment of 120 million yen and a net worth of 300–350 million yen. But controlled by, or at least connected with, the company was a huge industrial and financial empire of shipping, shipbuilding, mining, heavy industry, electricity, storehouses, and trading.[31]

Iwasaki was probably the boldest of all Meiji entrepreneurs. His efforts put him into the forefront of Japanese shipping and mining. He himself was not at all modest in assessing his own achievements and his contribution to Japan's economy. On his deathbed in 1885 he claimed before his friends that he was "The Man of the Far East," [32] and he regretted his untimely death because not even a third of his great plans were realized. His quest for power and greatness, combined with samurai patriotism, are reflected in his Mitsubishi family rule: "Do not take up small projects, engage only in large enterprises. Once you begin something, see to it that it becomes a success. Do not engage in speculation. Do business with a patriotic attitude." [33]

Although Iwasaki had gathered associates, all of them samurai — his company was called the "samurai company" — they did not gain prominence as independent business leaders until his death. It was his planning and his decisions that ruled the whole Mitsubishi concern. The first two paragraphs of its "constitution" spell out the dominant position of Iwasaki within the combine:

1. Although this enterprise assumes the name of a company and establishes company structure, in reality it is entirely a family enterprise and differs therefore greatly from a company

with joint capital. Therefore, all things that concern the company, praise and blame and all, are entirely up to the president.

2. All profits return to the person of the president and the losses, too, are borne by him alone.[34]

Almost all zaibatsu men shared this dictatorial attitude, although it was most openly expressed by Iwasaki and Yasuda Zenjirō. This trait contrasts strongly with Fukuzawa's democratic principles, although Fukuzawa was close to Iwasaki and supplied Mitsubishi with a number of its most talented men. Shōda Heigorō, one of his closest associates, had been a teacher at Keiō; so had Kondō Renpei, Toyokawa Ryōhei, and Asabuki Eiji. Iwasaki himself built a school to promote business education along Fukuzawa's lines, and his preference for Fukuzawa-trained clerks and managers was proverbial. But he himself retained the mentality of a strong-willed official, and his entrepreneurial talent, ambition, and competitive spirit made of him an unbending and stormy leader.

HIROSE SAIHEI, THE MODERNIZER OF SUMITOMO

Sumitomo, the third-ranking zaibatsu, had many features in common with Mitsui. They traced their lines back for a few centuries and were both wealthy merchant houses. Each owed its critical transition into modern enterprise to a great leader who, with a few farsighted and fundamental decisions and with political connections, turned the tide for his house. The strategic part played by Minomura in Mitsui was in many respects similar to that of Hirose Saihei (1828–1914) in Sumitomo; there were also important differences.

Sumitomo's wealth had been based on copper mining, especially since the beginning of the eighteenth century, when this house had succeeded in separating out copper from mixed ore.[35] Sumitomo became the official copper supplier for the bakufu. Its wealth increased, but for a hundred and fifty years no innovations were carried out and no business leadership was displayed. Sumitomo's once very profitable Besshi Copper Mine became a liability owing to flooding, and was kept operating only with the aid of government subsidies. When the subsidies were suspended because of the imminent outbreak of the Restoration war, the Sumitomo family considered selling the mine for 100,000 ryo. It was at this juncture that Hirose's influence and determination became crucial for Sumitomo.[36] His fight to keep the mine under Sumitomo became a promise to make it profitable again. The modernization of Besshi became Hirose's outstanding entrepreneurial achievement, and it meant for Sumitomo the start of a new era.

An adopted child of the manager of Besshi, Hirose Saihei had started working at the mine at the age of eleven. Having come up from the rank and file, he not only knew the problems better than anyone else but also loved the mine. Now as its manager he had to fight for its survival. When the government stopped its rice supplies for the 5,000 workers, he almost singlehandedly quelled their riots and succeeded in negotiating an extension of rice deliveries. He soon reorganized the food supplies for the mine, produced bean paste, soy sauce, and sake on the spot, built housing projects for the workers and schools for the children.[37] After he had succeeded in settling the disputed right of ownership of the Besshi Copper Mine between the government and Sumitomo in favor of the latter, he proceeded with its modernization, supported by Kawada Koichirō and Iwakura Tomomi. In order to avoid future difficulties that might arise from sudden investment needs or other contingencies, he began to accumulate a hundred-year stabilization fund. By 1926 this fund had reached 20 million yen.[38] With the help of foreign engineers, the output of Besshi was boosted from 420.7 tons of copper in 1868 to 601 tons in 1874 and 1,202 tons in 1885.[39]

Branching out from copper, Hirose extended the rising Sumitomo empire into allied fields and built up his own supply and sales branches. Large areas of woodland were purchased for lumber supply, and a machine-manufacturing and repair shop were affiliated with the mine. A foreign-trade department in Kobe handled Sumitomo exports, mainly copper but later coal, tea, raw silk, and other products. The Sumitomo banking branch grew during Hirose's expansion program and secured for him the supply of additional capital. Within twenty years of the Restoration, a solid basis for the Sumitomo empire had been laid by Hirose.

From then on, the development was rapid, notably because of the growth of the Sumitomo Bank and the Sumitomo Trust Company. By 1932 the Sumitomo zaibatsu comprised fourteen directly owned enterprises with a total capital stock of 380 million yen. In addition there were some seventy enterprises worth 2.5 billion yen in which Sumitomo had some 1.6–1.7 billion yen invested, receiving dividends of about 100 million yen a year.[40] In the fields of banking and heavy industry, the three zaibatsu — Mitsui, Mitsubishi, and Sumitomo — were about equal by the 1930s.

The first and most obvious reason for Hirose's achievement lies undoubtedly in an early acquaintance with his field of endeavor. He was like Asano, who loved his work "more than money and more than his life." Hirose tried to remain in copper mining; even when his leadership of

Sumitomo made him extend his sphere of interest to foreign trade and banking, he remained the "copper man." Outside of Sumitomo, he held important positions in the Osaka Copper Refining Company and the Sulphuric Acid Company, both closely connected with copper mining.[41]

Hirose's restless drive to innovate was fired by his keen interest in reading and learning, and his intimate acquaintance with Western technology. Through his close association with a French engineer employed in his mine, he himself became an expert in mining technology. Hirose was a man who fully believed in progress; it is said that he hated the prevailing stagnant and conservative atmosphere in Osaka business circles. According to him, complacency and nostalgic attachment to the past were the worst enemies of progress.[42] On this point he agreed completely with all representative innovators of the Meiji era. Hirose was a leading member of the Osaka Chamber of Commerce, where he cooperated with the entrepreneurial elite to rebuild Osaka as a city of flourishing industry and commerce.

At the time of the Besshi Copper Mine's great crisis Hirose had turned the good offices of government officials to advantage, but afterward he moved rapidly toward independence from government patronage and official ties. In this respect Hirose differed basically from Mitsui's Minomura, who had moved the Mitsui headquarters to Tokyo and had tied its destiny to the Meiji government. Sumitomo's main operating base has remained Osaka to the present day; it was modernized, but it did not move to the center of progress. Perhaps this is one reason why Sumitomo retained throughout its modern development a tendency toward conservatism, more so than did Mitsui or Mitsubishi.

YASUDA ZENJIRŌ, THE BANKER

The Yasuda zaibatsu ranked fourth among the empires of finance and industry, and its development from small beginnings was no less spectacular than that of Mitsubishi. Yasuda Zenjirō (1838–1921), who had left home at the age of twenty and gone to Edo to make a living, succeeded so well that when summing up his blessings in 1908, at the age of seventy, he controlled in his empire of finance: eleven banks, with 21.2 million yen in capital; three insurance companies, with 13.3 million; one construction company, with 5.0 million; three railway companies, with 10.63 million; and one electric company, with 1.0 million.[43]

Yasuda was appointed a member of the board of trustees of the Bank of Japan in 1882 and held the post for two years; at one time he was financial agent of the Ministry of Agriculture and Trade. But these official positions were not at all typical for Yasuda. In striking contrast to Iwasaki, Yasuda remained almost entirely independent of government support.[44] His success was due to genius, favorable circumstances, and his insatiable drive to win profits.

Born the son of a poor samurai, Yasuda Zenjirō began his trading career by selling flowers in his native village. He had learned early that money was more powerful than samurai swords, so he went to Edo where, in those days, a daring and clever man could become rich in a short time. Yasuda displayed a remarkable instinct for turning a penny and multiplied his initial five ryo through lending, trading, and exchange manipulations.[45] A few years after the Restoration, he was already a wealthy banker. But even at the height of his success, he remained miserly; on his inspection rounds of factories and on his Tokyo business trips, he would take the early cheap-rate streetcar and carry his lunch.[46]

But this man, who had set out to become rich by ruthlessly exploiting any opportunity, began later to display a remarkable degree of responsibility with respect to the use of his wealth, and thus came to rank among the great Meiji entrepreneurs. He became a tireless advocate of large and modern investments. Although we have good reason to doubt whether he was always motivated by a consideration of the public benefit in his investment decisions, his own large-scale ventures, and especially his financial backing of industrial undertakings, contributed in no small measure to the economic development of Meiji Japan. When a sulphur-mining company to which he had extended large loans continued to operate in the red and could not pay him back, he made a careful study of the technical possibilities and then took over the mine. He invested heavily by installing new machinery, putting up new buildings, and constructing a railway line to the mine site; the mine became a financial success.[47]

With regard to industry and large-scale innovations, Yasuda could at times forget his caution and appear reckless in his drive to have innovations carried out. Yasuda cooperated in many schemes of industrial pioneering with Asano Sōichirō, who was another almost reckless innovator. People used to say that lending to Asano or Amamiya was equivalent to "throwing one's money into a ditch." But Yasuda said that, if it were not for men like Asano, great enterprises would not be undertaken in Japan. He considered Asano as his "general manager" working with his money.[48] Asano, who had founded the Tōyō Shipping Company, once placed an order for three large ships with the Mitsubishi Shipyard in Nagasaki at a total cost of 15 million yen, although he had almost no money in reserve. Even Shibusawa refused to extend a loan to Asano, but Yasuda lent him 7.5 million yen in spite of the great risks that this newly established shipping company faced in its competition with foreign lines and with Mitsubishi.[49]

Toward the end of his life, Yasuda's innovating plans became almost fantastic in scope. He proposed to the Ministry of Railways that he electrify the entire Tōkaidō Railroad extending from Tokyo to Osaka, at an estimated investment of 100 million yen, but his plan was refused. Yasuda became very bitter at this rejection of his great "service to the country." [50] He had mapped out a plan to modernize the entire city of Tokyo and supply through his banks the estimated capital of some 800 million yen.[51] Over this, his last plan, he was assassinated by a fanatic because he would not contribute to the building of a "workers' hotel." [52]

The banker and entrepreneur Yasuda appears to have combined two attitudes not always found together in one man. He was, on the one hand, a pitiless "profit maximizer," especially in the early part of his career, and at times he displayed miserly traits. On the other hand, he had a genuine interest in general economic progress and in the things that would benefit the nation as a whole. Among the conditions essential to the establishment of an enterprise, he demanded, first of all, that "the purpose of the enterprise be good, that is for the public benefit, contributing to the welfare of the people and the progress of society." [53] Probably it is not wrong to attribute his zeal for innovations for the sake of Japan's advancement to his close association with the group of leading entrepreneurs. If this is true, we have here a good example of how a group spirit and status consciousness can influence the actions of men who otherwise might take a very different approach. It is also true, of course, that in such large-scale projects as the modernization of the city of Tokyo, Yasuda would have reaped his fair share of the profits, together with public acclaim for his services.

Yasuda, like Iwasaki, was a dictator within his own banking empire. It was difficult for him to find congenial men to whom he could delegate powers of decision. In this respect the zaibatsu builders were almost all alike. While Iwasaki saw to it that a few of his aides were groomed for independent entrepreneurial positions, the Yasuda concern was considerably handicaped after the death of its founder by the lack of capable managers.[54]

ŌKURA KIHACHIRŌ, THE TRADER AND INDUSTRIALIST

Ōkura Kihachirō (1837–1928) came of a rich landowner-merchant family of the Niigata district.[55] Disgusted and disillusioned by the social conditions in his village, especially by the overbearing behavior of the samurai, he left for Edo and there, at the age of eighteen and with twenty ryo as his starting capital, began his career as a businessman.[56] He was just as cold-blooded a profit seeker as Yasuda, and almost as successful. His business was trading in rifles, and he had no scruples about delivering arms to the Restoration army while living in Edo under the bakufu. Called to account by the bakufu, he replied that to a merchant money was the only thing that mattered, and he did not care whom he supported.[57] In 1872 he made a trip abroad, the first merchant to do so. Ōkura must have been greatly impressed by what he saw, for he returned to Japan a different man. He had apparently come to realize that money also meant responsibility toward his country in its quest for economic progress. Ōkura Kihachirō became an entrepreneur with a tremendous zest for new ventures that would profit both himself and Japan.

To him, as to Iwasaki, responsibility toward the nation did not preclude a ruthless drive to personal power and shrewd manipulation of government connections. Ōkura remained throughout his career a political merchant who thrived on government contracts, notably in connection with wars. In all military operations, from the Taiwan expedition to the Russo-Japanese War, he managed a lucrative army-supply business. His personal courage secured him a major contract in the Taiwan expedition. Other merchants refused the contract because they were afraid to sail with the expedition, but he accepted. The important fact about the profits gained from the army commissions is that Ōkura invested them in foreign trade, and later even more in large-scale industrial ventures.

In 1873 he founded the Ōkura Company with 150,000 yen in capital, gained chiefly from his arms trading. By the following year he had already established a branch of Ōkura in London, and he moved vigorously into foreign markets, to Korea and Southeast Asia, in an effort to expand Japan's trading position and his own power. But somehow Ōkura was not satisfied with trade alone. He was by character a pioneer and he was attracted to industry, particularly to untried fields. He disliked being an imitator and doing things that others could do equally well. When someone suggested that he invest in cotton spinning, he replied that there were already plenty of businessmen who were operating mills; he insisted that his mission was to start enterprises that others did not or could not undertake.[58]

Ōkura expanded into a wide industrial field, very much as the other zaibatsu did. The four central companies of the Ōkura concern, which were holding companies for a string of others, were: Ōkura Construction, Ōkura Trading, Ōkura Mining, and Ōkura Maritime Insurance. But Ōkura was different from the other top zaibatsu in that it did not build up its own banking branch. Ōkura is said to have declined to play both the lender and the borrower, the rich and the poor.[59] Because he lacked his own bank as a capital-supply line, he fell behind the first four zaibatsu; he lost control over a number of companies that he had initiated because expansion required new share capital, and his holdings were thereby reduced to a minority. This was the case in the Dai Nippon Beer Company and two electricity companies, among others.[60]

Ōkura experienced great difficulties in his pioneering efforts, particularly in his monopoly iron mining in China, which he started after the Sino-Japanese War. Army demand again eventually bailed him out, but he was not a man to become frightened by mounting difficulties. Prince Yamagata suggested to Ōkura at a time of crisis in his iron and steel enterprise that he apply for government subsidies, but he flatly rejected this possibility. He said that he had started out with the expectation of making profits eventually, and that he could take losses for some time. Ōkura was acclaimed by the public for his independence of the government in this instance, especially in view of his earlier ties and commissions.[61]

Ōkura extended his interests and investments over a wide range that included electricity, lumber, charcoal, pulp, chemicals, and land-reclamation schemes. Repeatedly he received the initial stimulus toward a new venture from abroad and then knew no rest until the project was carried out in Japan. Ōkura claimed that he disliked ties with the government and that his main desire was to further the cause of Japanese trade and industry.[62] We may not accept the first part of that claim at face value, but his contribution to Japanese economic growth was certainly outstanding.

FURUKAWA ICHIBEI,
THE BUILDER OF A MINING EMPIRE

Quite in the same fashion as Minomura and Yasuda, Furukawa Ichibei (1832–1919) rose from lowly origins to a position of dominance in the Meiji economy. His father was a poor soybean–cheese peddler in Kyoto. The boy had received a strong impression of social inequalities, which added to his ambitions to make good. At eighteen he left home and was variously employed; he then traveled frequently between Fukushima and Tokyo as an exporter of raw silk within the framework of the House of Ono. He built the first mechanical silk filature in Japan, one year before the government set up its Tomioka Mill in 1872.[63] Entrusted with the management of several mines in the Akita area while still the chief of the silk-export branch of Ono, he was ruined by the bankruptcy of Ono in 1874. At the age of forty-three he had to make a new start.

With the help of a loan from Shibusawa, he purchased the Ashio Copper Mine, which became the basis of his new success. There he innovated on a large scale. He dismissed the old clerks and employed a score of young Keiō graduates in 1884. He contracted with an English firm to deliver 673,120 kilograms of copper per year while he was still mining only 432,720 kilograms.[64] Under this self-imposed pressure he bought new machines, built a railroad to the mine, an electric power station, and, on the whole, made the Ashio mine one of the most modern and most efficient copper mines in Japan. He bought new copper and silver mines. By 1887 Furukawa was mining 39.8 percent of Japan's total copper output, and in 1897, only twenty-two years after he had started in copper mining, he owned or controlled ten copper mines, eight silver mines, one gold mine, and several other enterprises connected with mining.[65] At one time, when he was running a 50,000-yen loss but still kept expanding, people warned him to retrench; even Shibusawa suggested that he consolidated the mines before taking on new ones. But Furukawa insisted that he had to expand, that his only task and joy was copper mining, and that the profits were nothing but a bonus to him.[66]

In terms of general type, Furukawa seems to represent a blend between the merchant and the progressive entrepreneur. He had been associated for a long time with the House of Ono and continued to live in the merchant section of the city. Until a few years before his death, he retained the traditional merchant administration: he did not establish an office but discussed and worked out everything sitting together with his men, "smoking his tobacco," as in the old days.[67] On the other hand, he received many advanced ideas through close association with his friend Shibusawa. And yet, whereas Shibusawa was the tireless champion for the joint-stock form of enterprise, Furukawa was strongly opposed to the company form, because he hated to "bow to majority decisions." [68] Only one of all his ventures, railroad, was a genuine joint-stock enterprise. The aversion to majority decisions which characterized most zaibatsu builders was probably to a large extent based on the fear that the majority would only handicap the innovational programs, which had to be carried out very rapidly and boldly. Furukawa and Ōkura declined to follow the practice of successful businessmen in writing a "family constitution," a set of business rules to be followed by their successors. Both men insisted that men with imagination and initiative would need no rules, for these might do more harm than good by hamstringing new ventures and the enterprising spirit.[69]

ASANO SŌICHIRŌ, THE COURAGEOUS INNOVATOR

The beginnings of Asano's entrepreneurial career are very similar to Yasuda's.[70] Perhaps this was one of the reasons why these two zaibatsu builders, working their way up from poverty to great economic power, frequently cooperated and planned together. But they differed in their fields of action: Yasuda was a banker and remained, on the whole, true to this line; Asano Sōichirō (1849–1930) was an industrial innovator, a restless jack of all trades. He displayed his versatility from early youth. As the son of a rural physician, he received a classical samurai education; he ran away from home at the age of fourteen. At fifteen he was already the "employer" of a few girls in a rural manufacturing enterprise. Repeatedly he failed, but he always started something else. In 1871, at the age of twenty-four, he came to Tokyo almost penniless. He began his career there by selling ice water in the streets, switched to firewood trading, and used many other opportunities to make money. He even built toilets and collected night soil to sell it to peasants as fertilizer.

One day Asano discovered that unused coke was piling up at the gas works in Yokohama. He bought the whole pile and sold it to the Fukagawa Cement Works, where he had been told by an engineer that coke could be used for the furnaces. Asano's interest in cement production here received its first stimulus, and this marked the turning point in his life. He began to study cement production; when he later came to take over the Fukagawa Cement

Works he knew almost as much about the production techniques as an engineer working at the factory.[71] He is said to have been interested in cement above all because he considered it important "for the progress of civilization."

The Fukagawa Cement Works, established by the government in 1871, had stopped operations in 1879 because of technical difficulties. Asano rented the factory first and then purchased it for 125,000 yen in 1883. In these works the government had lost 86,801 yen in deficit operations from 1871 to 1879.[72] It felt that the losses would stop under private management and, according to Shibusawa, the government at any rate wanted to sell out the official enterprises in order to stimulate private initiative. Asano was able to make the purchase with the help of Shibusawa, who gave him a loan and induced his nephew Ōkawa, a trained engineer, to join the company.[73] From 1884 to 1889 the output of the Asano Cement Works increased fivefold. Asano installed new machinery, sent fourteen of his staff engineers and employees to Germany for further research and experience in cement manufacturing, introduced strict supervision, and streamlined the management.[74] The government subsidized Asano indirectly by placing large orders for cement. Owing to Asano's entrepreneurial talent and these government contracts, the Asano Cement Works, in contrast to other cement mills, operated very profitably, although precise figures are not available.

After the achievement of this decisive breakthrough, Asano knew no limits: he ventured into shipping, shipbuilding, and coal mining, built iron works, invested in electric power generation, and various other fields. As I have mentioned, his ambitious plans were largely supported by Yasuda. When Asano proposed to Yasuda reclamation of part of the sea between Tokyo and Yokohama,

Yasuda inspected the area and came to the conclusion that the plan was important "for the national economy" and that it should not be postponed. In that scheme Asano invested 1.5 million yen, Yasuda 0.8 million yen, Shibusawa 0.4 million yen, and a group of Tokyo nobles another 0.8 million yen.[75]

The remarkable enterpreneurial career of Asano reads like an American success story, "from newspaper boy to millionaire." The chief factor in this was Asano's entrepreneurial genius; the role of the government was of minor importance. Although there was no initial capital, Asano built a zaibatsu of his own. Initial large capital and favors received by the government were not common to all zaibatsu builders. What was common to all was their approach to the task: daring, talent, endurance, and a long time horizon. Asano was also, like Yasuda or any of the others, decisively a man of the new era, cut off by choice from adherence to established traditions, and a man who believed firmly in the modern way of doing things.

With Asano we may conveniently leave our examination of the zaibatsu builders. A few sketches more could be added, since there exists no commonly accepted line of demarkation between zaibatsu and nonzaibatsu, but this would not change the general picture that has emerged. There is a certain pattern that holds for all of the successful entrepreneurs of the period, despite incidental differences in their beginnings and in external circumstances.

Conclusions on the Zaibatsu Builders

It should have become clear by now that the zaibatsu of modern Japan did not result from bourgeois wealth in combination with government guidance and subsidies. The process was by no means as straight and simple as this.

The two zaibatsu that were built up on the basis of Tokugawa merchant capital made a sharp break with tradition,
and it was because of this break that they survived and
flourished. Where leadership in this direction was miss-
ing, as in the cases of the Ono and Shimada houses — both
of which shared many favors with Mitsui immediately
after the Restoration — initial capital accumulation and
government favors profited little in the long run.

The role of the government as a supporter of modern
ventures was very important indeed. But it was the indirect subsidies that were of first consequence: the government trading contracts, the depositing of official funds
without interest, the low-interest long-term loans, monopolies, tax incentives, and the like. These took the place of
the tariff protection which is usually necessary to shield
young industries in latecomer countries. But while tariff
protection across the board helps all firms in an industry,
whether they are efficient or not, the Meiji government
could pick its favorites on the basis of ability, which means
on the basis of success. Those which received more and
grew into giants were run by seasoned entrepreneurs who
worked with a passion for money, for personal power, and
for the country. Indirect subsidies of this kind, avoiding
the inefficiencies of both tariff protection and government
operation, promoted a concentration of capital that had
far-reaching effects on the entire course of Japanese economic development.

The sale of the government's own model factories to the
zaibatsu is sometimes said to have had an exaggerated
effect upon the rise of these empires of finance and industry. But in the general framework of the zaibatsu these
sales were of minor importance and did not constitute
nearly so big a help as the other indirect subsidies. Those
government sales that did eventually become top profit-

bearing assets did so only after further large-scale investments and innovations had been made by the zaibatsu men themselves. The Nagasaki Shipyard and the Fukagawa Cement Works were deficit propositions at the time of their sale and owed their success to Iwasaki's and Asano's talent and relentless energy.

The subordinate role of government sales to the zaibatsu can be seen from the following table, which indicates the purchasers and the years of the sales. Of the seven zaibatsu discussed above, only Mitsui, Mitsubishi, Furukawa, and Asano appear among the purchasers, not Sumitomo, Ōkura, and Yasuda. Besides the Nagasaki Shipyard, Mitsubishi bought two mines directly and one indirectly (at second hand) from the government. Only the Takashima Coal Mine, purchased at second hand from Iwasaki's old friend Gotō Shōjirō for twice the price he had paid to the government, became of great importance to Mitsubishi; and Gotō sold it because he kept losing money on it. Mitsui's purchase of the Miike Coal Mine was of strategic importance, but again it was a secondhand purchase masterminded by Masuda Takashi against strong opposition within the Mitsui ranks. The other two Mitsui purchases, Tomioka and Shinmachi, were not too important in terms of the Mitsui operation. Actually Mitsui's strategic turn to industry came under Nakamigawa quite independently of government sales. Furukawa bought the Innai and Ani mines from the government, but his main achievement and real source of profits was the Ashio mine.

On the whole, then, the government created the enabling conditions for these entrepreneurs by generally encouraging modern enterprise and by opening possibilities to accumulate or find capital, directly or indirectly. But the choice of project, the investment decisions, the energy and skill to carry them through to success, must be credited to

SALES OF GOVERNMENT ENTERPRISES
(*zaibatsu italicized*)

Enterprise	Year built or acquired	Sold by government to	Finally acquired by
Mines			
Sado (gold)	1869	1896, *Mitsubishi*	
Ikuno (silver)	1868	1896, *Mitsubishi*	
Kosaka (silver)	1869	1886, Fujita	
Innai (silver)	1875	1884, *Furukawa*	
Ani (copper)	1875	1885, *Furukawa*	
Miike (coal)	1873	1888, Sakaki	1890, *Mitsui*
Takashima (coal)	1873	1874, Gotō	1881, *Mitsubishi*
Horonai (coal)	1879	1889, Hokkaidō Tankō	
Kamaishi (iron)	1874	1883, Tanaka Chōbei	
Shipyards			
Yokosuka	1868	1872, Naval Ministry	
Nagasaki	1868	1884, lent to *Mitsubishi*	1887, *Mitsubishi*
Hyōgo	1871	1886, Kawasaki Shōzō	
Akabane Construction	1871	1883, Naval Armament Office	
Fukagawa Cement	1874	1883, lent to *Asano*	1884, *Asano*
Fukagawa Brick	1878	1884, *Asano*	
Shinagawa Glass	1876	1885, Nishimura Katsuzō	
Tomioka Silk Filature	1872	1893, *Mitsui*	
Shinmachi Spinning	1877	1887, *Mitsui*	
Senju Woolen Mill	1876	1888, army management	
Mechanical Thread	1873	1874, lent to Ueda Spinning Mill	
Aichi Spinning Mill	1878	1886, Shinoda Naokata	
Hiroshima Spinning Mill	1878	1882, Hiroshima prefecture	
Printing Office	1872	remained government-operated	

Source: Takahashi Kamekichi and Aoyama Jirō, *Nihon zaibatsu ron* (A treatise on the Japanese zaibatsu; Tokyo, 1938), pp. 54–55.

the zaibatsu builders. This sounds like common sense, yet it is often forgotten and the whole outcome viewed as a result of impersonal forces. The very differences in the start of these men, Mitsui and Sumitomo with considerable wealth, Yasuda, Ōkura, and Asano starting with nothing, Iwasaki building up an inherited han enterprise, indicate further that initial capital was not a necessary condition for becoming a zaibatsu builder or even a successful entrepreneur in Meiji Japan.

All the great Meiji entrepreneurs shared basic attitudes toward the new era: they believed in it; they worked for its implementation; they themselves were new men who had experienced at one point or another a final break with traditions, either leaving home and starting a new life, making a deliberate political decision to side with the new forces, or absorbing strong Western influences through travel and association with foreigners. The change from rugged moneymaking for the love of profit and power to more responsible entrepreneurial planning coincided with a newly perceived realization of their role in the national economy. After the uprooting of Asano, Yasuda, Ōkura, and to a lesser degree of the others — that is, after the rupture with "the past" — came the vision of a new order and a new ideal. This was strong enough to moderate, if not change, the initial profit maximizers into industrial pioneers with a sense of mission for the country and its economy. Their mutual association and cooperation, their esprit de corps, and the public and official acclaim that they won contributed in no small measure to make these zaibatsu builders great benefactors of modern Japan.

VII

FIFTY LEADING
ENTREPRENEURS

The detailed presentation of the zaibatsu builders enabled us to assess, among other things, the relative role
of government subsidies and of private initiative and personality in the entrepreneurial process. But it would be
misleading to take the few giants of industry and banking
as a basis for sweeping generalizations on all aspects of
Meiji entrepreneurship. How did the less successful but
still important innovators approach their task? This chapter contains an examination of fifty leading businessmen
— all entrepreneurs in the broad sense; from this sampling
we may be able to draw valid conclusions about Meiji
entrepreneurs in general.

I have selected fifty men whose innovating activities
achieved some prominence before the Sino-Japanese War
of 1894–95, since these years are usually taken to mark
the end of the pioneering industrial period. All of these
men were active in banking, trading, or industrial enterprise along modern lines, although quite a few had started
in other pursuits. My sole standard of selection was the
degree of success of each entrepreneur, and in the table
that appears here their names are arranged roughly in

order of the relative success and importance of each man. This approach is less than ideal; it is quite conceivable that some entrepreneur who failed was a most daring and progressive man, and that his failure was fortuitous or due to the fact that he was too far ahead of his time. Cases of this kind would enrich our insight into the difficulties that the pioneers of Meiji industry had to face. But, rightly or wrongly, the published biographies make little of those who failed, and we have to take what data we can get.

The number fifty has no magic significance; it was chosen because it is large enough to permit some generalization but not too large to allow a meaningful glimpse into the life of each man. The process of selection was laborious. The top twenty or thirty were easily found; they could almost be enumerated offhand, since they are the well-known figures whose achievements stand out and have found their way into Japanese economic-history books. There was no scarcity of biographical material on these men. The task of sifting out the others was more exacting. Some collections of short biographies of Meiji businessmen were helpful in indicating all those who could qualify. The *Dai Nihon jimmei jisho* (Biographical dictionary of greater Japan) presented the bare facts in brief and reliable summaries. Imposition of my two conditions — modern enterprise and 1895 as the upper time limit for at least initial success — caused the number gradually to dwindle to about fifty. In spite of careful weighing there is, of course, nothing absolute about the selection; a few could always be exchanged with other men without in any way changing the results that emerge from this analysis.

At no point in the preparation of this book have I felt my limitations so severely as in this chapter. The vast amount of material to be handled created unusual difficulties for both analysis and presentation. In the published biographies and sketches of these men, each emerges as an individual, as an arresting personality stubbornly resisting any attempt to fit him into a statistical array or to present him by figures. The same basic characteristics appear in most, but with differing colors and slants. The problem was to determine how many of these differences could be omitted without distorting reality and oversimplifying complex phenomena. Attitudes, motivations, and approaches to enterprise are something so personal that they can become all but meaningless when expressed in true but overly broad generalizations. It is necessary to preserve at least a part of each man's uniqueness. This chapter thus became something of a hybrid between a statistical analysis and biographical notes. But perhaps the shortcomings of one approach will be partly offset by the other, and in the end the reader may acquire a fairly comprehensive idea of what the entrepreneurs of the early Meiji era were really like.

The arrangement of the accompanying table needs no comment at this point; it will become clear as I proceed with the explanation of each column. The content of the table, and correspondingly of this chapter, falls into two parts. The first part gives background information for each of the fifty men; the second part presents data on their entrepreneurial activities.

FORMATIVE INFLUENCES

The Older and the Younger Group

The year of birth is given in column 2 simply to show the relative ages of the men. But by the same token this column enables us to time the major political and social events occurring during the early life of each entrepre-

SURVEY OF FIFTY LEADING ENTREPRENEURS IN THE EARLY MEIJI ERA

Name (listed in order of success) (1)	Birth		Formative influences (before age 20)		Entrepreneurial type (6)	Main fields of activity (7)
	Year (2)	Class (3)	Practical training (4)	City (5)		
Shibusawa Eiichi	1840	P	M, P	Tokyo	R	Banking, general industrial pioneering
Iwasaki Yatarō	1834	S	Official, M	Nagasaki, Tok.	R	Shipping, shipbuilding, mining, banking
Ōkura Kihachirō	1835	P	M	Tokyo	R	Trade, mining, heavy industries
Yasuda Zenjirō	1838	S	M	Tokyo	(R)	Banking, promotion of industry
Hirose Saihei	1828	S	Mining	Osaka	Cl	Mining, allied fields (Sumitomo)
Asano Sōichirō	1848	S	M	Tokyo	R	Cement, general industrial pioneering
Furukawa Ichibei	1832	M	M	Tokyo, Yok.	Cl	Mining
Godai Tomoatsu	1834	S	Official	Nagasaki, Tok.	Cl	Mining, indigo, general industrial pioneering
Kawasaki Shōzō	1837	M	M	Nagasaki	Cl	Shipbuilding, heavy industry
Tanaka Gentarō	1853	P	M	–	R	Banking, pottery, electricity ("Shibusawa of Kyoto")
Matsumoto Jūtarō	1844	P	M	Osaka	R	Banking, railways, promotion of industry in Osaka
Minomura Rizaemon	1821	S	M	Tokyo	(R)	Banking, modernization of Mitsui
Nakamigawa Hikojirō	1854	S	Student, teacher	Tokyo	R	Banking, Mitsui industries, spinning
Ōkawa Heizaburō	1860	P	M	Tokyo	Cl	Paper manufacturing, advising in other enterprises
Hara Rokurō	1844	P	Army, student	–	(R)	Banking, general promotion of industry
Kondō Renpei	1848	S	Student	Tokyo	(R)	Shipping, mining (Mitsubishi)
Masuda Takashi	1847	S	M	Tokyo, Yok.	(R)	Trade, mining, general industrial pioneering
Fujita Denzaburō	1842	M	M	–	R	Shipping, railways, general industrial pioneering
Kawasaki Hachiuemon	1837	M	M, official	–	Cl	Banking
Yamabe Takeo	1851	S	Student	Tokyo	Cl	Cotton spinning
Katakura Kentarō	1849	P	Student, P	Tokyo	Cl	Silk spinning
Kinbara Meizen	1832	P	P	–	R	Land improvements, banking, social-welfare schemes
Sakuma Sadaichi	1846	S	Army	Tokyo	Cl	Printing, libraries
Okuda Masaka	1847	S	M	–	R	Spinning, banking, railways ("Shibusawa of Nagoya")
Morimura Ichizaemon	1839	M	M	Tokyo	Cl	Trade
Ōtani Kahei	1844	P	M	Yokohama	(R)	Trade, banking

Name	Birth	Class	Training/Occupation	Location	Type	Industry
Toyokawa Ryōhei	1851	S	Student	Osaka, Tok.	Cl	Banking (Mitsubishi)
Shōda Heigorō	1847	S	Student, teacher	Tokyo	(R)	Shipping, shipbuilding, other (in Mitsubishi)
Suzuki Tōzaburō	1855	M (?)	M	—	Cl	Sugar refining
Kawada Koichirō	1836	S	Official, M	—	(R)	Shipping, banking (Mitsubishi)
Takashima Kazaemon	1832	M	M	Tokyo	R	Railways, gas, land reclamation
Amamiya Keijirō	1846	P	M	Yokohama	R	Trade, mining, railways
Nakano Buei	1838	S	Official	—	R	Railways, general industrial pioneering
Hirano Tomiji	1846	S	Shipbuilding	Tokyo	Cl	Shipbuilding
Tanaka Chōbei	1858	M	M	Tokyo	R	Mining, iron casting, gas
Hirose Sukesaburō	1844	M	M	—	R	Banking, railways, newspaper, education
Motoki Shōzō	1824	S	Interpreter	Nagasaki	Cl	Type printing
Tanaka Heihachi	1834	?	M	Osaka	(R)	Trade, banking
Magoshi Kyōhei	1844	S	M	Osaka	(R)	Beer brewing, cooperation with industrial pioneers
Nishimura Katsuzō	1836	S	Teacher, M	Nagasaki, Tok.	(R)	Leather, bricks
Kashima Manpei	1832	M	M	Tokyo	Cl	Cotton spinning
Abe Taizō	1849	S	Student	Tokyo	Cl	Insurance
Doi Michio	1837	S	Student	—	R	Textiles, banking, railways
Tanaka Ichibei	1838	M	M	Osaka	R	Trade, banking, railways, shipping
Hiranuma Senzō	1896	?	M	Tokyo	(R)	Trade, banking
Nakano Goichi	1842	S	Official	Tokyo	(R)	Sulphur production, participation in Osaka industries
Yonekura Ippei	1831	P	P	—	Cl	Internal tea and rice trade
Wakao Ippei	1820	M	P	Tokyo	(R)	Internal trade, railways, electricity
Imamura Seinosuke	1849	P	M	Yokohama	(R)	Railways, banking, participation in industrial projects
Asabuki Eiji	1849	P	Student	Osaka	(R)	Trade, cotton spinning, general promotion (Mitsui)

Totals

S: 23	M: 30	Tokyo: 27	R: 18		
P: 13	Other: 9	Osaka: 6	(R): 16		
M: 12	None: 11	Yokohama: 5	Cl: 16		
Unknown: 2	—	Nagasaki: 5	—		
—	50	None: 13	50		
50		—			
		56 (doubling counting)			

Notations. Class and training: S, samurai (including physicians); M, merchant; P, peasant. Entrepreneurial type: R, romantic; (R), semiromantic; Cl, classic. These types are defined in text.

[249]

neur. It is believed that most basic attitudes and concepts are fixed during the "formative years" of adolescence and early years of manhood. Not only his parents and the kind of education but also the political events that stir up public emotions may exert a lasting impact on a man's view of life and society. Because of the selected time limits we do not, of course, get much differentiation with respect to age groupings. Roughly, the men all lived through the same turbulent years of the pre-Restoration period, with its uprisings, the controversy over the opening of the ports, and the rallying resistance against the bakufu. They were all influenced by patriotic attitudes; if we try to find differences in this respect, we have to content ourselves with something other than black and white contrasts.

If we call the men born before 1840 the "older group" and those born in 1840 or later the "younger group," we meet a few rather surprising facts. Among the twenty-one entrepreneurs of the older group, we find all the founders of the zaibatsu except one, Asano. By "founders of the zaibatsu" I do not mean precisely the same men mentioned in the previous chapter; here I shall leave out Masuda and Nakamigawa, who entered Mitsui only after it had already taken its turn toward modern enterprise. Included are two who were not treated in Chapter Six: Kawasaki Hachiuemon and Kawasaki Shōzō, who founded zaibatsu of their own, although of somewhat smaller size than those discussed before. Another characteristic of the older men is their tendency to "go it alone," to maintain private ownership, in contrast to the company form so frequently and strongly urged by Shibusawa. A third feature of the older men is their semiofficial approach, characterized by ties with the government and the receipt of privileges and commissions from the government.

These three characteristics can probably be explained

by the way in which these men entered their entrepreneurial careers. They belonged predominantly to two
classes, officials and adventurer-merchants. The officials
like Godai, Hara, Motoki, Kawada, and, of course, Iwasaki were naturally inclined to continue the familiar approach, to maintain close political ties to the government
and to promote enterprise in the spirit of the *fukoku
kyōhei* (wealthy nation, strong army) in which they had
grown up in the han administrations. Even in the private
wing of the economy, these men remained half officials.

Doi Michio,[1] who abandoned his samurai status prior
to the Restoration and moved to Osaka to engage in trade,
occupied an official post under Godai which started him
off on his business career. Doi retained the official approach
all through his life. He became a promoter of modern
establishments, cooperated with others, and staged exhibitions to stimulate industrial advance. Examples of this
kind are numerous.

Those who made their start as adventurer-merchants
usually began in a very rough way, not caring about the
government or about anything except money. Men of this
type were Ōkura, Yasuda, Tanaka Heihachi, Takashima,
Morimura, Hiranuma, Nishimura, and Wakao. But in their
dealings these same men began to realize the weakness of
Japan's trading position. They then came under the influence of nationalism, which was particularly strong in
Tokyo, and so eventually combined their private moneymaking with public service by carrying out government
commissions. Increasingly they turned toward projects that
were in the public interest. Almost anyone who had participated in the fears, hopes, and enthusiasms of the Restoration became a patriot in those days, whatever social
group he belonged to.

Kashima Manpei[2] was a cotton merchant of Tokyo who

established the first private cotton-spinning mill because
he thought that this was the only way to drive down the
price of calicoes. In the face of a host of difficulties and
much resistance, he carried his plan through. He later had
machines constructed according to his own designs; they
cost him far more than imported ones would have, but
he insisted on making Japanese cotton spinning independent of imported machines. Kashima was not only a
successful spinner whose mill never had losses, but he was
also a bold and politically minded man. He advocated the
opening of the ports and carried on business dealings with
foreigners at a time when such actions could very well inspire assassination by fanatics.

Whether merchants or samurai, these men became involved in the political matrix and behaved like officials,
and they felt that their own work was almost as important
as that of the government leaders. Iwasaki's dictum, "I
am the Man of the Far East," and Takashima's remark,
"Even if Prince Itō should die, as long as Takashima lives
there is no need to worry about the affairs of the country," [3]
characterize the strong and prideful political make-up of
the men of the older group.

The former adventurer-merchants had amassed their
starting capital through boldness and shrewdness in foreign
trade or from government commissions. Therefore they
needed no joining of capital and remained lone-wolf entrepreneurs who built their own empires of trade and industry. The officials, too, could dispense with the cooperation
of shareholders, and to them especially the idea of bowing
to majority decisions must have been hard to accept. This
probably explains why the older men favored private ownership and why some of them built such large empires for
themselves.

The younger group, in contrast, tended more toward the

joint-stock form of enterprise, with less reliance on government help. This tendency cannot be pinned down with figures because the same man sometimes had one or two enterprises under his personal control and ownership, while he cooperated as a shareholder in a string of others. The same holds true with regard to government favors. Government subsidies and favoritism tapered off gradually. Nakamigawa best indicates this emerging trend, with his clear-cut economic rationality and exclusive reliance on other people's money — he could accumulate no capital in his position as a teacher. To what extent a genuine turn toward democratic ideas, majority rule, and cooperation were involved is difficult to say. The government became less generous in meting out favors, and the younger men had had little occasion to build up their own capital; so they were forced to depend on the capital of shareholders and on the cooperation of men like Shibusawa, Yasuda, Hara, and Masuda. The Chamber of Commerce and the leadership of Shibusawa welded the men together more firmly as an entrepreneurial group; cooperation in joining capital for large well-planned ventures thus became easier.

Class Origins

Of the fifty men in the table, twenty-three were of samurai origin, thirteen were peasants' sons, twelve were born as merchants; the class origins of the remaining two could not be ascertained. Some qualifications must be introduced here. A few of these attributions could be disputed and changed: for example, one might call Ōkura the son of a peasant or of a merchant, since his father was both, and the same could be said of two or three others; two or three country samurai could also be called peasants, since they differed in almost nothing but name from rich peasants who were commoners. Finally, the physicians, who were usually commoners, are here included in the samurai group because of the samurai-like education, occupation, and social privileges, which made them too unlike merchants and peasants to be grouped among them. Excluding country samurai and physicians, then, we would have seventeen or eighteen clear-cut samurai.

Even so, my sample seems to indicate that the samurai were best represented and that the merchants supplied relatively few leading entrepreneurs; perhaps this is what one would have expected from the start. But we must be careful not to draw the wrong conclusions from this. It by no means proves that the samurai as a class supplied more entrepreneurs than either the rich peasants or the merchants, relative to their total number. In fact, the sample points if anything in the opposite direction and indicates that, considering the total numbers of the three groups, the samurai were more poorly represented than the other two groups. Poor peasants and artisans, who hardly had a chance to become entrepreneurs, made up about 85 percent of Japan's population in the early Meiji era. Of the remaining 15 percent, about 7 percent of the population were samurai (according to the broad definition), some 5 percent merchants, and 3 percent rich peasants. Again, I emphasize that these percentages are approximations because the definitions and demarcations, especially between the merchants and rich peasants, and between ordinary peasants and rich peasants, cannot be clearly established. If we pay no attention to the relative size of the three groups, we can easily come to the conclusion that the samurai as a class were the innovators, and then build on this a theory like the one sketched at the beginning of Chapter Two. In order to make the case stronger in one direction or another, one has only to impose certain conditions on the sample. For instance, if we exclude the trading sector, we get a still stronger preponderance of samurai as against merchants, who in turn were better represented in the trading sector and in cotton spinning. All sectors were included in the sample, provided that the enterprises established by the entrepreneur were modern and that he joined in the efforts at pioneering so common to the modern business elite of the early Meiji years.

Some students of Meiji business maintain that industrial leadership and innovations were a near monopoly of the samurai class; they cite examples of the innovators within the Mitsui and Mitsubishi zaibatsu and a few others where samurai concentration was most pronounced. Then again we find assertions that merchants predominated as business leaders throughout the Meiji; these statements are based on a survey of those who held prominent positions in the largest businesses, including domestic trading and manufacturing of the traditional type. In the second approach the crucial distinction between innovating (entrepreneurship in the sense used here) and routine business is completely dropped. If such a point conveys anything at all it is that, by the middle of the Meiji, merchants and their capital were still dominant in the traditional sectors of business. This in turn strengthens my conclusions that merchants as a class were the least progressive group of all.

It was mentioned in Chapter Three that the entrepreneurs of peasant origin did not as a rule stay in their villages; they went to the city — usually Tokyo — early in their lives. Only two of the peasants here became entrepreneurs in their villages, Katakura and Kinbara. Katakura used his large landholdings as the financial basis for a silk filature, and Kinbara devoted his energies to land improvements and rural welfare projects. The others, such as Ōkura, Hara, Amamiya, Asabuki, and Shibusawa, left home, resolutely breaking the fetters of village traditions and limitations.

The merchants' sons in the sample similarly broke with family rules and guild restrictions and usually left their fathers' businesses to gain freedom of action. Whether peasants or merchants, they were restless young men, dissatisfied with society and with conditions at home. Of the merchants' sons, Hirose Sukesaburō and Suzuki had traveled and tried various new things before achieving entrepreneurial success; Fujita had been a political adventurer more interested in fighting battles than in his father's lucrative business and sake brewery.[4] Morimura was a poor man but he was disgruntled with the merchants' ways, and in his later career he never tired of scoring the low business morale and ethics of merchants in general.[5] Tanaka Ichibei had rejected the idea of continuing his inherited business as a wholesaler in Osaka and decided to become an entrepreneur of the modern type.[6] Most of the men with merchant backgrounds, then, were anything but the typical *shōnin* described in Chapter One.

My conclusion is that class origin was not of decisive importance in molding entrepreneurs. All three groups of samurai, peasant, and merchant descendants in the sample had cut the ties to their previous economic life — the samurai by force of events, the others usually by free choice. Economically, the men had to start all over again, at least insofar as their approaches and places of activity were concerned, although some entered existing enterprises which they either reorganized themselves or which had been modernized by a predecessor.

The surprisingly equal representation of the classes according to numerical strength — the rich peasants as a class being no exception — confirms the conclusion that the

socioeconomic forces peculiar to one class were of secondary importance in influencing entrepreneurial careers. The
voluntary cutting of ties to the past, which resulted in economic uprootedness, the migration to the centers of foreign influence, indicate that the political and ideological
forces at work in Tokugawa society before the Restoration
constituted the single most important factor in the making
of entrepreneurs. These forces were not confined to any
one class; any man who was able to follow the course of
events intelligently could be affected. Thus the economic
uprootedness and the new start in a new place are only indicators of the dynamics of political and social pressures.
The men were not uprooted ideologically, but belonged
to the first wave of a general trend. The entrepreneurs
were genuine children of the same national ferment that
brought forth the Meiji Restoration itself.

Book Learning and Practical Training

The subject of book learning as against practical experience was touched upon when I dealt with the introduction of new technologies at the plant level. It was
indicated there that the modern entrepreneurs displayed
a tendency toward a theoretical, bookish approach, in the
tradition of those who had built cannons and even blast
furnaces according to descriptions found in foreign books.
The samurai companies often foundered because of inexperience in business matters. It is interesting to see the
degrees of both book learning and practical experience that
prevailed among our fifty men. Column 4 of the table
indicates how many had received some business experience
before starting their independent entrepreneurial activities. At least thirty out of the fifty had worked in a merchant store, been peddlers, or done business of some sort
before the age of twenty.[7] If we count the officials and those

who had been employed in mining and shipbuilding before starting as entrepreneurs, we get thirty-nine out of
fifty with practical training. These men must have been
able to avoid the blunders of the usual samurai business
methods.

It would be valuable to have similar figures on the formal educational backgrounds of the men, but unfortunately the available biographical material is not precise
enough to permit this. How many years of study are required to make a man "educated" in our sense? And even
if the years of study were known, we would not know
how many interruptions and side jobs had helped to fill
that time. From my endeavor to gain information on this
subject, however, the general notion was confirmed that
the large majority of the fifty men, say 70 percent, did receive an above-average education, one comparable with
that of the samurai.[8] Chief among these, of course, are the
ten listed as students and teachers, of whom seven were
Fukuzawa men. The sample therefore confirms the previously established evidence that book learning was of great
importance and almost a necessary condition to becoming
an entrepreneur in the early Meiji years.

The ten student-entrepreneurs throw light upon another
interesting trend that emerged in these years. Of the ten,
only one, Abe, built up his own enterprise; the others
rose to power and achieved their pioneering success within
the framework of existing enterprises, mainly the Mitsui,
Mitsubishi, and Shibusawa combines. The reason is rather
obvious, of course; they were "drafted" from the classroom
into their jobs and rose to top positions because of their
knowledge, attitudes, and talents, as well as their friendly
connections with Fukuzawa, Iwasaki, Shibusawa, and
Inoue. These men started a tradition of close connections
with certain colleges and enterprises whereby graduates

of these colleges had the best chance of entering the big
concerns and rising to high positions in them. Thus the
well-known preferential treatment and support existing
between the *gakubatsu* (school clique) and the *zaibatsu*
(used here in the rather broad sense of leading enterprises)
really started in these years when the Keiō and shortly
afterwards the Waseda universities supplied the *zaibatsu*
with talented and progressive managers.

Places of Early Influence:
Tokyo, Yokohama, Nagasaki, Osaka

Places of origin, like class origins, seem to have had no
significance as a source of entrepreneurs. In the sample
the largest single contingent, seven in all, were born in Edo.
Considering that of the city's population about half were
samurai and half merchants, the number indicates nothing
significant. Actually the fifty men represent all parts of
Japan with only a slight preponderance from the southwestern han, notably Tosa, where Iwasaki and his associates originated. Dismissing place of birth as of no consequence in determining entrepreneurial careers, let us see
whether the places of early influence had any significance.

A glance at the table shows the following: twenty-seven
out of fifty had moved to Tokyo — or at least had spent
some time there — before the age of twenty; six had some
Osaka experience; five were in Nagasaki and five in Yokohama; thirteen had no experience in these cities before
reaching the age of twenty.

Nagasaki decisively stimulated five of the men to turn
to modern enterprise. All were born before 1838 and therefore belong to the older group. During their adolescence
Nagasaki was the only place where firsthand experience of
Western technology was available. The contact with foreigners and the shocking realization of Western economic

and military superiority became for all five the decisive
factor that set them on the path toward entrepreneurship.

Kawasaki Shōzō [9] conceived his great interest in shipbuilding there; when he saw the disparity between the
large foreign steamers and the small Japanese boats, he
decided then and there to spend his energies to improve
the Japanese situation and to work in shipbuilding instead
of trade. He eventually became a great shipbuilder and
the founder of the Kawasaki zaibatsu. Motoki Shōzō learned
Dutch and eventually became so inspired by books and
the art of printing that he made his own type and printed
a Dutch-Japanese dictionary. This was the start of his
career as a pioneer in printing.[10] For Iwasaki as well as for
Godai the sojourn in Nagasaki contributed much to the
formation of their progressive ideas. The case of Nishimura
is not quite so clear: he had studied chemistry in Nagasaki
and started brick manufacturing; then he ventured into
other things, and only later did he turn again to brick
manufacturing, but not as his main field of enterprise.[11]

Osaka as the background for six of our men has an altogether different meaning. To begin with, it is surprising
that the major city of commerce and capital is not better
represented. We saw how little Hirose Saihei, the mod-
ernizer of the Sumitomo zaibatsu, owed to Osaka's influence. Asabuki had taught English in Osaka; Toyokawa had
been there working for Iwasaki; but both Asabuki and
Toyokawa became entrepreneurs in Tokyo, after absorbing Fukuzawa's ideas in the Keiō college.

Magoshi Kyōhei left his native village for Osaka and
joined Kōnoike as a merchant apprentice. Dissatisfied with
this position, he became an innkeeper and then met
Masuda who had come from Tokyo. Masuda recognized
Magoshi's talents and spent a few evenings telling him
about the "new spirit of enterprise" that prevailed in

Tokyo. After reading the *Saikoku risshi hen* (Success story of Western countries), Magoshi decided to leave Osaka in 1872 and go to Tokyo to "breathe the new air." There he had his hair cut short, ate beef — "so far nothing unclean had ever entered his mouth" — and thus became a man of the new era.[12]

Matsumoto Jūtarō had come to Osaka at thirteen as a merchant apprentice, but he and Tanaka Ichibei became part of a team of Osaka modernizers who were acutely conscious of their alienation from the established traditions of that city. It would be wrong to deny that Osaka, too, received direct foreign influence, especially within the first few years after the opening of the port in 1868; but compared with Nagasaki, Yokohama, and especially Tokyo, Osaka remained in the backwaters of the new era and did not exercise a particularly strong stimulus upon entrepreneurship.

Tokyo and Yokohama were of course by far the most important cities for their effects on entrepreneurs. The two cities are close together and shared several important aspects in those years. There was first the golden opportunity for adventurers, the "free-for-all" after the opening of the ports and around the time of the Restoration. The cases of Ōkura, Yasuda, and Asano were often repeated. Youngsters who were dissatisfied with their social position or work at home left for Yokohama or Edo. Two further cases may be taken as illustrations.

Wakao Ippei, a peddler in raw silk and tobacco, came to Edo to "become a samurai"; when he failed he went home but later returned to try to become a scholar; again he could make no headway. Off and on he tried various types of trading, moving into the import-export business in Yokohama, dealing in raw silk, sugar, and cotton. Like Yasuda, he made a killing in paper-money exchange and secured handsome profits from government contracts during the Satsuma Rebellion. Then he moved up to respectable entrepreneurial tasks, built a silk-spinning mill for which he had the machines constructed according to his own designs, and finally became a member of the entrepreneurial elite in Tokyo, cooperating in a large variety of modern enterprises.[13]

Imamura Seinosuke, a poor peasant's son, left his home to start a new life in Yokohama before he was sixteen. He returned home, but three years later came back to Yokohama to make another start. He tried money exchanging and other businesses, but got nowhere; he moved to Tokyo and made some profit on the stock exchange. In 1884 he went to the United States and Europe, and the trip made a different man of this adventurer-merchant. He opened a small banking business in his house, but then went into railway building, founding, or at least cooperating in, twelve railway companies, occupied an important position in the Chamber of Commerce, and joined in many large-scale modern ventures.[14]

The rampant opportunities were but one advantage of coming to these cities; almost inevitably these men came into contact there with the new era and often also with foreigners. It was in Tokyo that Morimura Ichizaemon conceived the idea of becoming a "merchant of the *bummei kaika*," and he sent his younger brother to Fukuzawa who was to make of him a "soldier in the field of foreign trade." [15]

Sakuma Sadaichi, who had traveled far and wide within Japan, was struck in Tokyo by the new spirit of progress and distinguished himself by working to establish popular rural libraries, in order to spread civilization among the people. He was a quixotic man — first a samurai to the bone, who would choose a sword over a rifle, then doing an about-face to distinguish himself in enterprise. He kept Mill's *Principles of Political Economy* by his bed and read it every evening. When he was once asked what his faith was, he answered, "My faith is Mill." [16] But Sakuma was a typical patriot and samurai for whom Mill probably meant no more than belief in modern enterprise, not a liberal and laissez-faire ideology; therefore he did not differ from Shibusawa whose "bible" was the Analects of Confucius.

The very closeness of the government seat gave Tokyo, and to a lesser extent Yokohama, a unique advantage. At a time when newspapers were still a rarity and unknown outside the cities, the inspiring leadership of the dynamic Meiji leaders could not have the same stimulating impact in other cities. The programs and slogans originated in Tokyo and were discussed on the streets by everyone. The political and progressive climate of this city gave a strongly political cast to the Tokyo group of entrepreneurs; here the men could also gain easiest access to funds both from the government and through cooperation among themselves.

Summing up all the formative influences to which the fifty entrepreneurs were exposed, we notice a clear pattern. Neither class origin nor initial capital resources was of decisive importance; what mattered most was the new ideology, the new system of values, that each man had to absorb. If the entrepreneurs were to be innovators and pioneers, they had to be men of the new era, men who believed in the future of the Meiji Restoration. Capital was supplied from various sources, as has been shown in the case of the zaibatsu men. Certain key factors stand out which facilitated the necessary change in ideology or values: original dissatisfaction with conditions at home, which led these men to leave and become economically uprooted; learning, which became a vehicle for the new

ideas and an aid in grasping the complexities of the enterprise system; finally, a "center" from which the new ideas
radiated and attracted the dissatisfied and the dissenters.
The closeness between entrepreneurs and government officials stemmed from their sharing of a common task and a
common viewpoint. This made these entrepreneurs sometimes act like officials, and in spite of their "faith in Mill"
they were hardly touched by laissez faire and the spirit
of capitalism.

The Entrepreneurial Performance:
Biographical Notes

What did the fifty entrepreneurs do, in which lines did
they innovate? How did they approach their problems,
and what were the main difficulties they encountered?
There are many questions of this kind that we should like
to have answered. But generalizations are even more difficult here than in relation to the formative elements. It
seems best to let the variations as well as the similarities
among our men come out in brief notes on each of those
who have not yet been given particular attention. In order
to give to the whole a semblance of logic and to make possible short summaries of certain features, a grouping is used
as indicated by columns 6 and 7 of the table. Although
both columns pertain to all of the men, the biographical
note on each will appear only once, either under his "entrepreneurial type" or under his "main field of activity."

Romantic Type and Classical Type

A distinction according to range of innovating activity
is indicated by the terms *romantic type* and *classical type*.
The romantic type [17] is characterized by founding one company after another in rapid succession, moving from one

field of enterprise to another, leaving the details and continuation to others. The classical type is the opposite, the man who remains throughout his life within the field in which he is an expert. He may build subsidiary enterprises, even a whole industrial empire, but all of them will be essentially in the original line of his entrepreneurial success. In reality we find many mixed cases which will not fit entirely into either of these categories; in my table these are designated the *semiromantic type,* to show that they lean more toward the romantic type.

The classical entrepreneurs were not numerous during the early Meiji era. In the table only sixteen are thus labeled, and even they crossed the line on occasion. Those who remained in one field were the foreign-trade merchants Yonekura and Morimura, and the bankers Kawasaki Hachiuemon, Abe, and Toyokawa of Mitsubishi. In industry the classical entrepreneurs were the strongheaded pioneers who were fascinated by their one great task and carried it through. They acquired so much technical knowledge in the course of time that they broke the path for many followers. In cotton spinning there was the Tokyo merchant Kashima and the college graduate Yamabe, and in silk spinning Katakura. Furukawa and Hirose Saihei in mining, Ōkawa in paper manufacturing, and Kawasaki Shōzō in shipbuilding also came close to the one-line entrepreneurs.

Sakuma Sadaichi and Motoki Shōzō,[18] both mentioned earlier, were pioneers in printing. They both realized that civilization was inevitably connected with education, and education with printing. Each was absolutely dedicated to his task. Motoki was forty-five years old when he first succeeded in type printing, after innumerable trials. He resigned an official position and began a printing enterprise in Nagasaki with 4,000 yen; he moved to Tokyo in 1873

and later established branch offices in Osaka and Yokohama. Nor could Sakuma's determination be broken by
difficulties and losses. He once replied to a friend who
cautioned him to stop investing and save for his children:
"I was born naked and I intend therefore to die naked;
if I should die somebody else will take care of the education and upbringing of my children. But I have to continue
to work as long as my life lasts and to serve the interest of
others." [19]

Hirano Tomiji [20] lived for shipbuilding. In Nagasaki
he had become interested in this work; later he bought
the Ishikawajima Shipyard, which the government had
abandoned and partly dimantled, and began to construct
sailing ships and even steamers. In spite of his enthusiasm, he was in constant trouble, and it was Shibusawa who
kept him afloat. The total of Hirano's debt to Shibusawa
amounted to 100,000 yen. Hirano was supposed to pay
8 percent and to add "in the case of profits" half of the
profits. In about ten years of continued lending Shibusawa
only once received the interest payment. Yet he kept extending loans although, he reflected, as a commercial
banker he was really not supposed to do so. Both Hirano
and Shibusawa believed firmly in eventual success, and,
equally important for them, they felt the necessity to build
Japanese ships. The determination to stem the reliance on
imports was characteristic of Hirano. When there was a
debate about whether pipes for Tokyo's water mains should
be imported or produced in Japan, Hirano was lying ill
in bed; he got up and gave speeches against importation
of the pipes, and during one of these speeches he died.

Suzuki Tōzaburō [21] achieved his fame in sugar refining.
An uneducated sugar and candy retailer, he started to manufacture sugar. His struggle was a very long one; he first
succeeded in producing crystal sugar after some seven or

eight years of trials, but could find almost no buyers. He then decided to produce refined sugar because of his concern that all refined sugar was imported. Although some people encouraged him, he had to wait two years, until 1886, for financial cooperation. In 1890 he produced his first refined sugar; in 1895 he founded a refining company. He had worked alone; none of the great promoters and business leaders gave him any support until he achieved success. Only later, when he was already famous, did he cooperate with men like Inoue and Masuda. Suzuki and Hirano were very similar in approach; their natural strong interest in one kind of enterprise was enforced by the desire to compete with imports and to make Japan independent.

The romantic entrepreneurs were influenced in their approach to business by a strong sense of urgency: much had to be done, and few were ready to do it. The founders went from one task to another; often we find them involved in a string of uncoordinated ventures. They were not much concerned with details. Shibusawa once discussed his engagement in so many diverse projects. He agreed that "according to the principle of division of labor" one ought to engage thoroughly in only one kind of business. But, he added apologetically, "the conditions of the time left no other choice." [22] Magoshi had also been involved in a large variety of industrial ventures; but during a trip abroad he realized that there businessmen usually stuck to one line and therefore achieved great success. As a result of this new insight, he severed his ties with many establishments and concentrated almost exclusively on brewing beer. He became Japan's leading brewer.[23]

Amamiya Keijirō,[24] like so many others, began his business career in Yokohama with making money by any means that came to hand. After a trip abroad, he changed his approach and decided to become an entrepreneur. He imported machines and set up a flour mill, but had great difficulty in selling the flour because the Japanese were not used to eating bread. Amamiya had to sell part of his flour to Russia; then he imported high-grade wheat and distributed it free to peasants in an all-out drive to break down their prejudice. He also began making experiments in electric-power generation. Amamiya was the first and last man to open an iron mine entirely with private capital, investing over half a million yen in it, and he operated at a loss for years. Although he was president of a railway company, he urged nationalization of the railroads, apparently because the varying freight rates hurt industry and especially mining, in which he had invested heavily. Amamiya put his hand to a large variety of enterprises, founding, cooperating, consulting, and occupying honorary positions.

Tanaka Gentarō,[25] who was called "the Shibusawa of Kyoto," had supposedly conceived the idea of a career as an entrepreneur while studying English in Kobe, at the age of twenty-one. Tanaka did not experience a break with the past; his father had already opened a bank in Kyoto, and the son entered this business. In 1884 he founded the Kyoto Stock Exchange with his father. Because of his integrity and proverbial economic foresight (people used to say that Tanaka Gentarō would "light his lamp at noon already and turn it off at midnight"), he was able to achieve a position of influence and leadership in Kyoto. His chief concern was to innovate and to work for the modernization of Kyoto. He founded a string of enterprises, ranging from a previously mentioned pottery company to weaving and electricity. He is said to have founded the Kyoto Savings Bank mainly for the purpose of gathering capital for new enterprises. Anticipating prolonged difficulties with his electrical company, he insisted that the burden be shared by the whole population and so made a collection drive for capital contributions. For the twenty-odd enterprises that he founded he received no support from the government, but he cooperated closely with other industrial leaders, notably Shibusawa. As soon as an enterprise had been firmly established, Tanaka seems to have lost interest in it and gone on to new projects.

Takashima Kazaemon [26] was a man with a passion for promoting new things. The son of a village headman, he had left his home for Edo to make his fortune. He became a pioneer in a wide range of projects, sometimes under government auspices, sometimes in cooperation with others, sometimes on his own. He was active in railways, land reclamation, mining, utilities, and school building. Because of his deep interest in the railway program, the government appointed him to reclaim part of the sea between Tokyo and Yokohama to permit a straight connection for the Tokyo-Yokohama line. He employed about 3,000 workers on this project. In Hokkaido he reclaimed a large area of wasteland. In 1871 Takashima built a foreign-language school for 700 students with 30,000 yen of his own capital and urged Fukuzawa to teach in it. This man who had served a five-year sentence under the bakufu for establishing illicit trading relations with foreigners became a romantic entrepreneur with such a high degree of public responsibility that he would later compare his own importance to the country with that of Prince Itō.

Okuda Masaka [27] played a role in Nagoya similar to that of Tanaka Gentarō in Kyoto and was called "the Shibusawa of Nagoya." A dissatisfied official and a man with experience in trading operations, Okuda started his career as an industrialist with the foundation of the Owari Cotton Spinning-Mill in 1888. When the mill began to show

losses, he was advised to make good by speculative purchases and sales policies based on the rather violent price
fluctuations of raw cotton and yarns. He rejected such a
suggestion, maintaining that "an industrialist . . . has to
continue steadily with production, and his profits must
come from the progress of industry itself; profits from
speculation are despicable." [28] His disdain for salesmanship and pride in being an industrialist and a pioneer are
clearly expressed in these words. Okuda founded the
Nagoya Stock Exchange, became president of the Chamber of Commerce, spearheaded many new establishments
in banking, electricity, and gas, and founded a freight-car
construction company with 600,000 yen in capital.

Kinbara Meizen [29] was not an industrialist in the proper
sense, but he certainly was an innovator and a reformer.
As the son of a rich peasant, he decided to invest in agriculture on a large scale. His great projects included river
regulation, bridge building, and drainage systems. He
established a water-regulation school, pioneered in cattle
breeding, and built roads in rural areas; he also managed
a bank. Kinbara became well known for organizing an
institution for the care and rehabilitation of prisoners.
All his efforts seem to have been motivated principally
by a genuine and selfless patriotism and a desire to raise
the level of social well-being. Shibusawa, Morimura, Sakuma, and Kinbara are usually considered the most idealistic of the Meiji entrepreneurs. Whereas Shibusawa was
guided by Confucian ethics, Kinbara became a Christian,
and probably a good deal of his idealism was stimulated by
his new faith. He not only dedicated himself entirely to
his welfare schemes and rural innovations, but he asked
and received cooperation from the government, from
bankers and industrialists, and from the public through
collection drives.

These are only a few examples of entrepreneurs of the romantic type. The leading ones — Shibusawa, Godai, Asano, and Ōkura — have already been sufficiently discussed; others will receive attention in a different connection. But the general trend to bold innovations in many lines, to an almost headlong rushing from one task to another, is characteristic of the large majority of our fifty representative entrepreneurs.

The Bankers

Classification of these business leaders according to their field of activity presents a real difficulty because of the prevalence of the romantic type. With very few exceptions, we should call them all industrialists. Bankers and foreign-trade merchants usually ended up by establishing several industrial plants or founding railway companies or public-work projects. The subdivision here, then, should be taken loosely and not in any exclusive sense.

The bankers enjoyed high prestige in Meiji Japan owing to the success of the national banks. Banks were regarded as instruments for the building of modern industry. The foremost bankers extended long-term loans or invested directly in large projects with a long gestation period. Shibusawa, Yasuda, Nakamigawa, and others were not only great bankers; they were equally great as industrialists. Minomura, who should also be called a banker, was born too early to turn to industry. In addition to Shibusawa, Yasuda, Minomura, and Nakamigawa, we may classify seven others as primarily bankers: Hara, Toyokawa, Matsumoto, Kawasaki Hachiuemon, Hirose Sukesaburō, Kawada, and Abe.

Hara Rokurō, the son of a village headman, has been called one of the "big five" in the business world, together with Shibusawa, Yasuda, Ōkura, and Furukawa. Hara had

been a fierce *sonnō jōi* partisan in his native Choshu han
and had engaged in many battles. He decided to leave his
military career in 1871 while studying in the United States,
following the advice of a friend who stressed that the
foundation of a strong country lies not in its army but
in its trade and manufacturing.[30] He studied at Yale University for three years and in London for three more years.
Hara started his entrepreneurial career after his return
to Japan in 1877, with the foundation of the country's
hundredth bank; then he became co-founder of Japan's
first savings bank. From then on he moved out into an
unbelievably broad range of activities. We find him engaged in such fields as electricity, railways, spinning, shipping, mining and paper manufacturing. He now fought
for the competitive strength of his country with the same
determination with which he had previously battled riot-
ing peasants and bakufu forces.

Toyokawa Ryōhei [31] and Kawada Koichirō [32] were both
Mitsubishi men whose independent achievements are somewhat overshadowed by the genius of Iwasaki. Toyokawa
worked mainly in public relations for Mitsubishi. He had
valuable connections with Fukuzawa's college. As president of the Mitsubishi Bank and vice-president of the
Bankers' Association, he wielded great influence in the
promotion of the Keiō spirit. He insisted that the new
age needed new men. Kawada gained prominence as president of the Bank of Japan, in which position he is credited
with the reversal of official policy from promotion of agriculture to stress on trade and industry.

Hirose Sukesaburō [33] and Abe Taizō [34] were mainly
insurance men who championed this new line of business
in Japan. Hirose had been an accomplished and successful
merchant at the age of seventeen. He helped impoverished
fellow merchants in various ways and had a school built to

promote business education. He established a few banks, promoted railway construction, and in 1890 founded a newspaper; but his primary interest shifted to insurance. Abe was teaching English at Keiō at the age of twenty-one; at twenty-three he became an employee of the Ministry of Education. Later he went back to teaching and again returned to the ministry, which sent him on a trip to the United States. There he conceived the idea of introducing insurance into Japan, and after his return in 1881 he founded Japan's first insurance company, in cooperation with Mitsubishi's influential Shōda. Today Abe's Meiji Life Insurance Company is one of the largest in Japan. He traveled extensively, crisscrossing the country to spread the insurance idea and to establish branch offices.

Matsumoto Jūtarō [35] displayed from early boyhood an insatiable thirst for advancement in business. Dissatisfied with his slow progress in Kyoto, he went to Osaka at thirteen; there he could not become independent as quickly as he had hoped because of the strict guild rules, so he started anew on his own as a peddler. Next he turned to trading with imported goods and eventually became very successful as a manufacturer of woolen cloth. When he had amassed a handsome fortune, "he began to think of the public good." [36] After 1878 he applied himself to the reorganization of the Osaka money market. Through establishing and amalgamating banks, he rose to a dominant position, became president of the Osaka Bankers' Association, and used his financial strength and influence to promote modern industry in that city. After banking, Matsumoto's main fields of activity were railway building (he founded four railway companies and invested in others), cotton spinning, beer brewing, sugar refining, and education. He founded an "education insurance company" and opened the first nursery school in Japan. By 1898 his total yearly income was surpassed only in Osaka by that of Sumitomo.[37]

Kawasaki Hachiuemon [38] was a cautious banker with little direct interest in trading or industry. He was also one of the very few men who did not experience a major shift away from past activities. As a merchant in Mito han, he had been able to accumulate considerable capital through the operation of the bakufu mint. After the Restoration he continued in almost the same line as a prefectural money exchanger. Gradually he turned to modern banking, achieved great success, and rose to the stature of a zaibatsu builder. But he remained a fully conservative banker, quite in contrast to the others in the sample. His principles were honesty, diligence, thrift, and accumulation, which could have been taken straight from any of the Tokugawa merchant house rules. They compare unfavorably with the dicta of men like Iwasaki, Asano, Yasuda, and Ōkura insofar as daring and entrepreneurial vigor are concerned.

All the great bankers except Kawasaki Hachiuemon came to a turning point, after which they became not only interested in but completely absorbed by the task of national promotion. They sponsored modern banking, industry, and even education, more or less because they "began to think of the public good," realizing that their acquired wealth also meant a new responsibility for the progress of the economy.

The Men in Foreign Trade

The efforts of the government to establish trade companies soon after the Restoration ended in failure; no further attempts were made to organize the foreign-trade sector centrally, and the initiative was more or less left to individuals. But contemporary opinion attached great importance to competition with foreign countries, and the endeavors of a small group of pioneers must be understood against the background of that urgency — this helps to explain the unusual self-assurance and bold planning of these foreign-trade merchants. Ōkura and Masuda have already received sufficient attention in other connections. They were among the top men in foreign trade, though they both moved from trade increasingly into industry.

Morimura Ichizaemon [39] is probably the most interesting among these trade merchants because of his extraordinary idealism. At the age of thirteen he had vowed before a shrine never to deviate from the path of honesty, and he not only kept his promise faithfully but became a fighter for high business ethics. He started in great poverty, running a night stall in Tokyo. Gradually Morimura gained some ground, tried his luck in mining operations, then in fishing and salt production, and profited from government trade commissions. But, surprisingly, he severed his ties as an official merchant because of the corruption that prevailed in these commission deals. He then turned to foreign trade; he had his younger brother learn English and sent him to New York for further study; this brother opened a branch office of Morimura in New York. Morimura was extremely conscious of being different from most of the other merchants in his stress on absolute honesty. He eventually extended his activities to banking and cotton spinning; he also built several schools.

Ōtani Kahei [40] gained sufficient experience and money during his employment with the Smith Baker Company in Yokohama to start an independent tea-export business. He became very successful and, like Morimura, felt a responsibility toward Japan's trade position. He organized the Tea Traders' Association, staged and promoted exhibitions on foreign trade, and spoke frequently in various parts of the country on his two favorite subjects, the necessity of foreign trade and honesty in business. Ōtani argued that to the Westerners honesty was more valuable than life, and he held that a man should atone with his life for cheating because of the damage done to society.[41] Ōtani maintained a lively interest in civic affairs and actively promoted general welfare and education. For nine years he was a member of the Upper House.

Hiranuma Senzō and Yonekura Ippei displayed similar characteristics, and their careers can be sketched rather briefly. Hiranuma [42] was a merchant of fortune in the earlier part of his business life. Like Wakao, mentioned as a foreign-trade merchant in an earlier context, he made money by speculating in grain, stocks, and real estate in Yokohama, thus amassing over 10 million yen in capital. He was severely criticized for his usurious moneylending. In foreign trade he was very successful and eventually turned also to industrial investments in cotton spinning, railways, and electric companies. He, too, built a school and became known as a promoter of and contributor to public-welfare projects.

Yonekura Ippei [43] was born a merchant but participated in the *sonnō jōi* movement and was imprisoned. Later he became a prefectural official, resigned, and went to China to survey the market for Japanese products. He began with tea and lumber exports. In 1871 we find him in Tokyo establishing a bank, with a partner, with 500,000 yen in capital; then he built a paper mill. After 1872 he concentrated solely on the domestic and foreign rice trade; he organized and then controlled the Tokyo rice market.

There are a few common characteristics of these prominent foreign-trade merchants of the early Meiji era. These men usually had entered the port cities as penniless upstarts, who were not too particular about their methods of making money; and they made money, thanks to their talent and boldness and to the turbulent conditions of the time and their machinations with government officials. Then came a decisive turning point, their "conversion" from profit maximization by any method to a realization of responsibility to the country; they subsequently became merchants of the *bummei kaika*. In this capacity they insisted on honesty, reliability, and the honor of trade.

This same turn toward a new sense of responsibility as soon as a certain level of wealth and economic prominence had been acquired was seen among other men of the sample: Yasuda, Matsumoto, and Asano are typical. The newly acquired wealth, often gained by questionable methods, gave these men a real power over others; whether they wanted to or not, they became public figures. But it was almost impossible in Meiji Japan to be a public figure and to disregard the pressure of public opinion. Public opinion, in turn, acclaimed only those who combined wealth with progressive and responsible action, as indicated by the policies of the government itself. Public opinion and the new standards set by a few leaders like Shibusawa were, I believe, very real and effective factors in changing many men with talent and boldness into responsible entrepreneurs. For these men the problem of initial capital accumulation had been solved before their pioneering began; they could surmount initial difficulties in the new ventures and even sustain large losses for some time, compensated now by their sense of greatness and their firm belief in final success.

Also common to this group is the tendency to turn to industrial investments and to move gradually away from trade, to leave it to other men and to start, in the words of Ōkura, "enterprises that others do not or cannot undertake." It almost seems as if the foreign-trade merchants, in spite of their insistence on their honesty and patriotic motivations, could not otherwise establish a sufficiently striking contrast between themselves and men who were only interested in quick profits, as they in fact had been themselves. The real honor and entrepreneurial prestige were to be gained in modern industry and it was here that the cream of the Meiji business world tended to concentrate.

The Political Merchants

It does not seem necessary at this stage to marshal a set of representative men in order to illustrate the outstanding features of the Meiji industrial pioneers. The chapter on the zaibatsu builders showed the prevailing attitudes among the top industrialists; further examples were presented in the discussion of the classical and romantic types. The few remaining men in my sample who have not yet received any detailed attention will help to throw additional light on two aspects, or rather approaches, of the Meiji entrepreneurs. We saw in an earlier context that government connections and subsidies were particularly prevalent among the older group of men, while the younger group shifted gradually toward independence and the corporate form of enterprise. Thus official enterprise and the semiofficial entrepreneurs mark the beginning of the Meiji entrepreneurial development. The group of college graduates who moved to top managerial positions without substantial capital of their own signal a new stage.

The term "political merchant" (*seishō*) was new in the Meiji vocabulary, just as the word *jitsugyōka* was. But unlike the latter it carried a derogatory meaning; it branded the lobbyists who relied on their friends among officials to receive the coveted government contracts. The Satsuma Rebellion became a great boon to political merchants who obtained army delivery contracts or shipping monopolies. The outstanding examples here are Iwasaki, Ōkura, Masuda, and Matsumoto. Godai, too, remained very close to his former co-officials after he left office, and his half-million-yen loan from the government for an indigo plant was not the only favor he received. Even Yasuda and Shibusawa, who were extremely independent men, did not go entirely empty-handed when indirect subsidies were being offered. Yet Shibusawa was at no point criticized or called a political merchant; rather, he was praised for his independence from government help. The criticism of the political merchants was mainly directed either at those who were out only to make a "killing" under government cover, those who swarmed around the officials like bees around honey in order to gain favors, or, as in the case of Iwasaki, at ruthless monopoly power that thrived under the wing of a powerful faction within the government.

There was a system in the privileges that were handed out so liberally. It was thought that samurai and other newcomers with talent but no capital should be helped to build a basis, in terms of capital, for their entrepreneurial activity. These indirect subsidies were given as a matter of policy after the abolition of government enterprises, and one of the principal champions of the policy was Inoue Kaoru. He not only knew how to pick able men for Mitsui; other political merchants also relied on his good offices to secure privileges. Himself a man with keen insight into the economic problems that the entrepreneurs faced, Inoue usually knew whom to subsidize.

The policy of indirect subsidies to would-be entrepreneurs naturally raised a thorny ethical problem. How much favoritism and how much corruption were involved in this type of indirect stimulation to entrepreneurship? Old loyalties and the *hanbatsu* (han cliques) played an important role in determining the recipients of contracts. But when all is said and done, we must be careful not to apply the same standards to the early Meiji situation as we would to the present day. Not only was the need for indirect subsidy much greater at that time, but the Meiji government inherited a long-standing tradition from the Tokugawa rulers and the han. All had their *goyō shōnin* (official merchants) who made tremendous gains but at the same time had to be ready to be taxed heavily or to lend large sums on request. Thus the favors were coupled with a special duty; carrying on this tradition, the political merchants of the early Meiji were supposed to support the government and to be "taxed" by using their wealth, even at prolonged losses, for the building of modern industry.

Fujita Denzaburō is a good example of a political merchant both with respect to initial accumulation and the use of capital gained through government contracts. During the stage of accumulation, he does not seem to have been scrupulous in his methods; he was even accused of counterfeiting money.[44] This rich sake brewer's son, who knew a few top government officials from the time when he fought battles under their leadership, displayed unusual courage as well as shrewdness. He wanted and won huge profits from trade in army supplies and rice, and then was equally eager to reinvest these gains in industrial enterprises in Osaka. He built a large shoe factory, a sulphuric-acid plant, and spread out to many diverse investment activities in cooperation with his friend Nakano Goichi, and with Godai, Matsumoto, and a few others. Although he was the owner of some silver mines, he advocated the change to the gold standard as a necessity for the Japanese economy; he was acclaimed for this objectivity by contemporaries and thus proved that he was a political merchant who could think in terms of the national good.

Nakano Goichi [45] cooperated closely with Fujita. A samurai prodigy who became an official at fifteen, he had an adventurous career in military and administrative service and in trading under lucrative government commissions. He accumulated considerable wealth in army deliveries and then turned his interest to industry. He became one of the Osaka pioneers of modern enterprise and vice-president of the chamber of commerce. His vigorous entrepreneurial start came to a sudden end when he committed suicide in 1880, when only thirty-eight years old.

Kawasaki Shōzō [46] could have been included among the zaibatsu men of the previous chapter, since his shipyard was the nucleus of his empire of heavy industry. He had become interested in shipbuilding during his stay in Nagasaki, but for a considerable time had no opportunity to put his plans into action. He became friendly with Matsukata, who appointed him to make a survey of the Ryukyu Islands. From that position he was chosen to be vice-president of the Yūbin Jōkisen Company, which was the first of three attempts to break the shipping monopoly of Mitsubishi. Although Yūbin Jōkisen collapsed very shortly, Kawasaki's name was remembered among officials. With a government loan of 30,000 yen, he began in 1878 to rebuild the deserted Tsukiji Shipyard in Tokyo. He encountered innumerable difficulties of a technical nature, and few people believed he would ever succeed. When he had finally finished his first steamship, the *Hokkai Maru*, he had to make a vigorous effort to advertise. He invited over a thousand officials and businessmen to a party that actually cost him more than the *Hokkai Maru* itself.[47] It would lead us too far afield to follow the course of Kawasaki's rivalry with Mitsubishi, his purchase and extension of the Hyōgo Shipyard with government help, and the rise of his enterprises to zaibatsu dimensions. Connections with government officials and subsidies were of strategic importance to Kawasaki's success, but the basic reason was that, in his friend Baron Maejima's words, "he lived and died for shipbuilding." At the end of his life, in 1912, his yards had orders for large ships not only from Japan but also from China, Russia, and France.

Nakano Buei [48] remained a politician even after he had left his government post to become a businessman. He was a highly cultured and public-minded samurai who knew how to put his previous experience as a han administrator to good use in private business. The establishment of a horse-drawn railway in Tokyo led to his first major success. We find him later promoting and investing in railways, insurance, and even iron production. He was not so much an original innovator as a cooperator within the top group of Tokyo industrialists. As president of the chamber of commerce and the stock exchange, he exercised a moral leadership in the business community, and at the same time he kept his hand in politics, as an active member of the Liberal Party.

These few sketches of political merchants may suffice as illustrations of the way in which many entrepreneurs, and many lesser men who also tried, were able to use government connections and subsidies as stepping stones to business success. It was mentioned previously that in a certain sense all Meiji entrepreneurs were political merchants. The strict separation of the central and the private wing of the economy was slow to evolve in the politically emotional climate of the period.

The Graduates

The last group to be mentioned in this analysis of leading entrepreneurs is the managers who rose to prominence because of a college education. They constitute a separate group by virtue of their youth and because of their different approach. Among our fifty men these students-turned-entrepreneurs moved farthest away from officialdom and favoritism and also from the lone-wolf approach and the romantic approach. The heat of political emotions subsided gradually; the feeling of urgency that inspired many hasty ventures gave way to rational planning within the framework of a firmly established industrial nucleus. These newcomers from the classrooms of Fukuzawa's college were nonfeudal, nonpolitical, and eminently sensible and liberal-minded. Their emphasis was on technical knowledge and long-term planning.

We have already seen how in cotton spinning two of the Fukuzawa men achieved decisive breakthroughs: Yamabe in the Osaka Mill and Nakamigawa in his Kanegafuchi Mill. Another Fukuzawa man who is not in my sample, Okada Reikō, shared with Yamabe the leadership in cotton spinning; they both fought for rational tariff policies to make Japanese spinning competitive on the world market.[49]

Except for Abe, who applied himself to the promotion and foundation of insurance companies, the graduates in the sample were drafted into existing large companies because of their talents and educational achievements. They had no capital of their own, nor were they interested in gaining any through government favors. They relied on joint stock for their new companies, which they controlled not so much by the number of shares they held as by their entrepreneurial and technical know-how. The large zaibatsu were there to stay, but it became increasingly difficult to establish new ones; the time of tycoons in the style of Iwasaki, Yasuda, Ōkura, and Asano had come to a close. The new entrepreneurial talents were now absorbed into the existing industrial empires.

Asabuki Eiji [50] had first met his teacher Fukuzawa in Osaka. At that time he was still a fierce *jōi* man who was ready to kill Fukuzawa because the latter ate beef and advocated a complete opening of the country to Western influence. After reading Fukuzawa's books, Asabuki did an about-face: he sold his sword, went to Tokyo, and became Fukuzawa's student. From there he was invited to join Mitsubishi, and later he went to Mitsui. Apart from his managerial success, he became very valuable because of his progressive attitudes and his scouting of other graduates for these two zaibatsu.

Shōda Heigorō [51] had been a teacher at Keiō before joining Mitsubishi. He cooperated closely with Iwasaki in many ventures, but his outstanding achievements are undoubtedly the modernization of the Nagasaki Shipyard and the building of the famous Marunouchi Office Center in Tokyo. He had conceived the plan for such a center while abroad and, with the green light from Iwasaki, made his project a resounding success economically while at the same time contributing a good deal to the development of modern Tokyo.

Kondō Renpei,[52] like Shōda, had been a teacher before coming to Iwasaki. He took charge of the Mitsubishi Shipping Company in its fierce competitive battle with the government-sponsored Kyōdō Unyu Company; with Mitsubishi's victory, Kondō became president of the amalgamated Nippon Yūsen Company over which Iwasaki had gained control. Kondō was rated by his contemporaries among the top businessmen, and his advice was highly valued. It is maintained that he is primarily responsible for the fact that Japanese shipping became competitive with the great foreign lines at a comparatively early date. Although Kondō ventured into some other fields, notably mining, he remained chiefly a champion of shipping.

Ōkawa Heizaburō,[53] like Yamabe, was a Shibusawa protégé and occupied in paper manufacturing a leading position similar to that of Yamabe in cotton spinning. He worked for a while with Asano in his cement factory and then, as a paper-manufacturing expert, went into the Ōji Paper Mill established by Shibusawa. He had acquired his technical knowledge abroad and remained eager to keep abreast of the latest foreign manufacturing methods. When control of Ōji Paper went over to Mitsui, he left the mill and started out on his own. He was so successful that some writers call his "paper kingdom" a zaibatsu. Ōkawa occupied important positions in some eighty enterprises, by virtue not so much of his capital investments as of his expert knowledge and managerial talent.

With the trend of college graduates moving into key positions in Japanese industry, we arrive at a new stage. This is the postpioneering stage, which was marked by a close cooperation betwen the *gakubatsu* and the zaibatsu, by rational calculation based on large joint-stock capital and technical knowledge. The change was, of course, not abrupt. But different conditions and different problems called for a new type of businessman.

Along with the change in entrepreneurial types went a changing pattern of capital supply. The government subsidies tapered off, and the opportunities to profit from economic confusion in the port cities and from military actions disappeared. Cotton spinning was first to give indications of the new trend. After 1885, with the success of the Osaka Mill, we find a marked difference in the type of men who were founding the mills and supplying the capital. When the breakthrough had been achieved, the merchants staged their comeback and Osaka flourished once more.

It would be interesting to follow up these indicated

trends, to show how far the changes went and how they affected the growth of the young Meiji industries. But my study here comes to a close. I was concerned with the pioneering entrepreneurs, the men who established the foundations of industry, who built their factories in the face of formidable economic and technological difficulties. That Meiji industry succeeded and kept up its vigorous growth was to the credit of these bold innovators.

CONCLUSION

We have been walking through a forest of political and economic changes, of personalities and policies, of government initiative and private endeavor, of class movements, of productivity statistics. The Meiji industrialization was indeed a complex process. We have looked only at the beginning years. These pages can lead to no final conclusions concerning the decades of the most vigorous growth, after the turn of the century, but they do show that by the time of the Sino-Japanese War private modern industry had achieved a solid basis for rapid expansion.

In the course of this study I have tried to single out the trees from the undergrowth and to indicate a few major factors that accounted for the dynamics of the Meiji economy. There is no need to summarize them all. Instead, a few facts will be put into perspective, facts that relate to the process of the formation of entrepreneurs in the private economic sector and to the general spirit of enterprise in Japan.

Throughout the early period, capital was in critically short supply; the government coffers were chronically depleted, and the private sector initially offered only a trickle of funds for industrial investment. The bourgeoisie remained conservative almost until the turn of the century.

It had been deprived of its wealth by taxation and by the operations of the merchants of fortune, and as a group it thus grew ever more timid and cautious. The samurai were dispossessed of their sustenance and told to invest and work if they wanted to eat. The peasants, too, had to keep carrying a heavy burden after the monetization of the land tax. These were all elements in a radical and painful operation that was a prerequisite for the vigorous forward march of the entrepreneurs inside and outside of the government. The fact of the matter is that capital was neither sufficient nor, by and large, in the proper hands when that march started. It was requisitioned by the government and also seized by a ruthless group of successful businessmen of a new type. Potential capital was activated through the very process of change, violently and at times with little heed to ethical considerations. National resources that had been dormant or had existed in disguised forms, such as samurai stipends, were thrown into the determined effort of the government to compensate for two centuries of stagnation and to catch up with the West. The greatest resource of all was the totality of the physical and mental energies of a rejuvenated nation.

If there is any major lesson that Meiji Japan provides for today's backward countries, it may be this: they should not require their capital to be neatly arranged in usable form. The most important resource for development is the will to succeed. If it is possible to mobilize that resource, capital can often be requisitioned from many hidden sources, and it will be newly created by the increased efforts of planning entrepreneurs and a toiling population.

Two of the Meiji Japan's great assets in mobilizing resources were undoubtedly the stability and organization of her social system and, even more, the character of her people. These variables were not the product of short-term external influences; they were gifts of nature that developed over a long period of time. The Japanese inherited from their feudal period a strong sense of discipline, loyalty, public-mindedness, and national unity. These social characteristics, paired with a high degree of diligence and intelligence, were, and are, their national treasure.

But these qualities in themselves cannot explain the dynamic advances of the Meiji era. Intoxication with the idea of progress and the determination to bring Japan, in the shortest possible time, on an even keel with the Western world was in the last analysis based on a special emotional characteristic of the Japanese. Why did other nations not respond in a similar fashion — why not India, why not China? The Japanese are known for their relentless ambition, be it in science or industry or sports. They cannot easily swallow defeat. Foreigners often note that the Japanese can never quite rid themselves of a deep-seated inferiority complex. But that inferiority complex itself stems from the ambition to be first.

After the opening of the ports, the Japanese people were shocked into a realization of their own backwardness, which had been concealed from them by the closed-door policy and by the official contempt for the Western barbarians. At this point the national capital that consisted in loyalty to the leaders, discipline, intelligence, and capacity for hard work was harnessed for the one great effort: to catch up, and fast. The "New Deal in emotions" had indeed taken hold of the nation, and it is the major explanation for the irrational, noncapitalist, dynamic, and romantic approach of the pioneering entrepreneurs. The zaibatsu builders and the political merchants found ample justification for building their private empires with whatever kind of capital they could get. The samurai Ishikawa who founded a spinning mill with a view to making cannons, Kashima the cotton merchant who built his own spinning machines to be independent of the foreigners, tycoons like Iwasaki and Ōkura: all were carried away by a combination of personal ambition and nationalism, and public acclaim was one of their most coveted rewards.

The creation of a few centers of progress made possible a snowballing effect. Forces that otherwise might have dissipated themselves in rural areas were strengthened and coordinated in Tokyo, the headquarters of the avant-garde. It is sometimes suggested that, for the sake of economizing scarce capital, one should build small-scale factories in rural areas, where underemployed labor is close to its food supply and where no cost for city buildings and no leakage for food transport is involved.[1] Japanese factories, to some extent, were built in rural districts, but the entrepreneurial elite needed a center, and it was there that the industrial push gained momentum. It was not possible for the innovators to remain in their old traditional world; they needed and wanted a new place, a new atmosphere, new conditions. A man cannot be compartmentalized — he cannot easily be a changed man economically and remain socially and otherwise tradition-bound. This is the lesson we learn from the bourgeoisie of Osaka, and from the "uprooted" men who left their homes and who had their hair cut short and ate beef as sign of their drastic break with the past.

Just as individuals could not neatly separate their economic from their social and political lives, so it was with social groups and even with the nation as a whole. A single class could not monopolize entrepreneurship, which was but an offshoot of the nation's forward thrust. Initial differences with respect to experience and to capital accumulation were like minor hurdles easily scaled by those who had started to race. Class groupings and prior distributions of capital resources were thrown into confusion, and out of that confusion emerged the bold entrepreneurs who knew how to activate and even create new capital. And the strong-willed pioneers of industry themselves, like the political leaders, were only the standard-bearers of a nation on the march.

NOTES

BIBLIOGRAPHY

GLOSSARY

INDEX

NOTES

INTRODUCTION

1. The overthrow of the Tokugawa rule and the reinstatement of the emperor as *de facto* ruler of Japan was accomplished in 1867. In January 1868 the Meiji era began, lasting until the death of Emperor Meiji in 1912. It was followed by the Taishō era (1912–1926) and the present Shōwa era (1926–).

2. G. Myrdal, *Economic Theory and Underdeveloped Regions* (London, 1958), p. 100.

3. Albert O. Hirschman, *The Strategy of Economic Development* (New Haven, 1959), *passim*.

4. Joseph A. Schumpeter, *The Theory of Economic Development* (Cambridge, Mass., 1934), pp. 128–156.

5. Joseph A. Schumpeter, *Capitalism, Socialism and Democracy*, 3rd ed. (New York, 1950), pp. 131–134.

I. THE MERCHANT CLASS

1. Oda Nobunaga (1534–1582) began to build castles as places of safety and as a means to control the rebellious warlords. His retainer and successor, Toyotomi Hideyoshi (1536–1598), continued his building program. Samurai and also merchants and artisans were settled in the new castle towns and received many privileges as a stimulus to trade and craftsmanship; for example, no tax was levied on the merchants.

The word *chōnin* (townsman) refers to both craftsmen and merchants but is often used synonymously with *shōnin* (merchant).

2. The guild system was established by the Tokugawa in the seventeenth century; but an organization similar to the guild, the *za* (seat), had existed from the Kamakura period (1192–1332) onward.

The *za* were associations of merchants and artisans who lived on the large manors (*shōen*) and enjoyed the protection of the manorial lords.

3. Tokugawa Ieyasu won his decisive victory over the forces of Hideyoshi in the battle of Sekigahara in 1600. He was appointed shogun in 1603; Oda Nobunaga and Toyotomi Hideyoshi had never been shogun although they had unified the country and had actually ruled as such. The shogun was appointed by the emperor; his full title was *sei-i-tai-shōgun* (barbarian-subduing great general), which indicated the original purpose of his position. The idea that the shogun's government had a military and emergency character was kept up by calling it *bakufu* (tent government). Although the shogun had to be appointed by the emperor, the latter had no real political power during the bakufu rule.

The Tokugawa shogun established their government in Edo, hence the name Edo period for the time of the Tokugawa bakufu rule. It was preceded by the Kamakura (1192–1332) and the Muromachi (1338–1573) periods. The last decades of the Muromachi period are also known under the name of *sengoku jidai* (country at war); they were terminated by the rise of Oda Nobunaga.

4. Miyamoto Mataji, *Nihon girudo no kaihō* (The abolition of the Japanese guilds; Osaka, 1957), p. 8.

5. Yamaguchi Kazuo, *Bakumatsu bōeki shi* (History of foreign trade during the last years of the Tokugawa period; Tokyo, 1943), p. 291.

6. *Ibid.*, pp. 281–298.

7. See note 20.

8. Charles David Sheldon, *The Rise of the Merchant Class in Tokugawa Japan, 1600–1868: An Introductory Survey* (New York, 1958), p. 69. The passage is a translation from the *Seji kenbun roku* (Tales of worldly affairs).

9. When the Tokugawa moved the bakufu to Edo at the beginning of the seventeenth century, Edo was but a small hamlet; thanks to the large administration and the numerous samurai who now had to reside in Edo, it rapidly became the largest city in Japan. But it became the capital only after the emperor moved there in 1867, when it was renamed Tokyo (eastern capital), as distinguished from Kyoto (capital city).

10. The daimyo were the leaders and administrators of the feudal territories (han). This feudal administrative system was introduced by the Tokugawa. The 260-odd han varied in size and political importance and also in producing revenue for the daimyo. While the smallest yielded an equivalent of something over 10,000 koku of rice (1 koku equals 4.96 bushels), the large ones yielded between 200,000 and 1 million koku.

The Tokugawa shogun were extremely anxious to keep the daimyo under constant control. A daimyo could be transferred to another territory (unless his han was his inherited property or unless he was too powerful for such a drastic measure). Each daimyo had also to spend every second year in residence in Edo. This *sankin kōtai* system of alternate residence at the seat of the bakufu contributed greatly to the prosperity of the *chōnin* class while seriously weakening the han economies.

11. Miyamoto Mataji, *Ōsaka* (Tokyo, 1957), p. 9.

12. Kajinishi Mitsuhaya, *Shōgyō shihon oyobi kōrigashi shihon* (Trading capital and usury capital; Tokyo, 1949), p. 28.

13. For a very good description of the Tokugawa currency system, see John Whitney Hall, *Tanuma Okitsugu, 1719–1788, Forerunner of Modern Japan* (Cambridge, Mass., 1955), pp. 68–74.

14. Kanno Watarō, *Ōsaka keizai shi kenkyū* (Studies in the economic history of Osaka; Osaka 1935), pp. 171–173.

15. *Ibid.*, p. 134; also Kajinishi, *Shōgyō shihon*, pp. 29–30.

16. Kanno, *Ōsaka keizai*, p. 173.

17. Miyamoto Mataji, *Ōsaka chōnin* (The Osaka townsmen; Tokyo, 1957), p. 181.

18. Thomas C. Smith, *The Agrarian Origins of Modern Japan* (Stanford, 1959), p. 125.

19. Miyamoto, *Ōsaka chōnin*, p. 185.

20. The division into four classes had been preceded by the separation of the warrior class from the farming population under Hideyoshi, by the so-called *hei-nō-bunri* (separation of warriors and farmers) law. *Shi-nō-kō-shō* was but a popular expression for the rigid definition of status, of which these four were the main groupings. The Shinto and Buddhist ministers were a special group, and within the samurai class, too, there were subclasses.

21. Miyamoto, *Ōsaka*, p. 90.

22. The *myōji taitō* were the various privileges of the samurai class. The right to assume a family name was more easily granted; physicians usually used a family name and seem on the whole to have been rather close to the samurai class. Village headmen, too, were permitted family names. The right to carry a sword was less frequently given to commoners and was then often restricted with respect to the type of sword and the occasions when it could be carried.

23. Miyamoto Mataji, "Daimyō kashi no rishiritsu ni tsuite" (On the interest rates in daimyo lending), *Ōsaka daigaku keizaigaku* (Osaka University economics), 10.2:115–116 (November 25, 1960).

24. *Ibid.*, pp. 119–138.

25. Takegoshi Yosaburō, *Nihon keizai shi* (Japanese economic history; Tokyo, 1929), VI, 88.

26. E. S. Crawcour, "Some Observations on Merchants: A Translation of Mitsui Takafusa's *Chōnin kōken roku*, with an Introduction and Notes," *Transactions of the Asiatic Society of Japan*, 3rd series (Tokyo, 1962), 8:9–139 (December 1961). Mitsui Takafusa warned in these "observations" against daimyo lending, pointing out that once a merchant starts on this road he finds that there is no end to it: he has to lend further in order to receive interest on previous loans. But it is also evident from this document that if the daimyo did repay there was scarcely a better investment opportunity for merchant capital. The merchant house of Yoyoda had 100 million ryo in outstanding loans with daimyo before its property was confiscated by the bakufu at the beginning of the eighteenth century (*ibid.*, p. 23).

27. Miyamoto, *Ōsaka chōnin*, p. 207.

28. Honjō Eijirō, *The Social and Economic History of Japan* (Kyoto, 1935), p. 197.

29. *Ibid.*, p. 206. The rank of a samurai depended on the size of his fief, expressed in terms of koku of rice. The nominal amounts, however, were often much greater than what the daimyo would or could actually pay.

30. The expression is somewhat incorrect. Prior to the Restoration the movement was known mainly under the names *sonnō jōi* (revere the emperor, expel the barbarians) and *tōbaku* (overthrow the bakufu). Initially the Restoration itself was called *go isshin* (the new era), which then was changed to *ishin* (restoration).

31. See W. W. Rostow, *The Stages of Economic Growth* (Cambridge, Mass., 1960), *passim*; Pitirim Sorokin, *Social and Cultural Dynamics* (Boston, 1957), pp. 523–532.

32. Robert N. Bellah, *Tokugawa Religion* (Glencoe, Ill., 1957), p. 115.

33. The *oyakata-kogata* relationships existed also in the villages between the peasants' *oyakata-uchi* and *kogata-uchi* (parent-house and child-house); the peasant of the child-house had the marriages of his children arranged by the peasant of the parent-house, and a child-house peasant was careful not to outdo the peasant of the parent-house in any manifest way.

It is interesting that the same notions of *oyabun* and *kobun*, with similar almost feudal relationships between employers and underlings, persist even in present-day Japan. The extraordinary deference to the boss, to authority of any type, often puzzles foreigners. The boss is right because of his position; his views are not questioned although the same opinion or approach from a man in a lesser position may not stir a leaf. In the field of scholarship, quotations from authorities bear tremendous weight; current imported theories are often applied uncritically to conditions for which the theories

were never meant. It may perhaps be possible to trace these attitudes back to the deeply ingrained Confucian ideology of Tokugawa days.

34. Kanno Watarō, *Nihon kaisha kigyō hassei shi no kenkyū*
(Studies in the development of the company form of enterprise in
Japan; Tokyo, 1931), p. 648.

35. Miyamoto, *Ōsaka shōnin* (The Osaka merchants; Tokyo, 1958),
p. 123.

36. The *kanban* is the wooden nameplate on a store, often artis-
tically designed with calligraphy. The *noren* is a blue cloth hang-
ing over the entrance, still used today for restaurants and kimono
shops.

37. Miyamoto, *Ōsaka shōnin*, p. 108.

38. Miyamoto, *Ōsaka*, p. 109.

39. Miyamoto, *Ōsaka shōnin*, p. 123.

40. Tsuchiya Takao, *Nihon ni okeru keieisha seishin no hattatsu*
(The development of managerial mentalities in Japan: Tokyo,
1957), p. 34.

41. Miyamoto, *Ōsaka shōnin*, p. 131.

42. Shibusawa Eiichi, ed., *Meiji shōkō shi* (History of Meiji trade
and industry; Tokyo, 1911), p. 19.

43. Miyamoto, *Ōsaka*, p. 162.

44. The Genroku period was the classic period of culture and art
and of economic prosperity as a result of the national unification and
the long peace. The samurai turned to literature and philosophy;
the merchants prospered and spread luxury consumption.

45. See Bellah, p. 159.

46. *Ibid.*, p. 160.

47. *Ibid.*, p. 174.

48. For a brief and very clear account of the Meiji Restoration
itself, see Edwin O. Reischauer, *Japan, Past and Present* (New York,
1946), pp. 108–141.

49. Nomura Kentarō, *Ishin zengo* (Before and after the Restoration; Tokyo, 1941), pp. 106–113.

50. Inoue Kaoru (1835–1915) belonged to the Choshu group in
the Meiji government and became known particularly for his role
in economic planning and the encouragement of industry. He occupied leading positions in the Ministry of Finance, became foreign
minister in 1885, and held other ministerial positions off and on until
his death. He was the Mitsui zaibatsu's stanchest friend and saved
it from disaster several times. For an account of Minomura, see
Chapter Six.

51. Ōsaka shiyakusho (Osaka City Office), ed., *Meiji Taishō Ōsaka
shi shi* (History of Osaka City during the Meiji and Taishō eras;
Tokyo, 1935), III, 359–360.

52. Terao Kōji, *Meiji shoki Kyōto keizai shi* (Economic history of Kyoto during the early Meiji era; Kyoto, 1943), pp. 557–562.

53. Kanno, *Nihon kaisha*, p. 325.

54. *Ibid.*, pp. 367–368.

55. Shibusawa Eiichi, ed., *Meiji shōkō shi*, pp. 212–213.

56. Takahashi Kamekichi, *Meiji Taishō sangyō hattatsu shi* (The history of manufacturing during the Meiji and Taishō eras; Tokyo, 1929), pp. 105–106.

57. *Ibid.*, p. 236.

58. Takegoshi, *Nihon keizai shi*, VI, 110.

59. *Commercial Reports of Her Majesty's Consuls in Japan, 1868* (London, 1869), p. 22.

60. Ōkubo Toshimichi (1830–1878) was one of the Satsuma clique and a chief organizer of the Restoration itself, together with Iwakura, Saigō, and Kido. In 1871 he went with the Iwakura group to Europe as minister of finance. The famous encouragement of industry (*sho-kusan kōgyō*) policy as well as the land-tax reform were mainly his work. He was assassinated in 1878 because of his dictatorial methods.

61. Honjō Eijirō, *Nihon no keizai to shisō* (Japanese economy and thought; Kyoto, 1943), pp. 336–350.

62. Kanno Watarō, "Tsūshō kaisha, kawase kaisha" (The trade and finance companies), in Honjō Eijirō, ed., *Meiji ishin keizai shi kenkyū* (Studies in the economic history of the Meiji Restoration; Tokyo, 1930), pp. 105–300.

63. Kanno, *Nihon kaisha*, pp. 606–607.

64. *Ibid.*, p. 49.

65. *Commercial Reports, 1869–1870*, pp. 12–13.

66. Katō Toshihiko, "Development of the Monetary System," in Shibusawa Keizō, ed., *Japanese Society of the Meiji Era*, tr. S. H. Culbertson and Kimura Michiko (Tokyo, 1958), p. 196.

67. Kanno Watarō, "Kokuritsu ginkō" (The national banks), in Honjō, *Meiji ishin keizai*, p. 337.

68. *Meiji zaisei shi* (The Meiji financial history), ed. Meiji zaisei shi hensan kai (The Meiji Financial History Editorial Board; Toyko, 1905), XIII, 245.

69. Tsuchiya Takao, *Nihon no seishō* (Japan's political merchants; Tokyo, 1956), pp. 155–156.

70. *Ibid.*, pp. 160–161.

71. Honjō, *Nihon no keizai*, pp. 383ff.

72. *Ibid.*, p. 384.

73. *Ibid.*, p. 387.

74. Ōsaka shiyakusho, ed., II, 842.

75. *Ibid.*, II, 624–625.

76. *Ibid.*, III, 363.

77. *Ibid.*, II, 478–479, 576–579, 516–517.

78. *Ibid.*, II, 527–530.

79. *Ibid.*, II, 631.

80. *Ōsaka fu shi* (History of Osaka prefecture), ed. Ōsaka fu (Osaka, 1903), II, 8–10.

81. *Ibid.*, II, 9–10.

82. Samuel P. Hayes, Jr., "Personality and Culture Problems," in Bert F. Hoselitz, ed., *The Progress of Underdeveloped Areas* (Chicago, 1952), p. 207.

II. THE SAMURAI CLASS

1. Herbert Norman, *Japan's Emergence as a Modern State*, 3rd ed. (New York, 1948), p. 82.

2. G. B. Sansom, *The Western World and Japan* (New York, 1951), pp. 110–111.

3. The samurai had existed since the ninth century as a distinct class of men of arms who combined warfare and farming. They farmed in times of peace and followed their manorial lords to battle. But Nobunaga and especially Hideyoshi drew these men together in the new castle towns and severed them from the farms. This division of society into the commoners who farmed and the samurai who were given stipends for the protection of peace marked the beginning of the feudal system, which reached its height under the Tokugawa bakufu.

4. See Nitobe Inazō, *Bushido, The Soul of Japan*, 17th ed. (Tokyo, 1911), *passim*.

5. Sakada Yoshio, *Hōken jidai kōki no chōnin seikatsu* (The life of the townsmen during the later part of the feudal era; Tokyo, 1950), pp. 6–7.

6. Fukuzawa Yukichi, *The Autobiography of Fukuzawa Yukichi*, tr. Kiyooka Eiichi (Tokyo, 1948), p. 11.

7. *Ibid.*, p. 3.

8. Honjō Eijirō, *Social and Economic History*, p. 216.

9. This system was introduced in 1635 and was kept in force until 1862. The daimyo traveled with large retinues of samurai; they also had to maintain expensive mansions in Edo for their families and for those samurai who had to remain there during the daimyo's year of absence.

10. Honjō, *Social and Economic History*, p. 217.

11. The use of the terms "lower samurai" and "higher samurai" is very common but leads to a great deal of ambiguity. It is usually asserted that the lower samurai were the carriers of the *sonnō jōi* movement and the Meiji Restoration. But Albert Craig has shown convincingly that the identification of the *sonnō jōi* movement with the lower samurai is meaningless, if not positively wrong. It is mean-

ingless if a classification is adopted that designates some 85–90 percent of all samurai as lower-class members, and it is historically wrong if the division is drawn between the groups of *shi* and *sotsu*, each constituting roughly half of the total. The term "lower samurai" in my context simply means those who were so poor that they had to resort to some economic activity for a living. Nothing is asserted about their numbers, yet they apparently comprised a majority of the samurai class. It will be shown, however, that this economic condition of itself did not make these lower samurai economic innovators. They had no monopoly on the political, ideological, or economic reconstruction of Meiji Japan. See Albert Craig, "The Restoration Movement in Chōshū," *The Journal of Asian Studies* 18.2:187–197 (February 1959).

12. Fukuzawa Yukichi, "Kyūhanjō" (The conditions in the old han), in *Fukuzawa Yukichi zenshū* (The Fukuzawa Yukichi collection, Tokyo, Jiji shinpōsha [The Jiji Newspaper Publishing Co.], 1926), VI, 677–680.

13. The peasant wives and daughters spun cotton and the samurai women silk; thus even here a distinction was maintained. The Yonezawa silk cloth, a samurai home-employment product, attained national fame.

14. Yamaguchi, "Opening of Japan," p. 37.

15. Yanagida Kunio, *Japanese Manners and Customs in the Meiji Era*, tr. Charles S. Terry (Tokyo, 1957), p. 95.

16. Cf. Craig, p. 188, esp. n. 4.

17. The samurai were told in official documents that in Western countries like England and France all people were equal and had to work for their sustenance and that in Japan, too, everyone should work to make Japan prosperous. Marius B. Jansen, *Sakamoto Ryōma and the Meiji Restoration* (Princeton, 1961), pp. 361–368, has a good description of the process of abolishing samurai privileges in Tosa han.

18. Takahashi Kamekichi, *Meiji Taishō sangyō hattatsu shi*, p. 101.

19. Kabushiki kaisha 77 ginkō (The 77th Bank, Ltd.), ed., *77 nen shi* (History of 77 years; Tokyo, 1954), pp. 11–13.

20. Takahashi, *Meiji Taishō sangyō hattatsu shi*, pp. 101–102.

21. Kikkawa Hidezō, *Shizoku jusan no kenkyū* (Studies in samurai employment; Tokyo, 1935), p. 49.

22. *Ibid.*, pp. 62–63.

23. Yanagida, p. 95.

24. Tsuchiya Takao, ed., *Meiji zenki keizai shi kenkyū* (Studies in the economic history of the first part of the Meiji era; Tokyo, 1944), p. 212.

25. A militarist group in the government under the leadership of Saigō Takamori tried to use the persisting tensions between Korea

and Japan to instigate war; they wanted to solve internal difficulties by the time-honored method of turning the attention of the dissatisfied toward an external enemy. The debate over Korea came to a head in 1873: Iwakura Tomomi and the men who had toured the Western countries with him were dead set against any military adventure; Saigō and a few of his followers resigned and returned to Satsuma. Saigō then became the leader of the dissatisfied elements in the Satsuma Rebellion.

26. The conscription law had been promulgated in 1873; the Satsuma Rebellion was thus the first opportunity to test the new army of peasant draftees who had been trained according to Prussian discipline. Their victory over Japan's best samurai was seen as a victory of the new era over all reactionary elements.

27. Akashi Teruo and Suzuki Norihisa, *Nihon kinyū shi, Meiji hen* (History of Japanese banking, Meiji volume; Tokyo, 1957), p. 49.

28. *Ibid.*

29. *Ibid.*, pp. 52–53.

30. *Ibid.*, p. 58.

31. The very word "national" (*kokuritsu*) helped to convey the idea of a public function and lent distinction. In the Japanese mind a *kokuritsu* institution is almost automatically superior to a *shiritsu* (private) one. The great prize for a student is his admission to a *kokuritsu* school, and it is not only because of its lower tuition and high academic standards.

32. Akashi and Suzuki, p. 52.

33. Kanno, *Nihon kaisha*, p. 352.

34. Takahashi Kamekichi, *Waga kuni kigyō no shiteki hatten* (The historical development of our country's enterprises; Tokyo, 1956), pp. 177–178.

35. Kabushiki kaisha 77 ginkō, ed., pp. 54–55.

36. *Meiji zaisei shi*, XIII, 256–257.

37. *Ginkō kyoku dai niji hōkoku* (The second report of the Banking Bureau), ed. Ōkura shō (Tokyo, 1879–80), p. 129. The nobility (*kazoku*) included after 1869 the former *kuge*, blood relations of the imperial family, and the former feudal lords (*kō*). According to the Nobility Law of 1884, the following ranking was established: *kō* (prince), *kō* (marquis), *haku* (count), *shi* (viscount), and *dan* (baron). Noble titles of lower rank were given to prominent persons in the government and other men of merit.

38. *Meiji zaisei shi*, XIII, 603–614.

39. *Ginkō benran* (Bank handbook), ed. Ōkura shō (Ministry of Finance; Tokyo, 1911), pp. 496–497.

40. *Meiji zaisei shi*, XIII, 10–11.

41. *Shibusawa Eiichi denki shiryō* (Biographical material on Shi-

busawa Eiichi), ed. Shibusawa Seien kinen zaidan ryūmonsha (The Shibusawa Seien Dragon Door Memorial Foundation; Tokyo, 1957–1958), IV, 293, 295–312; V, 313.

42. Kanno, *Nihon kaisha*, p. 670.

43. Iwakura (1825–1883) was a *kuge* and the main organizer of the overthrow of the bakufu; it was he who directed the coup d'état of 1867. He was opposed to the liberal democratic wing and stressed the prerogatives of the emperor.

44. Kikkawa, *Shizoku jusan*, p. 99.

45. Azuma Tōsaku, *Shizoku jusan shi* (History of samurai employment; Tokyo, 1942), p. 191.

46. Kikkawa, *Shizoku jusan*, p. 99.

47. *Ibid.*, pp. 373–387.

48. Azuma, pp. 694–696.

49. *Ibid.*, pp. 191–229.

50. Shizuoka had been the domain of the Tokugawa family before its victory over the Hideyoshi forces and so differed from the daimyo trusteeships of the han. After his victory of 1600, Ieyasu took over direct control of Osaka, Nagasaki, and many other important places, harbors, and mines. The Tokugawa family thus owned a territory of one million koku. The direct political control of the bakufu extended over one fourth of Japan, via the collateral families (*shinpan*) of Owari, Kii, and Mito.

51. Azuma, pp. 6–7.

52. *Ibid.*, pp. 5–60.

53. *Ibid.*, p. 19.

54. *Ibid.*, pp. 386–387.

55. *Ibid.*, p. 382.

56. Kikkawa, *Shizoku jusan*, p. 68.

57. Azuma, pp. 351–352.

58. Ragnar Nurkse, *Problems of Capital Formation in Underdeveloped Countries*, 4th ed. (Oxford, 1955), pp. 37–38.

III. RURAL ENTREPRENEURSHIP

1. For an extensive and excellent treatment of Tokugawa agriculture, see Smith, *Agrarian Origins*.

2. Tsuchiya Takao and Ono Michio, *Kinsei Nihon nōson keizai shiron* (A historical treatise on the Modern Japanese rural economy; Tokyo, 1933), pp. 62–63.

3. Sekiyama Naotarō, *Nihon no jinkō* (The population of Japan; Tokyo, 1959), p. 70.

4. Cf. Takahashi Shinichi, *Yōgakuron* (OnWestern studies; Tokyo, 1939), pp. 90–92.

5. Kobayashi Yoshimasa, *Nihon shihonshugi no seisei to sono kiban* (The emergence of Japanese capitalism and its foundation; Tokyo, 1949), p. 43.

6. In the last decades of the Tokugawa period scholars frequently wrote against land reclamations, insisting that because of them yields on the old lands declined. Deforestation caused floods; old fields were either neglected or even deserted, because of the easier rent terms on the new land and because new land did not fall under the bakufu restrictions with respect to division and sale. *Nihon keizai shi jiten* (Dictionary of Japanese economic history), ed. Keizai shi kenkyūkai (Tokyo, 1954), I, 869.

7. See W. G. Beasley, "Feudal Revenue in Japan at the Time of the Restoration," *Journal of Asian Studies*, 19.3:255–272 (May 1960). The reports of the han are not uniform, but vary with respect to what is or what is not included in the total value product of the han; some apparently included cash crops while others enumerated them separately. The very terse reports which have no comments attached are therefore not easy to interpret. Japanese economic historians do not seem to rely much on the evidence from these sources.

8. Kobata Jun, "Kinsei keizai no hattatsu" (The development of the modern economy), in Kobata Jun, ed., *Kinsei shakai* (Modern society; Tokyo, 1952), IV, 216.

9. Land reclamations and improvements on a large scale were first undertaken by the bakufu under the shogun Yoshimune in the first half of the eighteenth century. Though later shogun imitated Yoshimune's policies, it was merchant capital that came to dominate land reclamations. See Hall, pp. 63–65; also Miyamoto Mataji, "Tokugawa ki Ōsaka kinkō no nōgyō keisei" (Management of agriculture in the vicinity of Osaka during the Tokugawa period), in Miyamoto Mataji, ed., *Shōgyōteki nōgyō no tenkai* (The spread of the commercialization of agriculture; Osaka, 1954), p. 12.

10. Miyamoto, *ibid.*, 14–15.

11. *Ibid.*, pp. 15–16.

12. Miyamoto, *Ōsaka chōnin*, p. 168.

13. Miyamoto, *Ōsaka shōnin*, p. 98.

14. *Jinushi sei no keisei* (The formation of the landlord system), ed. Meiji shiryō kenkyū renrakukai (Meiji Historic Material Research Association; Tokyo, 1957), pp. 150–151.

15. Egashira Tsuneharu, *Ōmi shōnin* (The Omi merchants; Tokyo 1959), pp. 110–127; also Kanno, *Ōsaka keizai*, pp. 104–120.

16. Smith, *Agrarian Origins*, p. 83.

17. Egashira, pp. 105–108.

18. Fujita Gorō, *Nihon kindai sangyō no seisei* (The creation of Japan's modern industry; Tokyo, 1948), pp. 247–248.

19. Horie Eiichi, *Meiji ishin no shakai kōzō* (Structure of society at the time of the Restoration; Tokyo, 1954), p. 110.

20. *Ibid.*, p. 107.

21. Yasuoka Shigeaki, "Shōgyōteki hatten to nōson kōzō" (The process of commercialization and village structure), in Miyamoto, ed., *Shōgyōteki nōgyō*, p. 112.

22. Yamaguchi Kazuo, *Meiji zenki keizai no bunseki* (Analysis of the economy of the early Meiji era; Tokyo, 1956), p. 34.

23. Smith, *Agrarian Origins*, p. 69.

24. Horie, p. 105.

25. Tsuchiya Takao, ed., *Hōken shakai hōkai katei no kenkyū* (Studies in the disintegration process of feudal society; Kyoto, 1927), pp. 391–483.

26. Horie, pp. 108–109.

27. *Ibid.*, p. 151.

28. Yasuoka, p. 71.

29. Horie, p. 155.

30. Smith, *Agrarian Origins*, p. 73.

31. Fujita, p. 241.

32. Smith, *Agrarian Origins*, p. 174.

33. Fujita, p. 101.

34. Horie, p. 164.

35. Smith, *Agrarian Origins*, pp. 121–122.

36. *Ibid.*, p. 147.

37. Shōji Kichinosuke, *Henkaku ni okeru nōmin shisō no mondai* (The problem of peasant thought during the period of change; Tokyo, 1952), p. 27.

38. Nishinoiri Aiichi, *Asano, Shibusawa, Ōkawa, Furukawa Concern tokuhon* (The Asano, Shibusawa, Ōkawa, Furukawa Concern reader; Tokyo, 1937), pp. 97–100.

39. Hara Kunizō, ed., *Hara Rokurō ō den* (Biography of the Honorable Hara Rokurō; Tokyo, 1923), I, 8–13.

40. *Dai Nihon gaikoku bōeki* (The foreign trade of great Japan), ed. Nōshōmushō shōmukyoku (Ministry of Agriculture and Trade, Department of Trade; Tokyo, 1911), p. 6.

41. Thomas C. Smith, *Political Change and Industrial Development in Japan: Government Enterprise, 1868–1880* (Stanford, 1955), p. 57. Smith gives here a very good account of the first phase of Japanese mechanical silk reeling.

42. The House of Ono, as a partner of the First National Bank, borrowed from it 1.3 million yen as additional capital for its silk-reeling investments. When, on government order, the reserves had to be replenished, Ono was found insolvent and went into bankruptcy in 1875. *Nihon keizai shi jiten*, I, 181.

43. Shōji Kichinosuke, *Meiji ishin no keizai kōzō* (The structure

of the economy of the time of the Meiji Restoration; Tokyo, 1958), pp. 306-308.

44. *Zaikai bukko ketsubutsu den* (Biographies of outstanding men in the business world), ed. Jitsugyō no shakaisha (The Business World Co.; Tokyo, 1936), I, 342-348.

45. *Nihon sangyō shi taikei, sōron hen* (An outline history of Japanese industry, summary volume), ed. Chihō shi kenkyū kyōgikai (Regional History Research Association; Tokyo, 1961), p. 243.

46. Azuma, pp. 191-229.

47. *Ibid.*, p. 639.

48. Ōkubo Shigetarō, ed., *Gumma ken sangyōka meikan* (Biographical directory of silk industrialists of Gumma prefecture; Maebashi, 1910), *passim*.

49. Sata Kaiseki, a Buddhist monk and scholar, made himself the spokesman of the dissatisfied elements; he wrote in favor of shutting out foreign goods completely, and he organized rallies and formed associations to fight against imports of Western goods. Honjō Eijirō, ed., *Meiji ishin keizai shi kenkyū* (Studies in the economic history of the Meiji Restoration; Tokyo, 1930), pp. 761-765.

50. Hattori Shisō and Shinobu Seizaburō, *Meiji senshoku keizai shi* (Economic History of Meiji dyeing and weaving; Tokyo, 1937), pp. 104-120.

51. Kinugawa Taiichi, *Honpō menshi bōseki shi* (History of Japanese cotton spinning; Osaka, 1937), III, 49-85.

52. *Ibid.*, II, 215-216.

53. *Ibid.*, IV, 237-239.

54. *Ibid.*, IV, 205.

55. *Ibid.*, V, 31.

56. *Ibid.*, IV, 78-85.

57. *Ibid.*, IV, 362.

58. Yamaguchi, *Meiji zenki keizai*, p. 14. The figures are surprising, at least to me. Professor William Lockwood first pointed out to me the importance of the traditional manufacturing sector.

59. Egashira, *Ōmi shōnin*, p. 105.

60. Yamaguchi, *Meiji zenki keizai*, p. 108.

61. As an illustration of this gradual decline of vegetable-oil production, Furushima traces the records of a rich farmer and oil producer in the Kinki area. From 1868 to 1893 the amount of vegetable oil produced kept declining from 68 koku to 21 koku, and oil extraction was finally stopped completely in 1897. Furushima Toshio, *Kisei jinushi sei no seisei to tenkai* (The emergence and spread of the parasitic landlord system; Tokyo, 1952), p. 109.

62. Takahashi Kamekichi, *Meiji Taishō sangyō*, p. 254.

63. Tōbata Seiichi and Ohkawa Kazushi, eds., *Nihon no keizai to nōgyō* (Japanese economy and agriculture; Tokyo, 1956), I, 65.

64. Tsuchiya Takao and Okazaki Saburō, *Nihon shihonshugi hattatsu shi gaisetsu* (An outline history of the development of Japanese capitalism; Tokyo, 1937), p. 205.

65. Tōbata and Ohkawa, p. 375.

66. *Nihon keizai shi jiten*, I, 556.

67. Ohkawa Kazushi et al., *The Growth Rate of the Japanese Economy since 1878* (Tokyo, 1957), p. 51.

68. *Ibid.*, p. 58.

69. *Jinushi sei no keisei*, p. 101.

70. Furushima, p. 92.

71. *Ibid.*, p. 103.

72. *Ibid.*, p. 104.

73. See R. P. Dore, "The Meiji Landlord: Good or Bad?" *Journal of Asian Studies*, 18.3 (May 1959). Dore gives a survey of the research and the variations in the evaluation of the landlords by Japanese economic historians. The bone of contention is whether the "parasitic landlords" were forerunners of capitalism or whether they strengthened feudal control over the land. The Marxist school labels them a feudalistic element; according to the Marxists, the Meiji Restoration itself was a feudal and not a bourgeois revolution. For a more comprehensive treatment of the development of tenancy during the Meiji period, see R. P. Dore, *Land Reform in Japan* (Oxford, 1959), pp. 57–68.

74. Furushima, pp. 99–108.

75. Henry Rosovsky and Kazushi Ohkawa, "The Role of Agriculture in Modern Japanese Economic Development," *Economic Development and Cultural Change*, Research Center in Economic Development and Cultural Change, University of Chicago, 9.1:2.51 (October 1960).

76. *Ibid.*, p. 45.

77. *Ibid.*, p. 46.

78. The same conclusion is reached by Lockwood, although he maintains that agricultural productivity was not promoted, but rather hindered, by the landlords. Certainly many disadvantages, social and economic, have to be attributed to the landlord system. William W. Lockwood, *The Economic Development of Japan: Growth and Structural Change, 1868–1938* (Princeton, 1954), pp. 194–196.

IV. THE INITIATIVE FROM THE CENTER

1. Conveniently summarized in Henry Rosovsky, *Capital Formation in Japan, 1868–1940* (Glencoe, Ill., 1961), pp. 57–58.

2. Sansom, *The Western World and Japan*, is one of the best references.

3. Francis Xavier had the highest praise for the Japanese, calling

them by far the most intelligent and ethically most noble of all the newly discovered peoples. He was most impressed by their aristocratic demeanor, their sense of honor and their honesty, the purity of their family life, and the relatively high standards of popular education. Elisabeth Graefin Vitzthum, ed., *Die Briefe des Francisco de Xavier, 1542–1552* (Munich, 1950), pp. 154–155.

4. In the Nagasaki area some 40,000–50,000 had secretly remained Christian and some of them were discovered by a French missionary in 1865. Subsequently, however, the government once more applied the old persecution decrees and banished over 3,000 from Nagasaki to Honshu. But the Iwakura mission of 1871 met hostile demonstrations in several places in Europe and the United States, which denounced them as persecutors of Christians. Consequently, Iwakura cabled to his government demanding immediate repeal of the banishment. In 1873, finally, the old laws were repealed and the public signs denouncing the "wicked religion" were removed. See *Katorikku daijiten* (The Catholic cyclopedia), ed. Jōchi daigaku (Sophia University), 2nd ed. (Tokyo, 1952), I, 716–718.

5. The Bansho shirabesho (place to study barbarian books) changed its name several times after the Restoration, and finally became in 1877 Tokyo University.

6. Two examples will illustrate the nervous attitude of the bakufu toward Western studies. During the great famines of the 1830s the bakufu had sought the advice of students of Western learning and implemented some of their suggestions. But when a few of these men dared to caution against driving British ships from Japanese shores, and advocated at least a partial scrapping of the closed-door policy, they were imprisoned and ended their lives as suicides. When in 1848 an enthusiast presented the German physician in Nagasaki, Philipp Franz von Siebold, with a map of Japan, he was beheaded as a traitor and 37 of his companions were imprisoned.

But such individual examples cannot prove that the bakufu was in general opposed to Western learning. While initially favoring it, with some reservations, it reversed its stand drastically in 1843, banning all Western studies except medicine; this measure resulted from an increased awareness of a foreign menace, notably pressures from Russia in the north. After the opening of the ports the bakufu supported Western studies again. Confucian scholars were divided in their appraisal of Western studies: many were unconditionally opposed, sensing in them a threat to the fundamental values of Confucianism and Japanese tradition. But those who took a positive attitude, according to the "Western science, Japanese ethics" principle, had a decisive influence on Meiji ideology.

For a thorough discussion of the relation between Western studies and Confucian philosophy in the late Tokugawa, see Warren W.

Smith, Jr., *Confucianism in Modern Japan: A Study of Conservatism in Japanese Intellectual History* (Tokyo, 1959), pp. 20–40; Albert M. Craig, *Chōshū in the Meiji Restoration* (Cambridge, Mass., 1961), pp. 128–137; Kosaka Masaaki, *Japanese Thought in the Meiji Era*, tr. David Abosh (Tokyo, 1958), pp. 9–13.

7. In principle there was no difference between Sakuma and Yoshida. Sakuma clearly recognized the technical and even scientific superiority of the West but considered Westerners ethical barbarians. See Sansom, *The Western World*, pp. 253–256. To stress ethical or cultural superiority in the face of technical or military inferiority is nothing new; it happened in Europe repeatedly, notably between the Germans and the English.

8. Yoshida Shōin was beheaded in 1859 because of his antibakufu agitation. One item in the text of his death sentence reads: "He planned to give his opinion regarding foreigners to the Bakufu" (Sansom, *The Western World*, p. 274). On Yoshida Shōin, see also H. van Straelen, *Yoshida Shōin, Forerunner of the Meiji Restoration* (Leiden, 1952).

9. Itō Hirobumi (1841–1909) had taken part in the Iwakura mission to the West, and after the assassination of Ōkubo became minister of the interior. He established the cabinet system in 1885 and became the first prime minister of Japan.

10. Yamagata Aritomo (1838–1922) became, under Itō in 1885, minister of the interior; then he almost took turns with Itō as prime minister. But Itō and Yamagata represented two opposite factions. Itō stood for strong government under civilian control, while Yamagata was a thorough militarist who originated the Japanese militarist tradition that continued until the Second World War.

11. Shinagawa Yajirō (1843–1900) was active in the Ministry of Agriculture and Trade after 1881, and co-organizer of the Kyōdō Unyu Kaisha against Iwasaki's Mitsubishi Company. He was envoy to Germany and finally minister of the interior under Matsukata.

12. Fujii Jintarō, *Outline of Japanese History in the Meiji Era*, tr. H. K. Colton, and K. E. Colton (Tokyo, 1958), p. 24. The Charter Oath was the result of thorough discussions by the Meiji leaders; it outlined briefly the political course to be followed by the government. The oath was read by the emperor in the presence of all daimyo and the members of the new government.

13. The years between 1868 and 1872 were characterized by the strong efforts of the Meiji government to establish Shinto as an official state religion, directed primarily against Buddhism; but these efforts foundered because of the revival and strong resistance of Buddhism, and partly also because of foreign pressure to repeal the ban on Christianity. In 1872 freedom of religion was declared, but the strong official support of Shintoism remained and was closely

linked with Japanese nationalism. See Delmer M. Brown, *Nationalism in Japan: An Introductory Historical Analysis* (Berkeley, 1955), pp. 101–103.

14. Ōkuma Shigenobu (1838–1922) was a Saga samurai and opposed to the *han batsu* (han clique of Satsuma, Choshu, and Tosa) in the Meiji government. He was one of the economic planners, a most outspoken exponent of the railway-building program, and a friend and protector of Iwasaki. In 1889 he lost his right leg in an attack by antiforeign fanatics. He became, after his resignation from the Ministry of Finance in 1881, the main benefactor of Waseda University and acted for a while as its president.

15. Ishii Mitsuru, *Nihon tetsudō sōsetsu shi wa* (Historic narrative on the building of the Japanese railways; Tokyo, 1952), pp. 147–148.

16. These efforts at times took almost ridiculous forms. At the height of the Westernization fever, dance parties were held to promote Western civilization. On April 20, 1887, Prime Minister Itō gave a grand masquerade dance in his official residence in which some 400 distinguished Japanese and foreign guests took part, among them cabinet members like Yamagata, Inoue, and businessmen like Shibusawa and Ōkura. Fujii, p. 313.

17. This fact has probably induced Hattori to argue that the *bummei kaika* was a kind of enlightenment similar to that under Frederick the Great in Prussia, manipulated from above. Hattori Shisō, *Meiji no shisō* (The thought of the Meiji era), Vol. 6 of his *Chosaku shū* (Collected writings; Tokyo, 1955), pp. 166–185.

18. Sansom, *The Western World*, p. 383.

19. Ishii Ryōichi, *Population Pressure and Economic Life in Japan* (Chicago, 1937), pp. 31–37. On the widespread practice of infanticide during the Tokugawa period, see G. B. Sansom, *Japan, A Short Cultural History*, rev. ed. (New York, 1943), pp. 516–517.

20. Tanaka Toyojirō, *Meiji no senkakusha kindai no ijin kō Godai Tomoatsu den* (Biography of the Meiji pioneer and great man of the modern age, Lord Godai Tomoatsu; Osaka, 1921), pp. 347–355.

21. It was the time of the bombardment of Kagoshima in 1863 and of the battle of Shimonoseki in 1864; these events marked a climax of antiforeign sentiment. Satsuma and Choshu han brought the country to the brink of war. But after the lesson learned during these two engagements with foreign superior warships, these two han eventually became the most pro-Western of all.

22. Fujii, p. 43. The disregard of status in this program is noteworthy because up to this point the samurai had been considered the only social group qualified for leadership. And foreign studies were aimed at training an intellectual elite.

23. Tuge Hideomi, *Historical Development of Science and Technology in Japan* (Tokyo, 1961), p. 100.

24. Tsuchiya, ed., *Meiji zenki keizai*, p. 7.

25. Tsuchiya, *Nihon no seishō*, p. 76.

26. Ishii Mitsuru, *Nihon tetsudō sōsetsu*, pp. 139–140.

27. Karazawa Tomitarō, *Nihon kyōiku shi* (History of Japanese education; Tokyo, 1953), pp. 207–208; also Sansom, *The Western World*, p. 460.

28. Egashira Tsuneharu, "Saga-han ni okeru yōshiki kōgyō" (Western-style industry in Saga han), in Honjō Eijirō, ed., *Bakumatsu keizai shi kenkyū* (Studies in the economic history of the late Tokugawa period; Tokyo, 1935), pp. 76–78.

29. Tuge, p. 97. Tuge's total of technicians according to nationalities is 519, while the total according to fields of activity is 560. Apparently there is some double counting in the latter division.

30. *Ibid.*, p. 97.

31. *Meiji zenki zaisei keizai shiryō shūsei* (Collection of material on the finance and economy of the first part of the Meiji era), ed. Ōuchi Hyōe and Tsuchiya Takao (Tokyo, 1931), XVII, 347.

32. The technicians' salaries must be considered in relation to the comparable salaries of Japanese officials. Tuge, p. 97, quotes $500 as the monthly salary of a minister in the departments of the Ministry of Industry, and the salary of the chief of foreign employees in the Department of Railways was about $2,000 per month; he goes on to say that there were some 200 foreign engineers whose salaries were about as high. This would amount to a total of $2.4 million, or about 3.5 million yen per year, at a time when the total budget of the Ministry of Industry was only half a million yen. Actually, 500–600 yen per month is probably closer to the average salary of a foreigner in Japan in the 1880s. In 1876 a French engineer employed at the Tokyo and Yokohama Gas Works received 600 yen per month (*Shibusawa Eiichi denki shiryō*, XII, 409). The monthly income of a carpenter or smith was about 20–25 yen per month, and presidents of local banks earned some 50 yen per month. According to Rathgen, there were in the late 1880s in the whole of Japan only 63 people with annual incomes of 30,000 yen or higher. Karl Rathgen, *Japans Volkswirtschaft und Staatshaushalt* (Leipzig, 1891), pp. 426–429.

33. *Sangyō kyōiku 70 nen shi* (Seventy years of industrial education), ed. Monbushō (Ministry of Education; Tokyo, 1956), pp. 12–13. A few more agricultural schools were opened in the following years in Niigata, Gifu, and Hiroshima prefectures.

34. For a good survey of the government's efforts in the field of agriculture, see R. P. Dore, "Agricultural Improvements in Japan: 1870–1900," *Economic Development and Cultural Change*, vol. 9, no. 1, pt. 2, pp. 93–107.

35. *Sangyō kyōiku 70 nen*, pp. 22–26.

36. *Ibid.*, p. 17.

37. *Ibid.*, pp. 18–19.

38. Tuge, p. 98.

39. *Meiji unyu shi* (History of Meiji transportation), ed. Unyu nippōsha (The Japan Transport Publication Co.; Tokyo, 1913), Chap. 3, p. 73. Each chapter is paginated separately.

40. Inoue Masaru, Viscount, "Japanese Communications, Railroads," in Ōkuma Shigenobu, ed., *Fifty Years of New Japan*, tr. and ed. Marcus B. Huish, 2nd ed. (London, 1910), I, 435–436.

41. Nakayama Yasumasa, ed., *Shinbun shūsei Meiji hennen shi* (Chronological history of the Meiji era compiled from newspapers; Tokyo, 1936), IV, 126–127.

42. Kinugawa, Vols. I–III, *passim*.

43. *Ibid.*, II, 369–428.

44. Takegoshi Yosaburō, ed., *Ōkawa Heizaburō kun den* (Biography of Mr. Ōkawa Heizaburō; Tokyo, 1936), pp. 98–100.

45. *Shibusawa Eiichi denki shiryō*, XII, 150–189.

46. Hara, ed., III, 333.

47. Ōnishi Rihei, *Asabuki Eiji kun den* (Biography of Mr. Asabuki Eiji; Tokyo, 1928), pp. 86–87.

48. The problems of traveling in Japan during the Tokugawa period are aptly and imaginatively described in Oliver Statler, *Japanese Inn*, Pyramid paperback ed. (New York, 1962).

49. Ishii Mitsuru, p. 154.

50. *Meiji unyu shi*, Chap. 1, p. 50.

51. *Nihon tetsudō shi* (History of the Japanese railways), ed. Tetsudō shō (Ministry of Railways; Tokyo, 1935), I, 92–93.

52. *Ibid.*, p. 113.

53. Computed from Rosovsky, *Capital Formation*, p. 25.

54. Takahashi Kamekichi and Aoyama Jirō, *Nihon zaibatsu ron* (A treatise on the Japanese zaibatsu; Tokyo, 1938), p. 43.

55. *Nihon tetsudō shi*, I, 972–973.

56. Computed from Rosovsky, *Capital Formation*, pp. 25–26.

57. The close connection between the economic reforms and military objectives has been made very clear by Egashira Tsuneharu in the following three chapters in Honjō, *Bakumatsu keizai*: "Kōchi-han ni okeru bakumatsu no shinseisaku" (The new policies in Kōchi han in the last years of the Tokugawa period), "Saga-han ni okeru yōshiki kōgyō" (Western-style industry in Saga han), "Takashima tankō ni okeru nichiei kyōdō kigyō" (The joint Anglo-Japanese enterprise at the Takashima coal mine).

58. Egashira Tsuneharu, "Kōchi-han," pp. 119–120.

59. *Meiji unyu shi*, Chap. 3, p. 9.

60. Rosovsky, *Capital Formation*, pp. 165, 198–199.

61. *Ibid.*, p. 25.

62. This is an overstatement; actually the militarists stressed very strongly in the railway debates the need to build railways for the sake of army transportation. But railways were a long-range project while ships could be bought quickly.

63. *Ibid.*, pp. 199–200.

64. Takahashi and Aoyama, pp. 52–53.

65. *Meiji unyu shi*, Chap. 3, pp. 19–22.

66. *Ibid.*, Chap. 3, pp. 68–69, 183.

67. Matsukata Masayoshi (1835–1924) was one of the Satsuma men in the government and became known for his work on the land-tax reform under Ōkubo. During 1878 and 1879, while in Europe, he became well acquainted with financial matters. After his return he moved into the Ministry of Finance and took over from Ōkuma in 1881. In 1896 he served as prime minister.

68. Thomas Smith, *Political Change, passim.*

69. *Meiji zenki zaisei keizai*, XVII, 133–137.

70. Thomas Smith, *Political Change*, p. 48.

71. The Senju Woolen Mill was not sold out but was transferred to army management in 1888. It was one of the most important government enterprises and supplied the army with uniforms. Also retained were the Yokosuka Shipyard and the Akabane Construction Plant, both under the minister of the navy. The government did not want to depend for its military supplies on private industry.

72. Arizawa Hiromi, ed., *Gendai Nihon sangyō kōza* (A compendium of present-day Japanese industry; Tokyo, 1959), I, 59.

73. Takahashi and Aoyama, p. 56.

74. Ohkawa et al., p. 245.

75. Wada Hisajirō, *Asano Cement enkaku shi* (The history of Asano Cement; Tokyo, 1940), pp. 74–75.

76. Takahashi and Aoyama, p. 59.

77. Tsuchiya, ed., *Meiji zenki keizai*, p. 78.

78. *Ibid.*, p. 92.

79. Ohkawa et al., p. 79.

80. *Ibid.*, p. 79.

81. Kajinishi Mitsuhaya, *Nihon ni okeru sangyō shihon no keisei* (The formation of industrial capital in Japan; Tokyo, 1949), I, 37.

82. Yamaguchi, *Meiji zenki keizai*, pp. 93–94.

83. *Ibid.*, p. 100.

V. THE SPIRIT OF ENTERPRISE IN THE PRIVATE SECTOR

1. Mori Arinori (1847–1889) had been sent to England by his daimyo, Shimazu, prior to the Restoration; after 1868 he was employed in various embassies and became one of the most liberal-

minded men in the Meiji government. Under Itō he was Japan's first education minister and started a thorough educational reform. He was assassinated on the day of the promulgation of the constitution, in 1889, apparently because some fanatics feared he might introduce Christianity as a state religion.

2. This, of course, does not mean that the English universities educated their students primarily for business; it is a matter of emphasis on values, and in England where economics was first developed as a field of study, business pursuits tended to be valued more highly and to receive more attention than in the Prussian-oriented academic world. On the "Prussian" type of education in Japan, see Chitoshi Yanaga, *Japan since Perry*, consulting ed. Ralph E. Turner (New York, 1949), pp. 102–103.

3. Kosaka Masaaki, *Japanese Thought in the Meiji Era* (Tokyo, 1958), p. 83.

4. Shibusawa Eiichi, *Jitsugyō kōen* (Lectures on enterprise; Tokyo, 1913), II, 36–38.

5. Fukuzawa, *Autobiography*, p. 224.

6. *Fukuzawa Yukichi zenshū*, IX, 165–182.

7. Kurihara Shinichi, *Meiji kaika shiron* (An historical essay on Meiji civilization; Tokyo, 1944), pp. 11–12.

8. Tanaka Sōgorō, *Iwasaki Yatarō den* (Biography of Iwasaki Yatarō; Tokyo, 1955), pp. 205–209.

9. Kyugoro Obata, *An Interpretation of the Life of Viscount Shibusawa* (Tokyo, 1937), pp. 43–59.

10. Suzuki Gorō, *Suzuki Tōsaburō den* (Biography of Suzuki Tōsaburō; Tokyo, 1956), pp. 104–107.

11. Shibusawa spoke on many occasions, often extemporaneously, and most of these speeches and casual remarks were preserved for posterity by his admiring followers. His biographical material is now being edited; 42 volumes were printed in 1962, and more are to follow. This collection, *Shibusawa Eiichi denki shiryō*, contains over 4,000 speeches and talks of various descriptions by Shibusawa. For a good selection of speeches, see Shibusawa Eiichi, *Shōgyō dōtoku kōwa* (Discourses on business ethics) and *Jitsugyō kōen.*

12. Minamoto Yoshiie (1041–1106) was a general of the House of Genji in its long struggle against the Heike. He was called by his people the greatest samurai of Japan.

13. *Ryūmon zasshi* (Ryūmon periodical), ed. Ryūmonsha (The Dragon Door Company; Tokyo, May 1889), pp. 45–46.

14. Godai Ryūsaku, *Godai Tomoatsu den* (Biography of Godai Tomoatsu; Tokyo, 1933), p. 486.

15. Usaki Kumakichi, *Toyokawa Ryōhei* (Tokyo, 1922), p. 130.

16. Godai, p. 471.

17. Shibusawa Eiichi, *Jitsugyō kōen*, I, 227.

18. *Ibid.*, p. 199.

19. Shibusawa Eiichi, *Shōgyō dōtoku*, p. 16.

20. Tsuchiya Takao, *Nihon no keieisha seishin* (Managerial attitudes in Japan; Tokyo, 1959), p. 82.

21. *Ibid.*, p. 76.

22. Alexander Gerschenkron, "Economic Backwardness in Historical Perspective," in Bert F. Hoselitz, ed., *The Progress of Underdeveloped Areas* (Chicago, 1952), pp. 59–61.

23. *Ginkō tsūshinroku* (Bank correspondence records), ed. Ginkō shūkaijo (The Banking Center; Tokyo, January 20, 1886), pp. 514–515.

24. *Ginkō benran*, pp. 208–210.

25. *Nihon keizai tōkei sōkan* (Survey of Japanese economic statistics), ed. Asahi shinbunsha (Asahi Newspaper Co.; Tokyo, 1930), p. 457.

26. *Meiji 16 nen Tōkyō fu tōkeisho* (Statistics of Tokyo prefecture for Meiji 16 [1883]), ed. Tokyo fu; Tokyo, 1883), pp. 171–172.

27. *Meiji 14 nen tōkeihyō* (Statistical table of Meiji 14 [1881]), ed. Tokyo fu; Tokyo, 1881), pp. 155–157.

28. *Meiji 16 nen*, pp. 155–157.

29. *Meiji 14 nen*, pp. 129–139.

30. Tachikawa Tokuji, ed., *Meiji kōgyō shi, tetsudō hen* (History of Meiji industry, railway volume; Tokyo, 1932), p. 278.

31. *Meiji unyu shi*, p. 126.

32. *Meiji bunka zenshū, keizai hen* (The Meiji culture collection, economy volume), ed. Meiji bunka kenkyūkai (Research Council on Meiji Culture; Tokyo, 1957), p. 492.

33. Takahashi Kamekichi, *Meiji Taishō sangyō*, pp. 152–153.

34. Tsuchiya and Okazaki, pp. 248–249.

35. Kikkawa Hidezō, *Meiji ishin shakai keizai shi kenkyū* (Studies in the social and economic history of the Meiji Restoration; Tokyo, 1943), pp. 309–317.

36. Kinugawa, III, 207–209.

37. Arizawa, I, 66.

38. Kinugawa, II, 369–428.

39. *Ibid.*, IV, *passim*.

40. *Shigyōkai 50 nen* (Fifty years of the Paper Manufacturers' Association), ed. Hakushinsha (The Progress Co.; Tokyo, 1937), pp. 309–317.

41. *Ibid.*, p. 12.

42. Shibusawa Eiichi, *Jijoden* (Autobiography; Tokyo, 1938), p. 845.

43. Takegoshi, *Ōkawa*, pp. 98–100.

44. *Shigyōkai 50 nen*, pp. 27–28.

45. *Nihon Cement kabushiki kaisha 70 nen shi, hon hen* (Seventy-year history of Nihon Cement, Ltd., main volume), ed. Nihon Cement kabushiki kaisha shashi hensan iinkai (Editorial Committee for the History of Nihon Cement, Ltd.; Tokyo, 1955), p. 7.

46. Utsunomiya Saburō, as a leading expert on physics and chemistry, went with the Iwakura mission to Europe, and in 1875 visited the Philadelphia exhibition to study the latest cement production techniques. He had been entrusted with the technical direction of the Fukagawa Cement Factory. Wada Hisajirō, *Asano Cement*, pp. 25–32.

47. Nishida Hirotarō, *Meiji kōgyō shi, kagaku kōgyō* (History of Meiji industry, chemical industries volume; Tokyo, 1925), p. 461.

48. *Ibid.*, pp. 471–472.

49. Onoda Cement seizō kabushiki kaisha (Onoda Cement Manufacturing Company), ed., *Sōgyō 50 nen shi* (Fifty years after the founding; Tokyo, 1931), p. 108.

50. *Shibusawa Eiichi denki shiryō*, XI, 443–445.

51. German technicians who were called to demonstrate the use of imported machines were able to blow 350 bottles per hour while the Japanese workers made only 80. *Ibid.*, p. 451.

52. *Ibid.*, pp. 440–441.

53. *Meiji zenki zaisei keizai*, XVII, 133–137.

54. *Nihon tekkō shi, Meiji hen* (History of Japanese iron and steel, Meiji volume), ed. Nihon tekkō shi hensan iinkai (Editorial Committee for the History of Japanese Iron and Steel; Tokyo, 1945), p. 118.

55. *Ibid.*, p. 117.

56. *Ibid.*, pp. 117–118.

57. *Shibusawa Eiichi denki shiryō*, X, 668.

58. *Ibid.*, pp. 608–621.

59. Shibusawa Eiichi, *Jijoden*, pp. 551–553.

60. Asano Taijirō, *Asano Sōichirō* (Tokyo, 1939), appendix, pp. 5–6.

61. *Shibusawa Eiichi denki shiryō*, XI, 412–414.

62. *Nihon Cement*, pp. 6–7.

63. Shibusawa Eiichi, *Shōgyō dōtoku*, p. 3.

64. Max Weber, *The Protestant Ethic and the Spirit of Capitalism* (New York, 1956), p. 53.

65. I am indebted to Professor Reinhard Bendix for pointing out to me this functional equivalence between the Puritan spirit of capitalism and the mentality of the Meiji entrepreneurs.

66. *Shigyōkai 50 nen*, p. 9.

67. Gerschenkron, "Economic Backwardness in Historical Perspective," p. 24.

VI. THE ZAIBATSU BUILDERS

1. Katsuda Teiji, *Ōkura, Nezu Concern tokuhon* (The Ōkura and Nezu Concern reader; Tokyo, 1937), pp. 112–113.
2. *Ibid.*, p. 125.
3. *Ibid.*, p. 64.
4. Takahashi and Aoyama, p. 43.
5. Tsuchiya, *Nihon no seishō*, p. 67.
6. Takahashi and Aoyama, pp. 50–51.
7. *Ibid.*, p. 58.
8. The Mitsui constitution provided that the six-member families would be under the leadership of the oldest, Hachirōemon. When he retired, the next in line, Hachirōbei, would become Hachirōemon and the third move into second place. The individual member of the large family concern was assigned only a fixed sum that he could spend. If anyone refused to obey these regulations, he was forced into retirement and his name was taken off the family list. Honjo, *Social and Economic History*, p. 306.
9. Wada Hidekichi, *Mitsui Concern tokuhon* (The Mitsui Concern reader; Tokyo, 1937), p. 39.
10. Tsuchiya, *Nihon no seishō*, p. 76.
11. All three houses of Mitsui, Ono, and Shimada held large deposits of government funds with no rulings on reserves. In 1874 the government suddenly introduced a one-third reserve requirement, and at the same time started to call in deposits from Ono, which had overinvested and could not meet its obligations; Ono went into bankruptcy, and Shimada closed spontaneously. Mitsui, however, had been warned beforehand by Inoue, and Mitsui had thus gained time to prepare the needed reserves. Takahashi and Aoyama, p. 49; also Shibusawa Eiichi. *Jijoden*, pp. 396–401.
12. Wada Hidekichi, pp. 86–87.
13. Tsuchiya, *Nihon no seishō*, pp. 115–116.
14. Masuda Takashi, *Jijo Masuda Takashi ō den* (Autobiography of Masuda Takashi; Tokyo, 1939), p. 175.
15. *Ibid.*, p. 292.
16. *Ibid.*, p. 176.
17. Shiroyanagi Hidemitsu, *Nakamigawa Hikojirō den* (Biography of Nakamigawa Hikojirō; Tokyo, 1950), p. 211.
18. Tsuchiya Takao, *Zaibasu o kizuita hitobito* (The zaibatsu builders; Tokyo, 1955), p. 43.
19. Shiroyanagi, *Nakamigawa*, pp. 212–213.
20. *Ibid.*, p. 238.
21. *Ibid.*, p. 288.
22. *Ibid.*, p. 259.
23. Tsuchiya, *Zaibatsu*, p. 50.

24. Quoted in Kada Tetsuji, *Meiji shoki shakai keizai shisō shi* (History of social and economic thought during the early Meiji era; Tokyo, 1937), p. 713.

25. *Ibid.*, pp. 715–716.

26. Tanaka Sōgorō, *Iwasaki*, p. 130.

27. Iwai Ryōtarō, *Mitsubishi Concern tokuhon* (The Mitsubishi Concern reader; Tokyo, 1937), pp. 102–103.

28. Tsuchiya, *Nihon no seishō*, p. 106.

29. Kajinishi Mitsuhaya, *Nihon shihonshugi hattatsu shi* (History of the development of Japanese capitalism; Tokyo, 1957), p. 141.

30. Iwasaki's protector and former han official, Gotō Shōjirō, had bought the mine from the government for 500,000 yen but lost heavily. Iwasaki was eventually persuaded by Fukuzawa to purchase the mine for 900,000 yen, thus bailing Gotō out of his heavy debts. Shiroyanagi Hidemitsu, *Zaikai taiheiki* (Documents of prosperity in the financial world; Tokyo, 1948), pp. 169–189.

31. Iwai, pp. 201–204.

32. Tanaka Sōgorō, p. 301.

33. Iwai, p. 238.

34. Mitsubishi honsha hensan kyoku (Editorial Section of the Mitsubishi Head Office), ed., *Shashi* (The company history; Tokyo, 1917), No. 14, p. 1135.

35. Tsuchiya, *Zaibatsu*, pp. 126–127.

36. *Ibid.*, p. 144.

37. *Ibid.*, p. 145.

38. Tsuchiya, *Nihon no seishō*, pp. 176–177.

39. Tsuchiya, *Zaibatsu*, p. 146.

40. Nishino Kiyo, *Sumitomo Concern tokuhon* (The Sumitomo Concern reader; Tokyo, 1937), p. 40.

41. Hirose Mitsumasa, *Saihei iseki* (The glorious achievements of Saihei; Kyoto, 1926), pp. 170–171.

42. *Ibid.*, p. 76.

43. Tsuchiya, *Zaibatsu*, p. 175.

44. A notable exception occurred after the downfall of Ono and Shimada, when the government kept part of its money free of interest with the Yasuda Bank; in 1875 the Yasuda Bank held 180,000 yen of government money. Takahashi and Aoyama, p. 50.

45. In 1869 the inconvertible government bills had stood at 38:100 against specie money. Parity was then restored by government decree. Yasuda received news of the government move beforehand and bought up large amounts of bills at the low market rate, selling them a few days later at an almost 300 percent profit. Tsuchiya, *Zaibatsu*, p. 160.

46. Obama Toshie, *Yasuda Concern tokuhon* (The Yasuda Concern reader; Tokyo, 1937), p. 227.

47. Oda Shigeo, *Ningen Yasuda Zenjirō* (The man Yasuda Zenjirō; Tokyo, 1953), pp. 108–109.

48. *Ibid.*, p. 220.

49. Obama, pp. 235–237.

50. Oda, p. 214.

51. Yasuda wanted to collect the 800 million yen as deposits in his many branch banks throughout the country, paying 6.2 percent and receiving 8.5 percent on the loan for the project, thus gaining a 2.3 percent difference for his expenses and for profit. *Ibid.*, pp. 212–213.

52. *Ibid.*, p. 208.

53. *Ibid.*, pp. 139–140.

54. Obama, pp. 223–224.

55. Yokoyama Sadao, *Ningen Ōkura Kihachirō* (The man Ōkura Kihachirō; Tokyo, 1929); and Kadono Shigekurō, *Ōkura Tsuruhiko ō* (The Honorable Ōkura Tsuruhiko; Tokyo, 1924).

56. Tsuchiya, *Zaibatsu*, p. 183.

57. Hattori Shisō, *Kindai Nihon jinbutsu keizai shi* (A biographic economic history of modern Japan; Tokyo, 1955), I, 110.

58. Kadono, p. 450.

59. Katsuda, pp. 29–30.

60. *Ibid.*, p. 54.

61. Yokoyama, pp. 234–236.

62. *Ibid.*, pp. 168–170.

63. Tsuchiya, *Zaibatsu*, p. 200.

64. Konda Bunjirō, ed., *Furukawa Ichibei ō den* (Biography of the Honorable Furukawa Ichibei; Tokyo, 1926), p. 185.

65. Tsuchiya, *Zaibatsu*, pp. 204–206.

66. Konda, appendix, pp. 8–9.

67. Tsuchiya, *Zaibatsu*, p. 207.

68. Konda, p. 207.

69. *Ibid.*, letter appendix, p. 3; and Yokoyama, pp. 237–238.

70. Asano, *passim.*

71. Tsuchiya, *Zaibatsu*, p. 213.

72. Wada Hisajirō, pp. 86–87.

73. Shibusawa Eiichi, *Jijoden*, pp. 622–623.

74. Wada Hisajirō, pp. 104–106.

75. Asano, pp. 526–532.

VII. FIFTY LEADING ENTREPRENEURS

1. *Zaikai bukko ketsubutsu den*, II, 130–133.

2. Hattori and Shinobu, pp. 104–120; and Kinugawa I, 271–332.

3. *Dai Nihon jinmei jisho* (The great Japan biographical diction-

ary), ed. Dai Nihon jinmei jisho kankōkai (The Great Japan Biographical Dictionary Editorial Board; Tokyo, 1926), p. 1481.

4. Tsuchiya, *Nihon no seishō*, pp. 191–205.

5. *Zaikai bukko katsubutsu den*, II, 522–527.

6. *Ibid.*, pp. 2–6.

7. The age of twenty is not to be taken with mathematical exactness. In some cases the man may have actually been twenty-one or twenty-two when he moved to a new place or started a new career.

8. The difference between Western and Confucian studies does not matter too much at this late stage. Many Confucian scholars advocated the opening of the country as ardently as any Western scholar could have done; more often than not Western and Confucian studies were pursued by the same man.

9. Yamamoto Mitsuhiko, *Kawasaki Shōzō* (Tokyo, 1918), pp. 49–50.

10. *Zaikai bukko ketsubutsu den*, II, 506–511.

11. Ōsawa Shōzō, ed., *Nishimura Katsuzō ō den* (Biography of the Honorable Nishimura Katsuzō; Tokyo, 1921).

12. Ōtsuka Eizō, *Magoshi Kyōhei ō den* (Biography of the Honorable Magoshi Kyōhei; Tokyo, 1935), pp. 38–43.

13. Naitō Fumijirō, *Wakao Ippei* (Tokyo, 1914).

14. *Zaikai bukko ketsubutsu den*, I, 133–138.

15. Tsuchiya, *Nihon no keieisha seishin*, p. 178.

16. Toyohara Matao, *Sakuma Sadaichi shōden* (Short biography of Sakuma Sadaichi; Tokyo, 1904), pp. 166–167.

17. See Fritz Redlich, *History of American Business Leaders* (Ann Arbor, 1940), I, 19.

18. *Zaikai bukko ketsubutsu den*, II, 506–511; and *Dai Nihon jinmei jisho*, p. 2672.

19. Toyohara, p. 221.

20. *Shibusawa Eiichi denki shiryō*, XI, 599–665.

21. Suzuki, *passim*.

22. Shibusawa Eiichi, *Jijoden*, pp. 841–843.

23. Ōtsuka Eizō, p. 154.

24. Amamiya Keijirō, "Amamiya Keijirō shi kokkai jigyō keireki dan" (A narrative of the patriotic enterprises of Mr. Amamiya Keijirō), and "Amamiya Keijirō shi kiroku" (Records on Mr. Amamiya Keijirō), MSS (Tokyo University Library, n.d.).

25. Miura Toyoji, *Tanaka Gentarō ō den* (Biography of the Honorable Tanaka Gentarō; Kyoto, 1934).

26. Uemura Chōsaburō, *Donshō Takashima Kazaemon ō den* (Biography of the Honorable Donshō Takashima Kazaemon; Tokyo, 1914).

27. *Zaikai bukko ketsubutsu den*, I, 247–249; and Kinugawa, IV, 309–326.

28. Kinugawa, IV, 322.

29. Tsuchiya, *Nihon no keieisha seishin*, pp. 194–231; and Tsuboya Zenjirō, *Jitsugyōka hyakuketsu den* (Biographies of 100 outstanding entrepreneurs; Tokyo, 1893), VI, 177–186.

30. Hara, ed., I, 109.

31. Usaki, *passim*; and Tsuchiya, *Zaibatsu*, pp. 96–104.

32. Tsuchiya, *Zaibatsu*, pp. 77–85.

33. *Zaikai bukko ketsubutsu den*, II, 306–309.

34. *Ibid.*, pp. 5–10; and *Dai Nihon jinmei jisho*, pp. 92–93.

35. Matsumoto ō dōzō kensetsu kai (Association for the Erection of a Bronze Statue of Matsumoto), ed., *Sōgon Matsumoto Jūtarō ō den* (Biography of the magnificent Matsumoto Jūtarō; Tokyo, 1922).

36. *Ibid.*, p. 18.

37. Miyamoto Mataji, "Matsumoto Jūtarō," *Ōsaka kōgyōkai geppō* (Monthly bulletin of the Osaka Industrial Association), No. 14 (May 15, 1960), p. 16.

38. *Zaikai bukko ketsubutsu den*, I, 378–382.

39. Tsuchiya, *Nihon no keieisha seishin*, pp. 168–193.

40. Modeki Gentarō, *Ōtani Kahei ō den* (Biography of the Honorable Ōtani Kahei; Tokyo, 1931).

41. *Ibid.*, p. 517.

42. *Zaikai bukko ketsubutsu den*, II, 288–291.

43. *Ibid.*, pp. 624–626.

44. Iwashita Seishū, *Fujita ō genkōroku* (Records of the words and deeds of the Honorable Fujita; Tokyo, 1913); Shiroyanagi Hidemitsu, *Nihon fugō hassei gaku* (A study of the emergence of the Japanese rich; Tokyo, 1920), pp. 18–103.

45. *Dai Nihon jinmei jisho*, p. 1892.

46. Yamamoto, *passim*.

47. *Ibid.*, pp. 101–102.

48. Usuda Sadakei, *Nakano Buei ō* (The Honorable Nakano Buei; Tokyo, 1934).

49. Kinugawa, II, 99–109.

50. Ōnishi, *passim*.

51. Tsuchiya, *Zaibatsu*, pp. 104–114.

52. *Ibid.*, pp. 85–95.

53. Takegoshi, *Ōkawa*, *passim*.

CONCLUSION

1. Nurkse, *Problems of Capital Formation in Underdeveloped Countries*, pp. 38–39.

BIBLIOGRAPHY

Akashi Teruo 明石照男 and Suzuki Norihisa 鈴木憲久.
Nihon kinyū shi, Meiji hen 日本金融史, 明治編
(History of Japanese banking, Meiji volume). Tokyo, 1957.

Amamiya Keijirō 雨宮敬治郎. "Amamiya Keijirō shi kokka
jigyō keireki dan" 雨宮敬次郎氏国家事業経
歴談 (A narrative of the patriotic enterprises of Mr.
Amamiya Keijirō. MS, apparently autobiographical; Tokyo
University Library, n. d.

------"Amamiya Keijirō shi kiroku" 雨宮敬治郎氏記録
(Records on Mr. Amamiya Keijirō). MS; Tokyo University
Library, n. d.

Arizawa Hiromi 有沢広巳 , ed. Gendai Nihon sangyō kōza
現代日本産業講座 (A compendium of present-day
Japanese industry), vol. 1. Tokyo, 1959.

Asano Taijirō 浅野泰治郎 Asano Sōichirō 浅野総一郎.
Tokyo, 1939.

Azuma Tōsaku 我妻東策. Shizoku jusan shi 士族授産史
(History of samurai employment). Tokyo, 1942.

Beasley, W. G. "Feudal Revenue in Japan at the Time of the Meiji
Restoration," Journal of Asian Studies, 19.3:255-272
(May 1960).

Bellah, Robert. Tokugawa Religion. Glencoe, Ill., 1957.

323

Brown, Delmer M. Nationalism in Japan: An Introductory
   Historical Analysis. Berkeley, 1955.

Commercial Reports of Her Majesty's Consuls in Japan, 1868 and
   1869-1870. London, 1869 and 1871.

Craig, Albert M. "The Restoration Movement in Chōshū," The
   Journal of Asian Studies, 18.2:187-197 (Feb. 1959).

------Chōshū in the Meiji Restoration. Cambridge, Mass., 1961.

Crawcour, E.S. "Some Observations on Merchants: A Translation
   of Mitsui Takafusa's Chōnin kōken roku, with an Introduction
   and Notes," Transactions of the Asiatic Society of Japan,
   3rd ser., 8:1-139 (Dec. 1961). Tokyo, 1962.

Dai Nihon gaikoku bōeki 大日本外国貿易 (The foreign trade
   of great Japan), ed. Nōshōmushō shōmukyoku 農商務省
   商務局 (Ministry of Agriculture and Trade, Department
   of Trade). Tokyo, 1911.

Dai Nihon jinmei jisho 大日本人名辞書 (The great Japan
   biographical dictionary), ed. Dai Nihon jinmei jisho kankōkai
   大日本人名辞書刊行会 (Great Japan Biographical
   Dictionary Editorial Board). Tokyo, 1926.

Dore, R.P. Land Reform in Japan. Oxford, 1959.

------"The Meiji Landlord: Good or Bad?" Journal of Asian Studies,
   18.3:343-355 (May 1959).

------"Agricultural Improvements in Japan: 1870-1900," Economic
   Development and Cultural Change, vol. 9, no. 1, pt. 2,
   pp. 69-91 (Oct. 1960). Research Center in Economic Development and Cultural Change, University of Chicago.

Egashira Tsuneharu 江頭恒治 "Kōchi-han ni okeru bakumatsu no shinseisaku" 高知藩における幕末の新政策 (The new policies in Kochi han in the last years of the Tokugawa period); in Honjō Eijirō, ed., Bakumatsu keizai shi kenkyū, pp. 101-131.

------"Saga-han ni okeru yōshiki kōgyō" 佐賀藩における洋式工業 (Western-style industry in Saga han); in Honjō Eijirō, ed., Bakumatsu keizai shi kenkyū, pp. 59-100.

------"Takashima tankō ni okeru nichiei kyōdō kigyō" 高嶋炭鉱における日英共同企業 (The joint Anglo-Japanese enterprise at the Takashima coal mine); in Honjō Eijirō, ed., Bakumatsu keizai shi kenkyū, pp. 23-58.

------Ōmi shōnin 近江商人 (The Ōmi merchants). Tokyo, 1959.

Fujii Jintarō. Outline of Japanese History in the Meiji Era, tr. H. K. Colton and K. E. Colton. Tokyo, 1958.

Fujita Gorō 藤田五郎. Nihon kindai sangyō no seisei 日本近代産業の生成 (The creation of Japan's modern industry). Tokyo, 1948.

Fukuzawa Yukichi 福沢諭吉. Fukuzawa Yukichi zenshū 福沢諭吉全集 (The Fukuzawa Yukichi collection), vols. 6, 9, 10. Tokyo: Jiji shinpōsha 時事新報社 (Jiji Newspaper Publishing Co.), 1926.

------"Kyūhanjō" 旧藩状 (The conditions in the old han); in Fukuzawa Yukichi zenshū, VI, 677-696.

------The Autobiography of Fukuzawa Yukichi, tr. Kiyooka Eiichi. Tokyo, 1948.

Furushima Toshio 古島敏雄. Kisei jinushi sei no seisei to tenkai 近世地主制の生成と展開 (The emergence and spread of the parasitic landlord system). Tokyo, 1952.

Gerschenkron, Alexander. "Economic Backwardness in Historical Perspective," in Bert F. Hoselitz, ed., The Progress of Underdeveloped Areas, pp. 3-29.

Ginkō benran 銀行便覧 (Bank handbook), ed. Ōkura shō 大藏省 (Ministry of Finance). Tokyo, 1911.

Ginkō kyoku dai ni ji hōkoku 銀行局第二次報告 (The second report of the Banking Office), ed. Ōkura shō. Tokyo, 1879-1880.

Ginkō tsūshinroku 銀行通信録 (Bank correspondence records), ed. Ginkō shūkaijo 銀行集会所 (The Banking Center). Tokyo, Jan. 20, 1886.

Godai Ryūsaku 五代龍作. Godai Tomoatsu den 五代友厚伝 (Biography of Godai Tomoatsu). Tokyo, 1933.

Hall, John Whitney. Tanuma Okitsugu, 1719-1788, Forerunner of Modern Japan. Cambridge, Mass., 1955.

Hara Kunizō 原邦造, ed. Hara Rokurō ō den 原六郎翁伝 (Biography of the Honorable Hara Rokurō. 3 vols.; Tokyo, 1923.

Hattori Shisō 服部之總, ed. Kindai Nihon jinbutsu keizai shi 近代日本人物経済史 (A biographic economic history of modern Japan), vol. 1. Tokyo, 1955.

------Meiji no shisō 明治の思想 (The thought of the Meiji era); Chosaku shū 著作集 (Collected writings), vol. 6. Tokyo, 1955.

Hattori Shisō and Shinobu Seizaburō 服部之總·信夫清三郎 Meiji senshoku keizai shi 明治染色経済史 (Economic history of Meiji dyeing and weaving). Tokyo, 1937.

Hayes, Samuel P. Jr. "Personality and Culture Problems," in
Bert F. Hoselitz, ed., The Progress of Underdeveloped
Areas, pp. 203-229.

Hirose Mitsumasa 広瀬満正 . Saihei iseki 宰平遺蹟 (The
glorious achievements of Saihei). Kyoto, 1926.

Hirschman, Albert O. The Strategy of Economic Development.
New Haven, 1959.

Honjō Eijirō 本庄榮治郎 . The Social and Economic History
of Japan. Kyoto, 1935.

------ Nihon no keizai to shisō 日本の経済と思想、
(Japanese economy and thought). Kyoto, 1943.

------, ed. Meiji ishin keizai shi kenkyū 明治維新経済史
研究 (Studies in the economic history of the Meiji
Restoration). Tokyo, 1935.

------, ed. Bakumatsu keizai shi kenkyū 幕末経済史研究
(Studies in the economic history of the late Tokugawa period).
Tokyo, 1935.

Horie Eiichi 堀江英一. Meiji ishin no shakai kōzō 明治維
新の社会構造 (Structure of society at the time of
the Restoration). Tokyo, 1954.

Hoselitz, Bert F., ed. The Progress of Underdeveloped Areas.
Chicago, 1952.

Inoue Masaru, Viscount. "Japanese Communications, Railroads,"
in Ōkuma Shigenobu, Fifty Years of New Japan, I, 424-446.

Ishii Mitsuru 石井満. Nihon tetsudō sōsetsu shi wa 日本鉄
道創設史話 (Historic narrative on the building of
the Japanese railways). Tokyo, 1952.

Ishii Ryōichi.   Population Pressure and Economic Life in Japan.
　　Chicago, 1937.

Iwai Ryōtarō 岩井良太郎 .   Mitsubishi Concern tokuhon
　　三菱コンツェルン 讀本 (The Mitsubishi Concern reader).
　　Tokyo, 1937.

Iwashita Seishū 岩下清周 .   Fujita ō genkōroku 藤田翁言
　　行録 (Records of the words and deeds of the Honorable
　　Fujita).   Tokyo, 1913.

Jansen, Marius B.   Sakamoto Ryōma and the Meiji Restoration.
　　Princeton, 1961.

Jinushi sei no keisei 地主制の形成 　(The formation of the
　　landlord system), ed.   Meiji shiryō kenkyū renrakukai
　　明治史料研究連絡会 (Meiji Historic Material
　　Research Association).   Tokyo, 1957.

Kabushiki kaisha 77 ginkō 株式会社七十七銀行 (The 77th
　　Bank Ltd.), ed.   77 nen shi 七十七年史 (History of seventy-
　　seven years).   Tokyo, 1954.

Kada Tetsuji 加田哲二 .   Meiji shoki shakai keizai shisō shi·
　　明治初期社会経済思想史 (History of social
　　and economic thought during the early Meiji era).   Tokyo,
　　1937.

Kadono Shigekurō 門野重九郎 . Ōkura Tsuruhiko ō 大倉
　　鶴彦翁 (The Honorable Ōkura Tsuruhiko).   Tokyo, 1924.

Kajinishi Mitsuhaya 楫西光速 .   Nihon ni okeru sangyō shihon
　　no keisei 日本における産業資本の形成 (The
　　formation of industrial capital in Japan), vol. 1.   Tokyo,
　　1949.

------Shōgyō shihon oyobi kōrigashi shihon 商業資本及び 高利貸資本 (Trading capital and usury capital). Tokyo, 1949.

------Nihon shihonshugi hattatsu shi 日本資本主義発達史 (History of the development of Japanese capitalism). Tokyo, 1957.

Kajinishi Mitsuhaya et al. Nihon ni okeru shihonshugi no hattatsu, nenpyō hen 日本における資本主義の発達,年表編 (The development of capitalism in Japan, chronology volume). Tokyo, 1953.

Kanno Watarō 管野和太郎. Nihon kaisha kigyō hassei shi no kenkyū 日本会社企業発生史の研究 (Studies in the development of the company form of enterprise in Japan). Tokyo, 1931.

------"Kokuritsu ginkō" 国立銀行 (The national banks); in Honjō Eijirō, ed., Meiji ishin keizai shi kenkyū, pp. 301-357.

------"Tsūshō kaisha, kawase kaisha" 通商会社,為替会社 (The trade and finance companies); in Honjō Eijirō, ed., Meiji ishin keizai shi kenkyū, pp. 105-300.

------Ōsaka keizai shi kenkyū 大阪経済史研究 (Studies in the economic history of Osaka). Osaka, 1935.

Karasawa Tomitarō 唐沢富太郎. Nihon kyōiku shi 日本教育史 (History of Japanese education). Tokyo, 1953.

Katō Toshihiko. "Development of the Monetary System," in Shibusawa Keizō, ed., Japanese Society of the Meiji Era, pp. 181-235.

Katorikku daijiten カトリック大辞典 (The Catholic cyclopedia), ed. Jōchi daigaku 上智大学 (Sophia University), vol. 1. 2nd ed.; Tokyo, 1952.

Katsuda Teiji 勝田貞次 .　Ōkura, Nezu Concern tokuhon
大倉.根津コンツェルン讀本 (The Ōkura and Nezu Concern
reader).　Tokyo, 1937.

Kinugawa Taiichi 絹川太一 .　Honpō menshi bōseki shi
本邦綿糸紡續史　(History of Japanese cotton spinning).
7 vols.; Osaka, 1937.

Kikkawa Hidezō 吉川秀造 .　Shizoku jusan no kenkyū 士族授
産の研究　(Studies in samurai employment).　Tokyo, 1935.

------Meiji ishin shakai keizai shi kenkyū　明治維新社会
経済史研究　(Studies in the social and economic history
of the Meiji Restoration).　Tokyo, 1943.

Kobata Jun 小葉田淳 .　"Kinsei keizai no hattatsu" 近世経済
の発達 (The development of the modern economy); in
Kobata Jun, ed., Kinsei shakai 近世社会 (Modern society),
vol. 4.　Tokyo, 1952.

Kobayashi Yoshimasa 小林良正 .　Nihon shihonshugi no seisei to
sono kiban 日本資本主義の生成とその基盤
(The emergence of Japanese capitalism and its foundation).
Tokyo, 1949.

Konda Bunjirō 昆田文次郎 , ed.　Furukawa Ichibei ō den 古
河市兵衛翁伝 (Biography of Furukawa Ichibei).
Tokyo, 1926.

Kosaka Masaaki.　Japanese Thought in the Meiji Era, tr. David Abosh.
Tokyo, 1958.

Kurihara Shinichi 栗原信一 .　Meiji kaika shiron 明治開化史
論 (An historical essay on Meiji civilization).　Tokyo,
1944.

Kyugoro Obata.　An Interpretation of the Life of Viscount Shibusawa.
Tokyo, 1937.

330

Lockwood, William W.   The Economic Development of Japan:
Growth and Structural Change, 1868-1938.   Princeton, 1954.

Masuda Takashi 益田孝. Jijo Masuda Takashi ō den 自叙益田
孝翁伝 (Autobiography of Masuda Takashi). Tokyo,
1939.

Matsumoto ō dozō kensetsu kai 松本翁銅像建設会
(Association for the Erection of a Bronze Statue of Matsumoto),
ed. Sōgen Matsumoto Jūtarō ō den 雙軒松本重太
郎翁伝 (Biography of the magnificent Matsumoto Jūtarō).
Tokyo, 1922.

Meiji 14 nen tōkeihyō 明治十四年統計表 (Statistical table
of Meiji 14 [1881]), ed. Tokyo fu. Tokyo, 1881.

Meiji 16 nen Tōkyō fu tōkeisho 明治十六年東京府統計書
(Statistics of Tokyo prefecture for Meiji 16 [1883]), ed.
Tokyo fu. Tokyo, 1883.

Meiji bunka zenshū, keizai hen 明治文化全集 経済篇
(The Meiji culture collection, economy volume), ed. Meiji
bunka kenkyūkai 明治文化研究会 (Research Council
on Meiji Culture). Tokyo, 1957.

Meiji unyu shi 明治運輸史 (History of Meiji transportation),
ed. Unyu Nipposha 運輸日報社 (Japan Transport
Publication Co.). Tokyo, 1913.

Meiji zaisei shi 明治財政史 (The Meiji financial history),
ed. Meiji zaisei shi hensan kai 明治財政史編纂会
(Meiji Financial History Editorial Board), vol. 13.
Tokyo, 1905.

Meiji zenki zaisei keizai shiryō shūsei 明治前期財政史料
集成 (Collection of material on the finance and economy

of the first part of the Meiji era), ed. Ōuchi Hyōe 大内
兵衛 and Tsuchiya Takao 土屋喬雄 , vol. 17.
Tokyo, 1931.

Mitsubishi honsha hensan kyoku 三菱本社編纂局 (Editorial
Section of the Mitsubishi Head Office), ed. Shashi 社史
(The company history), no. 14. Tokyo, 1917.

Miura Toyoji 三浦豊二 . Tanaka Gentarō ō den 田中源太
郎翁伝 (Biography of the Honorable Tanaka Gentarō).
Kyoto, 1934.

Miyamoto Mataji 宮本又二 . "Tokugawa ki Ōsaka kinkō no
nōgyō keiei" 徳川期大阪近郊の農業経営
(Management of agriculture in the vicinity of Osaka during
the Tokugawa period); in Miyamoto Mataji, ed., Shōgyōteki
nōgyō no tenkai. 商業的農業の展開

------Nihon girudo no kaihō 日本ギルドの解放 (The abolition
of the Japanese guilds). Osaka, 1957.

------Ōsaka 大阪 . Tokyo, 1957.

------Ōsaka chōnin 大阪町人 (The Osaka townsmen). Tokyo,
1957.

------Ōsaka shōnin 大阪商人 (The Osaka merchants). Tokyo,
1958.

------"Matsumoto Jūtarō" 松本重太郎 ; in Ōsaka kōgyōkai
geppō 大阪工業会月報 (Monthly bulletin of the Osaka
Industrial Association), no. 14 (May 16, 1960).

------"Daimyō kashi no rishiritsu ni tsuite" 大名貸の利子
率について (On the interest rates in daimyo lending);
in Ōsaka daigaku keizaigaku 大阪大學經済學
(Osaka University economics), vol. 10, no. 2 (Nov. 25, 1960).

------, ed.　Shōgyōteki nōgyō no tenkai 商業的農業の展開 (The spread of the commercialization of agriculture). Osaka, 1954.

Modeki Gentarō　茂出木源太郎. Ōtani Kahei ō den 大谷嘉兵衛翁伝 (Biography of the Honorable Ōtani Kahei). Tokyo, 1931.

Myrdal, G.　Economic Theory and Underdeveloped Regions. London, 1958.

Naitō Fumijirō 内藤文治郎. Wakao Ippei 若尾逸平. Tokyo, 1914.

Nakayama Yasumasa 中山泰昌, ed.　Shinbun shūsei Meiji hennen shi 新聞集成明治編年史 (Chronological history of the Meiji era compiled from newspapers), vol. 4. Tokyo, 1936.

Nihon Cement kabushiki kaisha 70 nen shi, hon hen 日本セメント株式会社七十年史 本編 (Seventy-year history of Nihon Cement Ltd., main volume), ed. Nihon Cement kabushiki kaisha shashi hensan iinkai 日本セメント株式会社社史編纂委員会 (Editorial Committee for the History of Nihon Cement Ltd.). Tokyo, 1955.

Nihon keizai shi jiten 日本経済史辞典 (Dictionary of Japanese economic history), ed. Keizai shi kenkyūkai 経済史研究会. 2 vols.; Tokyo, 1954.

Nihon keizai tōkei sōkan 日本経済統計総鑑 (Survey of Japanese economic statistics), ed. Asahi shinbunsha 朝日新聞社 (Asahi Newspaper Co.). Tokyo, 1930.

Nihon sangyōshi taikei, sōron hen 日本産業史大系, 総論編 (An outline of Japanese industry, summary volume), ed. Chihō shi kenkyū kyōgikai 地方史研究協議会 (Regional History Research Association). Tokyo, 1961.

Nihon tekkō shi, Meiji hen 日本鉄工史 明治編 (History of Japanese iron and steel, Meiji volume), ed. Nihon tekkō shi hensan iinkai 日本鉄工史 編纂委員会 (Editorial Committee for the History of Japanese Iron and Steel). Tokyo, 1945.

Nihon tetsudō shi 日本鉄道史 (History of the Japanese railways), ed. Tetsudō shō 鉄道省 (Ministry of Railways), vol. 1. Tokyo, 1935.

Nishida Hirotarō 西田広太郎. Meiji kōgyō shi, kagaku kōgyō 明治工業史 化學工業 (History of Meiji industry, chemical industries volume). Tokyo, 1925.

Nishijima Tōshū 西嶋東州. Nihon shigyō hattatsu shi 日本 紙業發達史 (History of the development of Japanese paper manufacturing). Tokyo, 1942.

Nishino Kiyo 西野喜與. Sumitomo Concern tokuhon 住友 コンツエルン讀本 (The Sumitomo Concern reader). Tokyo, 1937.

Nishinoiri Aiichi 西野入愛一. Asano, Shibusawa, Ōkawa, Furukawa Concern tokuhon 浅野,渋沢,大川,古河,コン ツエルン讀本 (The Asano, Shibusawa, Ōkawa, Furukawa Concern reader). Tokyo, 1937.

Nitobe Inazō. Bushido, The Soul of Japan. 17th ed.; Tokyo, 1911.

Nomura Kentarō 野村兼太郎. Ishin zengo 維新前後 (Before and after the Restoration). Tokyo, 1941.

Norman, Herbert. Japan's Emergence as a Modern State. 3rd ed.; New York, 1948.

Nurkse, Ragnar. Problems of Capital Formation in Underdeveloped
   Countries. 4th ed.; Oxford, 1955.

Obama Toshio 小汀利得 . Yasuda Concern tokuhon 安田コンツェ
   ルン讀本 (The Yasuda Concern reader). Tokyo, 1937.

Obata Kyugoro. An Interpretation of the Life of Viscount Shibusawa.
   Tokyo, 1937.

Oda Shigeo 織田誠夫 . Ningen Yasuda Zenjirō 人間安
   田善次郎 (The man Yasuda Zenjirō). Tokyo, 1953.

Ohkawa Kazushi et al. The Growth Rate of the Japanese Economy
   since 1878. Tokyo, 1957.

Ohkawa Kazushi and Henry Rosovsky. "The Role of Agriculture
   in Modern Japanese Economic Development," Economic
   Development and Cultural Change, vol. 9, no. 1., pt. 2,
   pp. 43-67 (Oct. 1960). Research Center in Economic Development and Cultural Change, University of Chicago.

Ōkubo Shigetarō 大久保茂太郎 , ed. Gumma ken sangyōka
   meikan 群馬県蠶業家名鑑 (Biographical directory
   of silk industrialists of Gumma prefecture). Maebashi, 1910.

Ōkuma Shigenobu, Count, ed. Fifty Years of New Japan, tr. and
   ed. Marcus B. Huish, vol. 1. 2nd ed.; London, 1910.

Ōnishi Rihei 大西理平 . Asabuki Eiji kun den 朝吹英二君
   伝 (Biography of Mr. Asabuki Eiji). Tokyo, 1928.

Onoda Cement seizō kabushiki kaisha 小野田セメント製造
   株式会社 (Onoda Cement Manufacturing Company),
   ed. Sōgyō 50 nen shi 創業五十年史 (Fifty years after
   the founding). Tokyo, 1931.

Ōsaka fu shi 大阪府史 (History of Osaka prefecture), ed.
   Ōsaka fu, vol. 2. Osaka, 1903.

335

Ōsaka shiyakusho 大阪市役所 (Osaka City Office), ed.　Meiji
　　Taishō Ōsaka shi shi 明治,大正.大阪市史　(History
　　of Osaka City during the Meiji and Taishō eras), vols. 2, 3.
　　Tokyo, 1935.

Ōsawa Shōzō 大沢省三 , ed.　Nishimura Katsuzō ō den 西村
　　勝三翁伝 (Biography of the Honorable Nishimura Katsuzō).
　　Tokyo, 1921.

Ōtsuka Eizō 大塚榮三 .　Magoshi Kyōhei ō den 馬越恭平
　　翁伝 (Biography of the Honorable Magoshi Kyōhei).
　　Tokyo, 1935.

Ōtsuka Takematsu 大塚武松 , ed.　Hansei ichiran 藩制一覧
　　(Summary of han governments).　2 vols.; Tokyo, 1928-1929.

Rathgen, Karl.　Japans Volkswirtschaft und Staatshaushalt.
　　Leipzig, 1891.

Redlich, Fritz.　History of American Business Leaders, vol. 1.
　　Ann Arbor, 1940.

Reischauer, Edwin O.　Japan, Past and Present.　New York, 1946.

Rosovsky, Henry.　Capital Formation in Japan, 1868-1940.
　　Glencoe, Ill. , 1961.

Rostow, W. W.　The Stages of Economic Growth.　Cambridge, Mass. ,
　　1960.

Ryūmon zasshi 龍門雑誌 (Ryūmon periodical), ed. Ryūmonsha
　　龍門社 (The Dragon Door Company).　Tokyo, May 1889.

Sakada Yoshio 坂田吉雄 .　Hōken jidai kōki no chōnin seikatsu
　　封建時代後期の町人生活　(The life of the towns-
　　men during the later part of the feudal era).　Tokyo, 1950.

Sangyō kyōiku 70 nen shi 產業教育七十年史 (Seventy years of industrial education), ed. Monbushō 文部省 (Ministry of Education). Tokyo, 1956.

Sansom, G. B. Japan, A Short Cultural History. Rev. ed.; New York, 1943.

------The Western World and Japan. New York, 1951.

Schumpeter, Joseph A. Capitalism, Socialism and Democracy. 3rd ed.; New York, 1950.

------The Theory of Economic Development. Cambridge, Mass., 1934.

Sekiyama Naotarō 関山直太郎. Nihon no jinkō 日本の人口 (The population of Japan). Tokyo, 1959.

Sheldon, Charles David. The Rise of the Merchant Class in Tokugawa Japan, 1600-1868: An Introductory Survey. New York, 1958.

Shibusawa Eiichi 渋沢榮一. Jitsugyō kōen 実業講演 (Lectures on enterprise). 2 vols.; Tokyo, 1913.

------Jijoden 自叙伝 (Autobiography). Tokyo, 1938.

------Shōgyō dōtoku kōwa 商業道德講話 (Discourses on business ethics). Tokyo, n.d.

------, ed. Meiji shōkō shi 明治商工史 (History of Meiji trade and industry). Tokyo, 1911.

Shibusawa Eiichi denki shiryō 渋沢榮一伝記史料 (Biographical material on Shibusawa Eiichi), ed. Shibusawa Seien kinen zaidan ryūmonsha 渋沢青淵記念財団龍門社 (Shibusawa Seien Dragon Door Memorial Foundation), vols. 10-12. Tokyo, 1957-1958.

Shibusawa Keizō, ed. Japanese Society of the Meiji Era, tr. S.H. Culbertson and Kimura Michiko. Tokyo, 1958.

Shigyōkai 50 nen 紙業界五十年 (Fifty years of the Paper
    Manufacturers' Association), ed. Hakushinsha 博進社
    (The Progress Co.). Tokyo, 1937.

Shiroyanagi Hidemitsu 白柳秀湖 . Nihon fugō hassei gaku
    日本富豪発生學 (A study of the emergence of the
    Japanese rich). Tokyo, 1920.

------Zaikai taiheiki 財界大平記 (Documents of prosperity
    in the financial world). Tokyo, 1948.

------Nakamigawa Hikojirō den 中上川彦次郎伝 (Biography
    of Nakamigawa Hikojirō). Tokyo, 1950.

Shōji Kichinosuke 庄司吉之助 . Henkaku ni okeru nōmin shisō
    no mondai 変革における農民思想の門題
    (The problem of peasant thought during the period of change).
    Tokyo, 1952.

------Meiji ishin keizai no kōzō 明治維新経済の構造 (The
    structure of the economy of the time of the Meiji Restoration).
    Tokyo, 1958.

Smith, Thomas C.   Political Change and Industrial Development in
    Japan: Government Enterprise, 1868-1880. Stanford, 1955.

------The Agrarian Origins of Modern Japan. Stanford, 1959.

Smith, Warren W. Jr.   Confucianism in Modern Japan: A Study of
    Conservatism in Japanese Intellectual History. Tokyo, 1959.

Sorokin, Pitirim.   Social and Cultural Dynamics. Boston, 1957.

Statler, Oliver.   Japanese Inn.   Pyramid paperback ed.; New
    York, 1962.

Straelen, Henry van.   Yoshida Shōin, Forerunner of the Meiji
    Restoration. Leiden, 1952.

338

Suzuki Gorō 鈴木五郎. Suzuki Tōsaburō den 鈴木藤三郎伝 (Biography of Suzuki Tōsaburō). Tokyo, 1956.

Tachikawa Tokuji 立川得治, ed. Meiji kōgyō shi, tetsudō hen 明治工業史. 鉄道編. (History of Meiji industry, railway volume). Tokyo, 1932.

Takahashi Kamekichi 高橋亀吉. Meiji Taishō sangyō hattatsu shi 明治大正産業発達史 (The history of manufacturing during the Meiji and Taishō eras). Tokyo, 1929.

------Waga kuni kigyō no shiteki hatten 我国企業の史的発展 (The historical development of our country's enterprises). Tokyo, 1956.

Takahashi Kamekichi and Aoyama Jirō 青山二郎. Nihon zaibatsu ron 日本財閥論 (A treatise on the Japanese zaibatsu). Tokyo, 1938.

Takahashi Shinichi 高橋慎一. Yōgakuron 洋学論 (On Western studies). Tokyo, 1939.

Takegoshi Yosaburō 竹越与三郎. Nihon keizai shi 日本経済史 (Japanese economic history), vol. 6. Tokyo, 1929.

------, ed. Ōkawa Heizaburō kun den 大川平三郎君伝 (Biography of Mr. Ōkawa Heizaburō). Tokyo, 1936.

Tanaka Sōgorō 田中惣五郎. Iwasaki Yatarō den 岩崎弥太郎伝 (Biography of Iwasaki Yatarō). Tokyo, 1955.

Tanaka Toyojirō 田中豊次郎. Meiji no senkakusha kindai no ijin kō Godai Tomoatsu den 明治の先覚者近代の偉人侯五代友厚伝 (Biography of the Meiji pioneer and great man of the modern age, Lord Godai Tomoatsu). Osaka, 1921.

Terao Kōji 寺尾宏二 . Meiji shoki Kyōto keizai shi 明治
初期京都経済史 (Economic history of Kyoto
during the early Meiji era). Kyoto, 1943.

Tōbata Seiichi and Ohkawa Kazushi 東畑精一, 大川一司,
eds. Nihon no keizai to nōgyō 日本の経済と農業
(Japanese economy and agriculture), vol. 1. Tokyo, 1956.

Toyohara Matao 豐原又男 . Sakuma Sadaichi shōden 佐久
間貞一小伝 (Short biography of Sakuma Sadaichi).
Tokyo, 1904.

Tsuboya Zenjirō 坪谷善二郎 . Jitsugyōka hyakuketsu den
實業家百傑伝 (Biographies of 100 outstanding
entrepreneurs). 6 vols.; Tokyo, 1893.

Tsuchiya Takao 土屋喬雄 . Zaibatsu o kizuita hitobito 財閥
を築いた人々 (The zaibatsu builders). Tokyo, 1955.

------Nihon no seishō 日本の政商 (Japan's political merchants).
Tokyo, 1956.

------Nihon ni okeru keieisha seishin no hattatsu 日本における
経營者精神の発達 (The development of
managerial mentalities in Japan). Tokyo, 1957.

------Nihon no keieisha seishin 日本の経營者精神
(Managerial attitudes in Japan). Tokyo, 1959.

------, ed. Hōken shakai hōkai katei no kenkyū 封建社会
崩壊過程の研究 (Studies in the disintegration process
of feudal society). Tokyo, 1927.

------, ed. Meiji zenki keizai shi kenkyū 明治前期経
済史研究 (Studies in the economic history of the first
part of the Meiji era). Tokyo, 1944.

340

Tsuchiya Takao and Ono Michio 小野道夫 . Kinsei Nihon nōson
    keizai shiron 近世日本農村経済史論 (An historical
    treatise on the modern Japanese rural economy). Tokyo,
    1933.

Tsuchiya Takao and Okazaki Saburō 岡崎三郎 . Nihon
    shihonshugi hattatsu shi gaisetsu 日本資本主義発達
    史概設 (An outline history of the development of Japanese
    capitalism). Tokyo, 1937.

Tuge Hideomi. Historical Development of Science and Technology
    in Japan. Tokyo, 1961.

Uemura Chōsaburō 植村澄三郎 . Donshō Takashima Kazaemon
    ō den 呑象高嶋嘉左衛門翁伝 (Biography of the
    Honorable Donshō Takashima Kazaemon). Tokyo, 1914.

Usaki Kumakichi 鵜崎熊吉 . Toyokawa Ryōhei 豊川良平 .
    Tokyo, 1922.

Usuda Sadakei 薄田貞敬 . Nakano Buei ō 中野武栄翁
    (The Honorable Nakano Buei). Tokyo, 1934.

Uyehara, S. The Trade and Industry of Japan. Rev. ed.;
    London, 1936.

Vitzthum, Elisabeth Graefin, ed. Die Briefe des Francisco de
    Xavier, 1542-1552. Munich, 1950.

Wada Hidekichi 和田日出吉 . Mitsui Concern tokuhon 三井
    コンツエルン讀本 (The Mitsui Concern reader).
    Tokyo, 1937.

Wada Hisajirō 和田寿次郎 . Asano Cement enkaku shi 浅野
    セメント沿革史 (The history of Asano Cement).
    Tokyo, 1940.

Weber, Max. The Protestant Ethic and the Spirit of Capitalism. New York, 1956.

Yamaguchi Kazuo 山口和雄 . Bakumatsu bōeki shi 幕末貿易史 (History of foreign trade during the last years of the Tokugawa period). Tokyo, 1943.

------Meiji zenki keizai no bunseki 明治前期経済の分析 (Analysis of the economy of the early Meiji era). Tokyo, 1956.

------"The Opening of Japan at the End of the Shōgunate and Its Effects, " in Shibusawa Keizō, ed. , Japanese Society of the Meiji Era, pp. 1-46.

Yamamoto Mitsuhiko 山本実彦 . Kawasaki Shōzō 川崎正蔵 . Tokyo, 1918.

Yanaga Chitoshi. Japan since Perry, consulting ed. Ralph E. Turner. New York, 1949.

Yanagida Kunio. Japanese Manners and Customs in the Meiji Era, tr. Charles S. Terry. Tokyo, 1957.

Yasuoka Shigeaki 安岡重明 ・ "Shōgyōteki hatten to nōson kōzō" 商業的発展と農村構造 (The process of commercialization and village structure); in Miyamoto Mataji, ed. , Shōgyōteki nōgyō no tenkai. 商業的農業の展開

Yokoyama Sadao 横山貞雄 . Ningen Ōkura Kihachirō 人間大倉喜八郎 (The man Ōkura Kihachirō). Tokyo, 1929.

Zaikai bukko ketsubutsu den 財界物故傑物伝 (Biographies of outstanding men in the business world), ed. Jitsugyō no shakaisha 実業の社会社 . (The Business World Co.). 2 vols.; Tokyo, 1936.

GLOSSARY

Abe Taizō	阿部泰蔵	Echigoya	越後屋
Akabane	赤羽	Fujita Denzaburō	藤田伝三郎
Akebono shinbun	曙新聞	Fukagawa	深川
Akizuki	秋月	fukoku kyōhei	富国強兵
Ani	阿仁		
Arita	有田	gaku batsu	學閥
Asahi Maru	旭丸	Gakumon no susume	學問の勤め
Ashio	足尾		
bakufu	幕府	geisha	芸者
Bansho shirabesho	蕃書調所	Geishū	芸州
Besshi	別子	Genji	源氏
bummei kaika	文明開化	genkan	玄関
bushi wa kuwanedo takayōji		geta	下駄
武士は喰わねど高楊子		go isshin	御一新
chō	町	gonin gumi	五人組
chōnin	町人	gōnō	豪農
Chōshū	長州	Gotō Shōjirō	後藤象二郎
		goyō shōnin	御用商人
daimyō	大名	goyōkin	御用金
dan (shaku)	男 (爵)		
Dejima	出島	Hachirōbei	八郎兵衛
Dewa	出羽	Hachirōemon	八郎衛門
dō	堂	haku (shaku)	伯 (爵)
Doi Michio	土居道夫	han	藩

343

han batsu	藩閥	kaikoku	開国
hanchi	半知	Kaisei kan	開成館
hei-nō bunri	兵農分離	kaisha	会社
hibachi	火鉢	Kaitoku dō	懐徳堂
Hokkai Maru	北海丸	Kakeda	掛田
Hokkaidō tankō	北海道炭鉱	kakeya	掛屋
Hōrai	蓬莱	Kamaishi	釜石
Horonai	幌内	Kanakin	金巾
		kanban	看板
Ichikawa	市川		
Ikuno	生野	Kaneda Ichihei	金田市兵衛
Imamura Seinosuke	今村清之助	Kanegafuchi	鐘ヶ淵
Innai	院内	Kankōryō	勧工寮
Inoue Kaoru	井上馨	kanson minpi	官尊民卑
Inoue Masaru	井上勝	Kashima Manpei	鹿島万平
Ishida Baigan	石田梅巌	Kashimaya	加島屋
Ishikawa	石川	Katakura Kentarō	片倉兼太郎
Ishikawa Masaryū	石河正龍	Katō Yukichi	加藤勇吉
ishin	維新	Kawada Koichirō	川田小一郎
Itō Hirobumi	伊藤博文	Kawasaki Hachiuemon	
Iwaki	磐城	川崎八右衛門	
Iwakura Tomomi	岩倉具視	kazoku	華族
Iyo	伊予	Keiō gijuku	慶応義塾
		Kido Takayoshi	木戸孝允
Jitsugyō no Nihonsha	実業之日本社	Kii	紀伊
jitsugyōka	実業家	kimono	着物
jōkamachi	城下町	Kinai	畿内
		Kinbara Meizen	金原明善
Kaga	加賀	Kinki	近畿
Kagaya	加賀屋		

344

kisei jinushi	寄生地主	Maruya	丸屋
Kitsu	木津	Maruzen	丸善
kō (shaku)	公（爵）	Masuya	桝屋
kō (shaku)	侯（爵）	Matsukata Masayoshi	松方正義
Kōbu daigakkō	工部大學校	Matsumae	松前
kobun	子分	Meiji	明治
Kōgaku ryō	工學寮	Meirokusha	明六社
kogata	子方	Meiwa	明和
kogata uchi	子方家	Miike	三池
koku	石	Minamoto Yoshiie	源義家
kokuritsu	国立	Minomura Rizaemon	
Kondō Renpei	近藤廉平		三野村利左衛門
Kōnoike	鴻池	miso	味噌
Kosaka	小坂	Mito	水戸
Kōseikan	弘成館	Mitsui bussan	三井物産
kotatsu	炬燵	Mitsukoshi	三越
Kuga	久我	Miyake Sekian	三宅石菴
kuge	公卿	Mori Arinori	森有礼
kumiai	組合	Morimura Ichizaemon	
kuramoto	蔵元		森村市左衛門
kurayashiki	蔵屋敷	Motoki Shōzō	本木昌造
Kurihara Nobuchika	栗原信近		
Kuroda Kiyotaka	黒田清隆	myōgakin	冥加金
Kuwahara	桑原	myōji taitō	苗字帯刀
Kyōdō unyu kaisha	共同運輸会社		
kyōsō	競走	Nakano Goichi	中野梧一
		Nakatsu	中津
Maejima	前島	Nippon yūsen kaisha	
Marunouchi	丸ノ内		日本郵船会社

345

noren	暖簾
o-chōnin san	御町人さん
Oda Nobunaga	織田信長
Ōji seishi	王子製紙
Okada Reikō	岡田令高
Ōki Tamihira	大木民平
Ōkubo Toshimichi	大久保利通
Okuda Masaka	奥田正香
Ōkuma Shigenobu	大隈重信
Ōmi	近江
Ono	小野
Ōsaka kappan seizōsho	大阪活版製造所
Owari	尾張
oyabun	親分
oyakata	親方
oyakata uchi	親方家
rangakusha	蘭學者
rōnin	浪人
ryō	両
ryōgaeya	両替屋
ryōshu	領主
Saga	佐賀
Saigō Takamori	西郷隆盛
saikaku	才覚
Saikoku risshi hen	西國立志編
Sakaki	榊
sake	酒
Sakuma Shōzan	佐久間象山
samurai	侍
sankin kōtai	参勤交代
Sanwa	三和
sanyō	算用
Sata Keiseki	佐田介石
Satō Gentabei	佐藤源太兵衛
Satsuma	薩摩
Satsumaya Hanbei	薩摩屋半兵衛
sei-i-tai shōgun	征夷大将軍
seishō	政商
Seiyō jijō	西洋事情
Sekigahara	関ヶ原
sengoku jidai	戦国時代
Senju	千住
Senshū kaisha	先収会社
Settsu	摂津
shi	士
shi (shaku)	子 (爵)
shi-nō-kō-shō	士農工商
Shiba	芝
Shibaura	芝浦
Shimada	島田
shimatsu	始末
Shimazu Nariakira	島津斉彬
Shimonoseki	下関

Shinagawa	品川	tōfu	豆腐
Shinagawa Yajirō	品川弥二郎	Tokugawa Ieyasu	德川家康
shingaku	心學		
Shinmachi	新町	Tomioka	富岡
Shinoda Naotaka	篠田直方	tonya	問家
shinpan	親藩	Tosa	土佐
Shinshū	信州	Tōyō	東洋
Shintō	神道	Toyotomi Hideyoshi	豐臣秀吉
Shirakawa	白河	Tsukiji	築地
shiritsu	私立	Tsūshōshi	通商司
Shōda Heigorō	正田平五郎		
shōgun	將軍	Uchiike	内池
Shokkō gakkō	職工學校	Ueda	上田
shokusan kōgyō	殖産興業	Utsunomiya Saburō	宇都宮三郎
Shōnai	庄内		
shōnin	商人	Waseda	早稲田
sonnō jōi	尊王攘夷		
sotsu	卒	ya	屋
		Yamabe Takeo	山辺丈夫
Takashima	高嶋	Yamagata Aritomo	山県有朋
Tanaka Chōbei	田中長兵衛	Yamato	大和
Tanaka Heihachi	田中平八	yen	円
Tanaka Ichibei	田中市兵衛	Yokoyama Hisatarō	横山久太郎
tatami	畳	Yonekura Ippei	米倉一平
Tenpo	天保	Yūbin jōkisen kaisha	郵便蒸気船会社
terakoya	寺小屋	za	座
tōbaku	討幕	zaibatsu	財閥

INDEX

Abacus, 25

Abe Taizō, 272–273

Adoption of merchants by samurai, 21

Agriculture: cultivated area, 73–74; labor force, 109–110; productivity, Meiji, 109–110, 157; productivity, Tokugawa, 73–75; technology, 109, 110, 127–128

Aichi Cement Mill, 190–191

Akabane Construction, 150–151

Akita han, 64, 80

Amamiya Keijirō, 11, 267–268

Ancestors, authority of, 23

Ani Copper Mine, 152

Asabuki Eiji, 136, 226, 260, 284

Asano Cement Works, 153–154, 190, 238–239

Asano Sōichirō, 153, 192, 231–232, 238–240; attitudes, 197, 200–201

Ashio Copper Mine, 236

Bakufu: status quo policies, 7–8, 9, 17; Western learning, 115–116, 117

Balance of payments, 186. See also Imports

Bank of Japan, 149

Bankers' Association, 170

Banks: capital, 57; private banks, 57, 59; promotion of, 57–58; national (1872), 36, 56; national (1876), 56–57; zaibatsu banks, 212, 218, 219, 228, 230–232, 272

Bansho shirabesho, 116

Besshi Copper Mine, 227–228

Book learning. See Education

Bummei kaika: as new era, 114, 120, 164, 173; impact on entrepreneurs, 260–261, 262–263

Capital supply: for economic development, 3, 288; for Meiji indus-

try, 195, 211–214, 280, 285. See also Government subsidies

Capitalism, spirit of, 202–204

Cash cropping, 80–82

Castle towns, 7

Charter Oath, 118–119

Chōnin, 7. See also Merchants

Cement mills. See Aichi; Asano; Fukagawa

Classical entrepreneurial type, defined, 264–267

Commercial schools, 128. See also Education

Commutation of samurai stipends, 52–53, 54, 57

Company system, merchant reaction to, 31–32. See also Joint stock

Competition, aversion of merchants to, 30–31

Confucianism: ideology, 22, 204, 205–206; scholars, 26–27, 116–117; and Shibusawa, 174, 205–206

Consumption patterns, 101–102

Copper mining, 227–229, 236–237
    Mines: Ani, 152; Ashio, 236; Besshi, 227–228

Cotton spinning: advantages of Japan, 156; capital supply, 99, 100; depression, 99, 186–187; encouragement of, 96, 155–156; entrepreneurs in, 97, 98, 188, 252; efficiency, 97, 187; location of mills, 99; technology, 132 133, 161
    Mills: Hiroshima, 186; Ichikawa, 186; Kagoshima, 132; Kanegafuchi, 220–221; Osaka, 99, 188; Owari, 269–270; Sakai, 38

Cotton weaving, 100

Dai Ichi Bank. See First National Bank; Shibusawa

CPSIA information can be obtained
at www.ICGtesting.com
Printed in the USA
LVHW081617230419
615238LV00013B/328/P